FROM *SHANE* TO *KILL BILL*

New Approaches to Film Genre

Series Editor: Barry Keith Grant

New Approaches to Film Genre provides students and teachers with original, insightful, and entertaining overviews of major film genres. Each book in the series gives an historical appreciation of its topic, from its origins to the present day, and identifies and discusses the important films, directors, trends, and cycles. Authors articulate their own critical perspective, placing the genre's development in relevant social, historical, and cultural contexts. For students, scholars, and film buffs alike, these represent the most concise and illuminating texts on the study of film genre.

Published:
1   *From* Shane *to* Kill Bill: *Rethinking the Western*, Patrick McGee

Forthcoming:
2   *The Horror Film*, Rick Worland
3   *Hollywood and History*, Robert Burgoyne
4   *Film Noir*, William Luhr

FROM *SHANE* TO *KILL BILL*

RETHINKING THE WESTERN

PATRICK McGEE

Blackwell
Publishing

BLACKWELL PUBLISHING
350 Main Street, Malden, MA 02148-5020, USA
9600 Garsington Road, Oxford OX4 2DQ, UK
550 Swanston Street, Carlton, Victoria 3053, Australia

First published 2007 by Blackwell Publishing Ltd

1   2007

Library of Congress Cataloging-in-Publication Data

McGee, Patrick, 1949–
    From Shane to Kill Bill : rethinking the Western / Patrick McGee.
        p. cm.—(New approaches to film genre ; 1)
    Includes bibliographical references and index.
    ISBN-13: 978-1-4051-3964-9 (hardcover : alk. paper)
    ISBN-10: 1-4051-3964-1 (hardcover : alk. paper)
    ISBN-13: 978-1-4051-3965-6 (pbk. : alk. paper)
    ISBN-10: 1-4051-3965-X (pbk. : alk. paper) 1. Western films—United
States—History and criticism. I. Title. II. Series.

    PN1995.9.W4M37 2007
    791.43′6278—dc22

                                                            2005032201

A catalogue record for this title is available from the British Library.

Set in 11.5/13.5pt Bembo
by Graphicraft Limited, Hong Kong
Printed and bound in Singapore
by Fabulous Printers Pte Ltd

The publisher's policy is to use permanent paper from mills that operate a
sustainable forestry policy, and which has been manufactured from pulp
processed using acid-free and elementary chlorine-free practices.
Furthermore, the publisher ensures that the text paper and cover board
used have met acceptable environmental accreditation standards.

For further information on
Blackwell Publishing, visit our website:
www.blackwellpublishing.com

CONTENTS

ILLUSTRATIONS

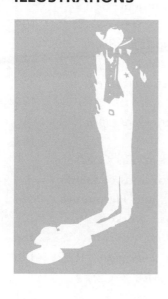

PREFACE

The tragic statement the film offers, while concerned with choices and failures in the distant (and largely mythical) American past, takes on particular resonance in the context of the Reagan administration, with its shameless bolstering of the rich camouflaged and given spurious validity by its "moral" crusade: the present political context makes Cimino's conception of the film, some years ago, curiously prophetic. For me, the sheer beauty of Heaven's Gate *– expressed through, but by no means confined to, its rich, elegiac images – makes all objections secondary. It seems to me, in its original version, among the supreme achievements of the Hollywood cinema.*
—Robin Wood (1986a: 317)

The epigraph above must seem bizarre and anomalous to those readers and moviegoers who know *Heaven's Gate* only by its reputation in the media. That reputation has been institutionalized by Steven Bach's *Final Cut* (1985), a work that has gone through several printings and a revised edition. It tells the story of Michael Cimino and the movie that destroyed a major Hollywood studio from the viewpoint of one of the corporate executives in charge of production. Critically, Bach tries to justify the aesthetic value of the original release of the movie, after it had been cut from nearly four hours to two and a half, as the best that could be redeemed from a production process gone awry. Robin Wood's comment above is the last sentence of an essay that offers a vindication of the movie, one which has never been answered, while the movie "continues to be treated as a fiasco" (1998: 267). It is not my intention to answer Wood's argument, except to say that I agree with it and will refer to it later. It is both an aesthetic and political vindication of the movie, and I cite it here as the starting point of a meditation on the Western movie that will take the form of cultural critique and social analysis.

For although the Western has often been described as a conservative film genre, one that stresses extreme versions of masculinity and individualism and that is certainly one of the inspirations for the cowboy mentality of the Reagan White House and now the second Bush Family White House, there has always been another side to the Western, another shadow that it casts, sometimes in the form of anti-Westerns like *Johnny Guitar*, *McCabe & Mrs. Miller* and, in its own way, *Heaven's Gate*, but also in the more traditional Westerns like *Shane* and many of John Ford's movies. Both *Shane* and *Heaven's Gate* are loosely based on the 1892 Johnson County War in Wyoming, which was a class conflict between corporate cattlemen and small ranchers; but these are not the only Westerns that represent class struggle as a conflict over the distribution of wealth. Through various displacements and disguises, such representations form a tradition within the genre, a tradition that includes some of the greatest Westerns ever made. More than any other film genre, the Western has repeatedly formulated the question of who has the right to wealth, the right to the power that wealth seems to bestow, and the right to freedom in the form that Marx specified as the definition of wealth. Freedom is the antithesis of wage slavery and manifests itself not as the abstract concept of an equal opportunity but as the social individual's autonomous and creative relation to time. Wealth is free time. All of these concepts – wealth, power, and freedom – must themselves be subjected to critical thought, something that Western movies rarely do, though such works can be seen as the unconscious utterances of mass culture, expressing the social desires that the members of such a culture harbor within themselves about the right to wealth and the justice of its distribution in contemporary society. Consequently, the Western movie has been particularly successful at articulating class resentments and the social contradictions that produce them in US culture, though it may also have had the effect of neutralizing critical knowledge of class as a system. For these reasons, this book participates in the shift away from the frontier myth in recent Western historiography and film criticism, which does not mean that it leaves the issue out of the account. As historian Patricia Limerick stresses, the frontier represented lines drawn on a map for "the definition and allocation of ownership" (1987: 27).

We start *in medias res* with a detailed analysis of George Stevens's *Shane* from a perspective that is more subjective than the other chapters, though it strives for a reading of the film that has objective validity. In my childhood, *Shane* was a minor event that cannot be separated from my blue-collar background and the context of the nuclear family that was the primary institution of my socialization in the fifties. In many ways, the movie is about class and the family and how these two social categories reinforce and yet contradict each other. In the nineteenth century, Friedrich Engels saw the family as "the economic unit of society" (Marx and Engels 1968: 591). More recently, scholars of the Western have seen the family as "the first economic unit of individualism in Westerns" (Durgnat and Simmon 1998: 76). In any case, the family as a structure reproduces not only the social relations of production, in the form of the class system, but also the contradiction between individual desire and social conformity, to which the Western frequently offers an imaginary resolution. Though it is impossible for me to write about *Shane* today without employing some critical and theoretical concepts, in the first chapter I have limited these concepts to what illuminates the kind of interpellation or hailing that the film performed in my history. The rest of the book gives that interpellation a larger framework through a series of immanent analyses. My purpose is to lay out the historical meaning of class struggle in the Western in a way that discloses not only the limits of the genre but also its positive political value as the expression of a social desire that is more or less disavowed by the public discourse of the United States. From our politicians and media gurus, whether conservative or liberal, we hear an ongoing diatribe against any criticism or even awareness of class as a systematic structure that defines and limits human beings. Such expressions are interpreted as class warfare, something to be avoided at all costs. Yet our mass culture never stops finding new ways of saying the unsayable.

The second chapter sketches the historical and theoretical conditions for understanding the cultural significance of the Hollywood Western from 1939 to the present. After that, the next four chapters complete the historical reading of the Western from 1939 to 1962, which could be called the Age of John Ford, beginning with *Stagecoach* and ending with *The Man Who Shot Liberty Valance*. Though these close analyses focus on direct and indirect representations of class conflict in individual works, they also suggest that the social relations designated by the term "class" cannot be reduced to a conflict between fixed social positions and forms of consciousness but refer to mobile social identities in an ongoing struggle and debate over distributions of wealth and social autonomy. There is no class before there is class struggle. From this perspective, gender, race, and other social categories constitute class formations in their movement to resist or revoke the dominant social relations. The last three chapters of the book look at the traditions that emerged after the demise of the classical Western. Perhaps in response to the social disillusionment that grew in the United States as a result of political strife, assassinations, riots, and the Vietnam War and other postcolonial wars of independence, these late Westerns from directors like Sam Peckinpah, Sergio Leone, Clint Eastwood, and others are more pessimistic than the films of the classical period. They demonstrate Theodor Adorno's view that "art today is scarcely conceivable except as a form of reaction that anticipates the apocalypse" (1997: 85). In effect, there is only one imaginary resolution to the social contradictions of capitalism, and that is death. Yet death becomes a figure of self-transformation as the ground of social change. None of these films is without significant contradiction, but they still foreground class struggle as the inevitable by-product of capitalism and the force within it that must bring about the end of history as we know it. In the Conclusion, on *Kill Bill*, the different modes of the Western's survival in the present suggest its relevance to the global culture of the new millennium.

I need to make a point about the understanding of genre that this text presupposes. Robin Wood has noted that "One of the greatest obstacles to any fruitful theory of genre has been the tendency to treat the genres as discrete. An ideological approach might suggest why they can't be, however hard they may appear to try: at best, they represent different strategies for dealing with the same ideological tensions" (1986b: 62). This study makes no claim to define the essence of the Western as a genre. Rather, it employs an ideological approach that allows for the examination of how some of the most popular and critically interesting Westerns ever made express ideological tensions that are associated with the class system and the antagonism of class subjects. These tensions are not unique to the Western, though the history of this genre and its political origins do suggest that it has a particular investment in exploring the relationship between class, wealth, and violence. Gangster films, for example, also explore the relation between wealth and violence, but they rarely focus on the conditions that lead to the formation of a class subject that is antagonistic to capitalism and its distribution of wealth in general.

If the Western can be considered one of the principle narratives in the discourse of mass culture on the right to wealth and the legitimacy of class, the reason for this lies in the history from which it emerged and to which it continues, almost obsessively, to respond. The belief in the necessity of class is the belief in a natural right to superfluous wealth in one form or another. The Western has sometimes supported this view, but its greatest achievements have interrogated that right and the social relations of capitalism itself. To study the Western is to contemplate violent conflict as both a fact of social history and a figure of social transformation. Such a study need not endorse violence or recommend it, but it must recognize violence as the expression of a social contradiction that will not go away without the transformation of the social relations that produce it. The Western movie cannot and will not answer the question of how to do that. Still, I would like to keep in mind for this project what Jean-Paul Sartre said of his own: "whatever an ideological project may be in appearance, its ultimate goal is to change the basic situation by becoming aware of its contradictions" (1968: 112).

I would never have finished this project without the support of my wife Joan, my son Sean, and my friends Tim Paulson, Mustapha Marrouchi, and Ben Lanier-Nabors. I am grateful to Louisiana State

University for supporting this work with release time and travel grants. I especially thank Mark Quigley of the UCLA Film and Television Archive, who enabled me to see films I could not have seen any other way, and Barbara Hall of the Margaret Herrick Library at the Academy of Motion Picture Arts and Sciences, who introduced me to the George Stevens Archive. Jayne Fargnoli and Ken Provencher of Blackwell have my gratitude for making the publication of this project go like a breeze.

CHAPTER 1

WHY SHANE NEVER COMES BACK

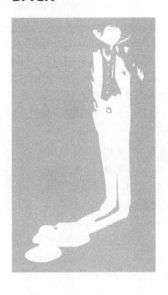

Alan Ladd's Face

The thing I remember most about seeing *Shane* as a boy is the face of Alan Ladd. It was the medium close-up shot at the beginning of the movie when he pauses on his horse and looks across the river at the boy on a fence. Shane's gaze is returned not only by the boy but by his parents, particularly the mother, played by Jean Arthur, who is framed by the kitchen window (Ills. 1–2). Ladd's face almost resolves the tensions between the masculine and the feminine that are starkly represented in the film by the contrast between the mother's gentility and rejection of guns and violence, on the one hand, and the rough, brutal faces of the Ryker brothers and their gunslinging cohorts, on the other. Structurally, Shane's face resembles the mother's, though his potential violence aligns him with Ryker. Despite the director's best efforts to make him appear so at times, Alan Ladd was not a towering figure in the tradition of other Western male heroes. If Shane was "not much above medium height" in Jack Schaefer's novel (1975: 2), Ladd was below

ILLUSTRATIONS 1–2 Shane and his mirror image. *Shane* (1953). Paramount Pictures. *Producer and director:* George Stevens *(shot/reverse shot sequence)*

medium height and made for a feminized version of the Western gunfighter.

Shane does not directly represent class division and conflict in the way that some later Westerns, like *Heaven's Gate*, would do. If it had, it probably would not have influenced me or anyone else of the fifties generation in the way it did. It was precisely the focus on the family, even its idealization, that made *Shane* something of an event in my childhood. As I noted earlier, both *Shane* and *Heaven's Gate* derive from the same historical background, which is the Wyoming Johnson County War of 1892. Neither of these films can be said to represent the events of that war accurately, though *Heaven's Gate* achieves some degree of authenticity in imagining the worst scenario for how the war might have gone. *Shane*, by contrast, reduces the conflict between the corporate cattlemen and the homesteaders of Johnson County to a more elementary struggle between a single rancher and a handful of families – between the rugged masculine individual and the more feminized community. There is no suggestion of any serious wrongdoing on the part of the homesteaders, no reference to rustling that was the accusation used by the big cattlemen to justify their invasion of Johnson County with the intent of executing a number of people from 19 to 70, depending on the source of the information (Smith 1966: 194). I will come back to the Johnson County War and its relation to the Western movie tradition throughout this study; but here I want to focus on what distinguishes *Shane* from *Heaven's Gate*, which is the articulation of class struggle through the mediation of the family.

In the areas of feminist and gender studies as well as queer theory, there have been frequent criticisms of essentialism as applied to the categories of gender and sex. According to this logic, whatever the necessary biological preconditions, no one is born a man or a woman, a homosexual or a heterosexual; rather these categories are constructed within a social context, and a subject takes on these identities through a complex process of social articulation or *suturing*. I use the later term not in its strict theoretical sense but rather in a more common-sense way that can still be related to its use in film theory and Lacanian psychoanalysis. To say that a subject must be sutured to an identity is to recognize a process that is not natural and that can never be complete. In the formation of a subject, the suture marks a relation that can always come undone, that breaks any continuity or ground of wholeness, and that must constantly undergo renewal through repetition (Butler 1991: 21). An error that sometimes haunts gender and class analysis is the assumption that a subject is necessarily determined in such a way as to assume a specific social identity such as homosocial masculinity or working-class consciousness. Even though the process of suturing is recognized, there is still the assumption that its outcome is inevitable and that it is added onto a more authentic and ethically legitimate social identity. In order to understand the historical impact of a movie like *Shane*, it is necessary to suspend these assumptions and try to imagine a world in which a subject that has no essential identity struggles to construct itself.

The opening shots of *Shane* illustrate this process. In the first shot after the credits, we see little Joey (Brandon De Wilde) stalking a deer with an unloaded gun. As he aims the gun, he notices (in the subjective reverse shot) Shane riding into the space between the antlers of the deer. The close-up of Joey's face as he concentrates on the distant rider may simply represent a child's curiosity, but these images link that curiosity with the aggressive drive and suggest that the child seeks the answer to a question about his place in the world that he can only formulate indirectly. In effect, Shane's image is what Lacan would call the answer of the real (Žižek 1992: 32). Joey's aggressive game is almost antithetical to the first images of the Starrett farm that immediately follow, images that suggest a natural utopia. Joey disavows his fantasy by running back to the farm where his father is chopping wood while his mother sings in the kitchen. In these opening shots, Joey moves away from the domestic space and virtually tries to subvert it through the fantasy of killing the deer; then he runs back into that space as if to verify his identification with his father's image and his mother's voice.

The first medium close-up of the father, Joe Starrett (Van Heflin), is at a low angle, which conveys his authority in the eyes of the boy. The father's impersonal gaze at the distant rider lacks the boy's aggressive curiosity. The boy runs to the fence; and then in the next shot the mother, Marian, walks past the kitchen window without looking out. Her singing voice pervades the scene. Joey climbs the fence; and then the camera cuts to a shot from behind the father, which shows him in full stature as he watches Shane nearing the farm in the distance. There is a contrast between the father's immobility and Shane's mobility, between Joe's large size and obvious physical strength and Shane's small size and relative physical weakness. In the next two shots, Shane's approach along the river is contrasted with the image of the mother in the window with her back to the camera. In the following long shot, Shane pulls up to the edge of the river and stops. In close-up, Joey gazes intently at Shane, while in a reverse medium close-up Shane looks back.

Critics and spectators usually assume that the viewpoint of the film more or less corresponds to that of the boy as it did in the novel. In the sequence I just mentioned, this reading is supported by the shot/reverse shot pattern: a close-up of Joey, the reverse shot in medium close-up of Shane, and another close-up of Joey that completes the circuit and would seem to suture the spectator to Joey's viewpoint. The parents reinforce Joey's gaze with their own, and there is no subjective reverse shot that reveals the family from Shane's perspective. In fact, Shane is clearly the object of the gaze and occupies the position that Laura Mulvey (1989: 19) attributes to women in classical Hollywood cinema (see Mitchell 1996: 160–3). Though Shane eventually plays an active role in the narrative of this film, for most of the time he is on the screen he functions as spectacle. In the opening sequence, he brings all narrative activity to a stop as everyone turns to look at him. After he leaves and Ryker and his men arrive, his sudden appearance at the side of the cabin is enough to disrupt Ryker's attempt to intimidate the Starretts. When he goes to town for the first time, he is scrutinized by everyone and is finally subjected to abuse by the cowhand Chris (Ben Johnson). Back at the Starrett place, the local homesteaders meet Shane with suspicion and then proceed to talk about him in the third person. Marian's look is more compassionate when she watches him through the window of the cabin as he stands in the rain. Even in the scene in which Shane shows Joey how to shoot, the emphasis is on how Shane looks to Joey and Marian rather than on what he can do with a gun. At the Fourth of July celebration, the emphasis is on how Shane looks to Joe as he dances with Marian. Finally, when Shane rides to the final confrontation, the camera focuses from different angles on the spectacular image of the man on a horse with triumphal music in the background. This sequence postpones the inevitable narrative conclusion – the moment when Shane acts – for as long as possible.

In that final ride, Joey's viewpoint seems dominant; but in most of its critical scenes the film articulates multiple viewpoints through complicated crosscutting. However, the dominant though not exclusive viewpoint is the one of which we are least aware, and that is the viewpoint of Shane. If the Starrett farm looks utopian, if the initial compositions and coloring create the feeling of a domestic paradise American-style, complete with home-baked pie, these images of the holy nuclear family reflect the viewpoint of someone on the outside, someone who has not had to "work, work, work," as Marian describes life on the homestead later in the movie. This suggests that the suturing process through which a spectator relates to a movie like *Shane* cannot be reduced exclusively to the configuration of shots in a technical sense. Suture theorists have always privileged the dominant shot/reverse shot structure, though they have also been willing to recognize that suturing is a function of the larger narrative process in cinema (Heath 1981: 19–112; Silverman 1983: 194–236). To that insight, I would add the understanding that spectators exist in history and that the way they insert themselves into the representations of mass culture responds to determinations that come from outside the medium of film itself.

What Shane Wants

Shane is a prototype of the Man with No Name played by Clint Eastwood in Sergio Leone's *Dollars* trilogy. It probably would be more appropriate to refer to this character as the Man with No

History. Ultimately, a man without a history has no real identity because identity is a function of history, of the stories we tell about ourselves, both as individuals and as members of a group. The gunfighter Wilson has an identity because his history precedes him, and even Shane knows about it. But when it comes to Shane, no one seems to know anything for certain. The cowhand who leaves town when he sees Shane can only explain his reaction as a form of superstition. Wilson doesn't know Shane the way Shane knows Wilson. Consequently, Shane is a nomad not only because he is mobile and without a domestic center like Joe Starrett's, but because he has no story that can explain his being.

Freud argued that the goal of life is death; and every individual's concept of his or her own life and its meaning or value is determined by the imagination of the end, of how our history must look from the perspective of our own death. The nomad is the force in every subject that pulls against the process of suturing and destabilizes any fully constituted identity and the determination of a specific end. In the movie, though we don't often see what Shane sees, we identify with the position from which he sees – with the nomadic subject as the condition of our seeing. I would argue that the appeal of cinema is not just that it gives us images that validate the social identities into which we have been born. Rather, it awakens in the spectator the nomad that questions every officially-sanctioned identity in the quest for a history that can resolve the contradictions inherent in his or her immediate social context.

When Shane and Joe work on removing the tree stump, their activity produces figures of labor that suggest Shane's identification with someone who produces value like Joe rather than someone who appropriates the value produced by the labor of others like Ryker. Marian's work in the kitchen and her partnership with Joe make her another figure of value-producing labor. Together they signify the productivity of the family as pure use value that transcends the principles of ownership and the patriarchal authority that defines the institutional structure of property. As a structure of feeling, these images express both Shane's desire to be a man and the force that divides such desire from its goal. He wants the family as use value, which produces affective wealth, but not as an institutional structure that tries to constrain human passions and desires. Joe is not such a high ideal of masculinity that neither the spectator nor Shane can imagine being able to step into his shoes, but as a patriarchal subject Joe appears to be fixed and immovable like the stump (and it is curious that, even after they have pulled up the stump, it remains in the yard, so that later Shane is driven up against it when he fights Joe for the right to take his place in the gunfight with Ryker and Wilson). Shane has a passion for Joe, but this passion makes it impossible for him to be like Joe. The nomad desires that which he is not, but the condition of that desire is distance from the identity that embodies the history he wants for himself. The object of his passion is never what he wants but the sign of what he wants, the thing that holds the place of desire in the world. It is the sign of something that can't be named but nonetheless conditions his desire and drives him onward toward the end that will make sense out of his quest but is always out of reach. He desires that which enables him to go on desiring, which could be called freedom.

Marian is attracted to Shane because she recognizes in him the nomadic desire that her history with Joe has disavowed but not completely repressed. Marian harbors the knowledge that Joe lacks, the knowledge that her desire exceeds her identity in the family structure. She loves Joe for being what she is not, for lacking the self-consciousness that is the condition of nomadic desire, for being at one with a history that centers on the family and its normalized gender identities. In this context, self-consciousness and the desire that exceeds the norms of patriarchal culture result in a figurative castration − in the feeling of incompleteness, of the necessity and impossibility of desire. Near the end of the movie, when Marian begs Joe to leave the farm and surrender to Ryker, Joe insists that Marian loves their place more than he does; but the truth is that Marian loves Joe's identity and the history it derives from more than she loves the place. She would rather move on and re-create that history than risk it. Marian knows that the land reduced to private property is never the true object of desire but the support of desire. Shane is similarly castrated. He doesn't want Joe's land; he doesn't even want to take Joe's place with Marian: he wants Joe's history. As a man without a history, he wants to protect Joe and his story from the death that Shane himself embodies. Shane desires a history and a story that he can never have because he can never surrender his desire for desire. Neither can Marian. Contrary to what so many critics have assumed, Shane and Marian are not potential lovers; but they are bound by their mutual passion for Joe as the embodiment of what they are not.

I realize that linking Marian and Shane as castrated subjects must seem counterintuitive and perverse to some readers. Obviously, the term "castrated" is harsh; but I only refer to the fact that as self-conscious desiring subjects, Shane and Marian can never be self-identical and, to that extent, complete in the way that Joe is. Unlike Shane at the beginning and ending of the movie, Joe doesn't wear a six-gun; but he is the symbolic phallus. The phallus in this context refers to the power of a social identity that contains and defines all social desire without allowing for any remainder or excess. The phallic man takes his identity for granted as the natural way of things and assumes that the dominant patriarchal narrative defines his life and its goals as it defines the life and goals of those around him. Still, Joe is not without knowledge of Marian's desire. As he prepares to face Ryker at the movie's climax, he tells Marian that he knows she will be taken care of if he is killed, better than he could himself, even though he has always known he could trust his wife under any circumstance. Structurally, Joe can never admit to the reality of desire. He merely takes it for granted that Shane can and will take his place in the nuclear family, that he will become the man he desires to be (thus putting an end to desire) and take on the function and the name of the father. As a man with only a first name, Shane has no patronymic signifier; and to that extent, he becomes the signifier of a desire for something that has no name. Shane's relation to Joe as the symbolic father is one of passionate ambivalence. Shane can never be Joe or successfully assume the function of the father or bear the name of the father without ceding his own desire, something he will never do. Joe himself has no desire – or rather has ceded his desire to the dominant patriarchal narrative, the "dominant fiction" (Silverman 1992: 30).

Shane and Marian both express ambivalence toward the symbolic phallus, though the spectator must look beyond the dialogue to realize this. Shane's most explicit phallic signifier is his gun. Critics frequently quote Shane's clichéd remark to Marian that "a gun is a tool, as good or bad as the man using it." When he utters these words, Shane looks self-complacent and a little pompous, but Marian retorts without hesitation that she would like to see every gun out of the valley. When she says this, Shane's complacency is punctured and his face expresses uncertainty and self-doubt, something you would never see in the face of John Wayne, at least not on this issue; but this hardly surprises the spectator who must have noticed Shane's ambivalence toward his weapon throughout the film. In fact, his attitude toward the gun matches his attitude toward Joe, Marian, and the family. He is proud of it and, at the same time, alienated from it. Shane's alienated relation to the family is also made explicit from the moment he contemplates entering their world. The morning after Shane's arrival Joey stumbles into the barn while playing, and encounters Shane. Then he blurts out that his father wants Shane to work for him but not to fight his battles. After the boy leaves, the worried expression on Shane's face conveys both his ambivalence about and attraction to the family. Director George Stevens never shows the moment when Joe formally asks Shane to work for him. Instead, the movie cuts from the worried expression on Shane's face in the barn to a scene that takes place after he has already accepted Joe's job offer. This scene is carefully composed to articulate Shane's new status as someone both inside and outside the family. In a set of shots, the camera is first positioned inside the parents' room and then inside the boy's room so that we see Shane framed by the doorways that constitute a threshold he may not cross. He is in the cabin but excluded from its more intimate space.

The sequence in which Marian watches Shane standing in the rain outside of Joey's bedroom window is one of the few in which we see family members from Shane's viewpoint. The shot/reverse shot structure suggests Shane and Marian's mutual identification with one another. Marian stands at the threshold between a feminine domestic space and the masculine violence of the outside world, but she cannot cross the threshold in order to bring Shane into her world anymore than Shane can cross over into the intimate space of the family. In response to Shane's vague reference to his own past, she says, "I think we know, (*pause*) Shane." The collective pronoun cannot refer to Marian and Joey; and though Joe cannot be utterly naïve about Shane's probable history, he doesn't appreciate, in the way Marian does, the contradictory nature of Shane's desire. Marian's long pause before she utters the name "Shane" signifies her implicit (though not necessarily conscious) understanding of what the name means: the absent patronymic of the subject without a history – that is to say, without a history to which he can admit and from which he can derive the pleasure of being a subject. The collective pronoun in the phrase "I think we know" ultimately refers to Shane and Marian. They know the truth that would fill the long pause before the utterance of Shane's name. That truth is the desire for desire.

As I suggested earlier, the phallus symbolizes a social identity whose power defines and regulates human desire. In *Shane*, the gun signifies masculine authority based on the use of force. Because Joe has a fully constituted patriarchal identity, he doesn't need a gun because his consciousness is not split and requires no symbolic representation in order to articulate itself. Joe's negative counterpart in the movie is not Shane but Ryker. The latter must carry a gun and hires additional gunmen because his authority has been threatened by Joe and the communal social structure Joe represents. Shane's relation to the gun is conflicted. When he first rides into the valley, there is a contrast in his physical appearance between the plain buckskins and the rather ornamental gun and flamboyant gunbelt. It is as if Shane needs to disavow his own problematic relation to the phallus and thus to masculine social identity. In the fight with Joe before the final showdown, Shane uses the gun to knock his opponent out when he is overpowered by Joe's greater strength. Finally, after the gunfight with the Ryker brothers and Wilson, Shane tells Joey that he has to leave the valley (and, by implication, the family and the social identities that the family encodes) because there is no going back on a killing. In effect, by using the gun, he has cut himself off from the object of his desire and made himself incomplete in relation to the history he has tried to assimilate. Yet Shane's personal failure is a sort of victory; for while he has lost the immediate object of desire, which would be a place in the family and in the history of the family, he continues to pursue or has already achieved the aim of his desire, a meaningful death.

Why Shane Wears a Blue Collar

Shane is symbolically castrated because he is conscious of the split between desire and demand, between the unnamable object of desire that is always out of reach and the immediate and fantastic goal of demand (McGee 1999: paras. 15–17). In a sense, both Ryker and Joe articulate a demand that is rooted in social fantasy. Both are proponents and defenders of private property as the basis of social relationships, though Joe is clearly the more flexible of the two because he doesn't think of private property as an end in itself but as the means to an end, as the condition of the nuclear family and the basis of community relationships. Joe spells out the difference between Ryker and himself at Tory's funeral: "he only wants to grow his beef and what we want to grow up is families." The family as a natural unit that regulates social desire, however, is itself a fantasy. It is not a fantasy as a social arrangement with pragmatic and emotional values, including erotic ones; but it takes on the structure of fantasy when it is imagined as the natural object and limit of all desire. In the final fight between Joe and Shane, it is the latter's task to challenge Joe's fantasy with force – to bring him to the realization that his social identity as a man and a father is limited. The horses and other farm animals go wild and kick against their pens and corrals because Shane is subverting the "natural" authority of the nuclear family.

Shane identifies with Joe Starrett and his family to such an extent that he puts on the symbolic blue collar and becomes, at least in appearance, a working-class subject, perhaps more than Joe is. It is not that Shane works for wages while Joe owns his property and works for himself, though these are expressions of a social difference. The key distinction is a difference in consciousness, a difference between Shane's alienation from and Joe's identification with the property system. Shane's critique of the property system is expressed by his actions, and it takes the conscious form of his understanding that the conflict between Ryker and the community of homesteaders led by Joe is not based on a disagreement over boundaries or the best method of raising cattle. It is based on the distribution of power and the use of force. For Joe, private property is a natural institution based on human reason; and he imagines that conflicts over property can be resolved through rational discourse that is itself a reflection of human nature. As he says to Ryker's men when they summon him to the final showdown, "I always figured on being reasonable." For Ryker, power and force determine ownership; and though he would prefer to get his way through persuasive words, he does not hesitate to resort to violence as the ultimate basis of social power.

After the homesteaders' Fourth of July celebration, Ryker confronts Joe at his place with a different history and a different understanding of property from the one that Joe has been promoting. Ryker claims that he and men like him "made this country, we found it and we made it. Work, blood, and empty bellies." To Joe's claim that the homesteaders have been in the right all along, Ryker responds by referring to "the men that did the work and ran the risks" by destroying the Indians and the rustlers. Joe responds that other men came to the West before Ryker and did more to tame the country than he did. Historically, Joe is right, though he shows no sympathy for the Native Americans who occupied and used the land before any of these so-called Westerners appeared on the scene. Even more than Ryker does, Joe assumes that the conquest of the West was a form of natural progress. According to Limerick, most Americans still support the view that Joe articulates: "Like the settlers themselves, we steadfastly believe in the social fiction that lines on a map and signatures on a deed legitimately divide the earth" (1987: 56). But Ryker has no intention of accepting such a legal fiction as the true basis of ownership.

Shane embodies the critique of private property and the class system in another sense. When Shane puts on a blue collar to work for Joe Starrett, it is a matter of free choice. Despite the fact that the Western is identified with conservative ideologies of self-making and individualism, this genre rarely supports the ideology of the work ethic (Cawelti 1999: 44, 53). On the contrary, the key to Western figures like Shane is their refusal of work in the ordinary sense of the word – their refusal of wage slavery that would mean the surrender of autonomy in the performance of any creative or transformative activity. Shane and many other Western heroes resemble the figure of the flâneur as it was described by Walter Benjamin in *The Arcades Project*. Though Benjamin's flâneur is the Baudelairean product of urban space and commodity culture, such a figure fits right into the character of the Western drifter for whom the vast expanses of the West constitute a marketplace. For Benjamin, the flâneur expresses contradiction by empathizing with "the soul of the commodity" and presenting himself to the marketplace not as a buyer but as merchandise, even though he controls his comings and goings in relation to buyers (1999: 42, 369). Upon his first appearance in the film, Shane conveys a knowledge of his own commodity status; and yet, at the same time, he implicitly protests that his price is beyond the governance of the marketplace, beyond the determination of value through comparison with any other commodity. He is a man for sale and in quest of a buyer, though he will never surrender his autonomy to the market and must make the deal on his own terms (10). He materializes the ultimate effect of commodity fetishism through which we imagine that if any commodity could speak it would say, "Buy me! For at any price I'm a bargain since I am unique and beyond value." Still, the significance of the Western flâneur's drifting, which also explains the attraction of the Great Plains as a mythological space in American history, lies in his "unconscious protest against the tempo of the production process" (338).

At the time of its emergence in the nineteenth century as a critical element of the American myth, the figure of the Great Plains signified an alternative to the wage slavery and industrialization of the East. The Western drifter supposedly treasured his idleness and purposeless existence, because, as Benjamin stresses, "The idleness of the flâneur is a demonstration against the division of labor" (427). When Ryker offers Shane a job, he turns it down without a moment's hesitation because, though he seeks the knowledge of his worth, he never accepts that value as his true measure and gives his labor only to the force in society that doesn't threaten his autonomy. When Shane works for Joe, he never plays the role of a subordinate; and at critical moments he takes Joe's place as head of the family and leader of the community. Nonetheless, Shane's natural state is that of creative idleness, of the refusal to work. His image perfectly illustrates what Benjamin calls the "dialectic of flânerie": "on one side, the man who feels himself viewed by all and sundry as a true suspect and, on the other side, the man who is utterly undiscoverable, the hidden man" (420).

Though Shane does not have the wealth of someone like Ryker, he emulates the autonomy and freedom that derives from wealth. His existence is a protest not only against the division of labor that constitutes the class system but against the distribution of wealth that is justified by the argument that those who have wealth have earned it through work. Shane knows implicitly that the basis of Ryker's wealth is not the work he did with other men to clear and tame the wild West but the physical force and political power that enabled him to take the land away from Indians and to defeat

ILLUSTRATION 3 Community in the foreground, power in the background. *Shane* (1953). Paramount Pictures. *Producer and director:* George Stevens

rustling and other forms of class antagonism with a freedom that went beyond any ethical principle of right. Though Shane has rejected the accumulation of wealth as the purpose of life, he has appropriated the condition of wealth through his mastery of the gun. Just as Shane's lifestyle both protests against and mimics that of men like Ryker, his potential violence threatens the class system with possible subversion by the very force that the system itself has created.

As the spokesman for the community, Joe wants to believe that it is law that determines entitlement and not the use of force. Yet the visual composition of the Tory funeral sequence suggests a contradiction between the practices of community and the exercise of power. In the establishing shot, the mourners in the graveyard are formed in a circle in the foreground, while the town in the background belongs to Ryker (Ill. 3); and that includes everything that the town represents to the homesteaders: commodities that enable them to work while providing physical comfort and social pleasure. The values of community and the values of power seem to be mutually exclusive.

Why Shane's Gun Sounds Like an Atom Bomb

Even before the funeral, Joe has been contaminated by Shane's presence just as Shane has been seduced by the fantasy of the nuclear family. The critical turning point for Joe is the fight with Ryker's men in Grafton's saloon after Shane has defeated Chris. In their victory, Shane and Joe have cemented their homosocial bond, but they have also betrayed their ethical identities. Shane has unleashed the destructive power that he apparently wanted to keep under control, while Joe has relied on force rather than reason to solve a problem. Even Marian has betrayed her principles of nonviolence when, after dressing the men's wounds, she says they were both wonderful. Another person has been transformed by the fight in the saloon: the cowboy Chris.

The most homoerotic moment in Schaefer's novel comes after Shane defeats Chris and is overcome by sadness: "He bent and scooped the sprawling figure up in his arms and carried it to one of the other tables. Gently he set it down, the legs falling limp over the edge." He gets a rag from the bar and "tenderly cleared the blood from the face" (1975: 61–2). In the movie, Shane performs none of these actions; yet Chris's transformation is critical to understanding Shane's identity. There are several medium shots of Chris sitting on the porch of the saloon during the Tory funeral sequence; and the expression on his face, especially in contrast with the boastful arrogance of Ryker's other men and Wilson's sadistic leer, suggests that his world has been turned upside down. Chris has become an alienated figure like Shane. This means that he no longer knows who he is or what the object of his desire is. Before his encounter with Shane, Chris was presumably confident in his masculine identity and had subordinated his desire to the social values of Ryker. He accepted without question the fantasy of power as an end in itself and, more specifically, Ryker's belief in his own physical force as the moral justification of his right to superfluous wealth. Chris associated the willingness to use physical force with masculinity and the right to private property. After he suffers defeat, he has no choice but to rethink his social identity. When Chris rides out to the Starrett place in order to warn Shane of Ryker's treacherous intention toward Joe, he can only explain his turnaround with the phrase, "I reckon somethin's come over me." Ironically, in this scenario, the spectator gets a glimpse of what Shane's own history must have been. While it seems unlikely that Shane ever led a life similar to that of Joe Starrett, he may have been a man like Chris, a gunman for hire to someone like Ryker, a servant to power and property. Something brought about a change, and more than likely it was an act of violence that disrupted Shane's perception of himself and the world.

The image of violence as socially transformative is not unique to the Western. Historically, as Richard Slotkin notes, violence has played a significant role in the US national ideology, particularly through the Myth of the Frontier:

> In each stage of its development, the Myth of the Frontier relates the achievement of "progress" to a particular form or scenario of violent action. "Progress" itself was defined in different ways: the Puritan colonists emphasized the achievement of spiritual regeneration through frontier adventure; Jeffersonians (and later, the disciples of Turner's "Frontier Thesis") saw the frontier settlement as a re-enactment and democratic renewal of the original "social contract"; while Jacksonian Americans saw the conquest of the Frontier as a means to the regeneration of personal fortunes and/or of patriotic vigor and virtue. But in each case, the Myth represented the redemption of American spirit or fortune as something to be achieved by playing through a scenario of separation, temporary regression to a more primitive or "natural" state, and *regeneration through violence*. (1992: 11–12)

In another context, Slotkin notes that "while the rhetoric we will be studying [that of the Frontier Thesis] is brimful of proposals for genocide and wars of extermination, there is in fact nothing exceptional about our history of violence." Just as our economic history belongs to "the larger patterns of western capitalism," our history of violence can be assimilated to "the general system of European expansion" (1985: 61). I would push this logic one step further, though this step is already implicit in many of Slotkin's readings of twentieth-century Western movies. If violence is the figure of social regeneration in American ideology and myth, it is also the figure of social resistance in the counternarratives of that myth.

In part, such a figure of revolt responds to the facts of social history. However effective the ideology and myths of the nation may be in governing the majority of the people through consensus, these hegemonic narratives are ultimately backed up by force. In the history of the United States, Native Americans, African Americans, women, gay people, the working class and other so-called minorities have learned that their efforts to transform their social and economic situations are usually met with violence and are perceived as violent. The classic example of violent resistance, as Slotkin demonstrates, is that of Native Americans. It can hardly be surprising that the original inhabitants of the North American continent would respond with violence to their conquest by the white settlers who claimed the "New World" as their own. Yet it is remarkable to what extent the concept of Indian or "savage" war came to dominate representations of class struggle, racial conflict, and gender divisions in this country. The evidence for this lies in all three volumes of Slotkin's masterful work on the Myth of the Frontier (1973, 1985, 1992). Though the Civil Rights Movement was remarkably nonviolent by comparison with other revolutions and revolts, it was nonetheless perceived by the supporters of the status quo and racial segregation as violent in its threat to social order. Typically, the violence of the state and the community against nonviolent or minimally violent protest is blamed on the victims. From the suffragettes and union organizers of the early twentieth century to the African-American, Gay Liberation, and antiglobalization protesters of more recent times, the victims of social oppression who challenge their oppressors are usually subjected to and identified with violence.

At the end of *Shane*, the violence unleashed in Shane has transformed everyone it touches. Chris leaves Ryker and becomes a wandering loner like Shane. Ryker, his brother, and Wilson are dead because the social order they embody has lived too long. Joe has been changed by his fight with Shane, though the spectator never sees the result of that transformation. The last image of Joe in the film is that of a defeated man reduced to almost infantile dependency on the woman who supports him. To some extent, this manifests Joe's necessary feminization, or rather the feminization of the patriarchal values that have guided him in his conflict with Ryker. Joe has put property and masculine identity above his concrete social ties. It is not only that he mistakenly thinks he can challenge Ryker's force or naively assumes that Shane can take his place in the family. Rather, he is willing to sacrifice his life for property as an abstraction and implicitly makes the family as a set of concrete social relationships into an abstraction of itself, into the nuclear family as an idealized model of natural social organization. When Marian tries to persuade him not to face Ryker because she's tired of "work, work, work," he says that "even if that was the truth, it wouldn't change things." As Countryman and von Heussen-Countryman have noted, this negation of his wife's labor and desire is "chilling" (1999: 64). Joe thinks he can transfer his family as property to Shane, but Shane knows that his own violence and alienated desire make that impossible. It has been noted before that the Starretts constitute a holy family as the names of the parents indicate: Joe for Joseph, Marian for Mary. Little Joey is not exactly Jesus; but at the end of the movie he could be said to have two fathers, one for this world and another for the world that lies in or beyond death.

In the long ride to town with its triumphal music, Shane has been transformed into a godlike figure; and little Joey has never been more in awe of his power. In this sequence, more than any other since the opening shots of the film, the spectator sees Shane from Joey's viewpoint. Even in the mobile low-angle front shots of his ride into town, he appears to the spectator as he must appear to Joey's imagination. These images (which will later inspire Clint Eastwood) transform Shane into the embodiment of a law that transcends human institutions and into the violent instrument of divine providence. The destruction he visits on Ryker and his men is performed with surgical skill; and were it not for the implication that Shane has been shot himself, perhaps fatally, there would be little in these scenes to suggest that he is a mortal human being (Ill. 4). In this context, Joey functions as the allegorical embodiment of a generation of young boys who have been imprinted with this phantasmic idealization of masculine identity and violence.

Though the idealization of masculinity that Shane signifies is pervasive, it is nonetheless ambivalent. As I have tried to suggest throughout this analysis, it is the manifestation of a contradiction. Shane can be read as the ultimate Cold Warrior who is the final line of defense against communism, with the Ryker brothers representing the communist totalitarians and their range war the authoritarian state's threat to hard-working entrepreneurs who believe in private property (see Corkin 2004: 127–63). This reading is certainly possible and may be close to the "dominant fiction" of post-World-

ILLUSTRATION 4 Immortal mortality. *Shane* (1953). Paramount Pictures. *Producer and director:* George Stevens

War-II America. When Shane or anyone else fires a gun in this movie, it sounds like the roar of a nuclear blast; and nuclear tests were among the signature events of the fifties. Shane may be the embodiment of the theory of nuclear deterrence; but if he is, he also signifies US society's fear of its own defense and of the men who transformed themselves into the agents of state violence. In the end, he cannot be part of the world he has made possible through his violence. The men like Joe who remain behind as the real fathers of a generation of Joeys must undergo a process of feminization by embracing the values that historically have been associated with women: peaceful coexistence in the community and domestic harmony in the family. Still, such a message cannot interpellate every constituent of mass culture without interference from different class positions and identities. Class itself is the structural violence of the capitalist social system that Shane cannot transcend, even in death. At once, it makes his coming back impossible and inevitable.

CHAPTER 2

THE POLITICAL ORIGIN OF THE WESTERN

Owen Wister Went West

Since Owen Wister's *The Virginian* is usually considered to be the first serious Western fiction, it can hardly be surprising that the historical events that lay behind it have played a role in the Western movie tradition. In this 1902 novel, the homesteaders are consistently called "rustlers" and "thieves"; and every reference to the Johnson County War of 1892 is couched in terms that justify the use of force by the corporate cattlemen. The so-called "thieves" are blamed for the ultimate collapse of the open-range cattle industry, since they "prevailed at length, . . . forcing the cattle owners to leave the country or be ruined." According to the narrator, the "cattle war" resulted from the thieves' "putting their men in office, and coming to own some of the newspapers," though ultimately the war brought ruin on the thieves since "in a broken country there is nothing left to steal" (Wister 1998: 327). Another novel published the same year as *The Virginian*, Frances McElrath's *The Rustler* (2002), offered a more "liberal" view of the same events (Lamont 2003), though one that also legitimated wealth over any force that would oppose it. Wister's representation won the day and became a blueprint for the ideologies that would emerge in the Hollywood Western.

The climax of the novel is the lynching of the Virginian's friend Steve for horse stealing and cattle rustling. In the movies, one accepts such an event as the expression of a mythical frontier justice; but *The Virginian* argues for vigilantism without appealing to myth. After Steve's hanging, his friend defends himself through reference to actual history, though history as seen from the viewpoint of corporate cattlemen: Steve "knew well enough the only thing that would have let him off would have been a regular jury. For the thieves have got hold of the juries in Johnson County" (1998: 268–9). Later Judge Henry, the Virginian's boss and future partner, justifies the practice of Western lynching when Molly Wood, the Virginian's fiancée, compares it to the lynching of black people in the South. In a rather twisted appeal to democratic theory, the Judge insists that ordinary citizens

> are where the law comes from, you see. For they chose the delegates who made the Constitution that provided for the courts . . . So you see, at best, when they lynch they only take back what they once gave. Now we'll take your two cases that you say are the same in principle. I think that they are not. For in the South they take a negro from jail where he was waiting to be duly hung. The South has never claimed that the law would let him go. But in Wyoming the law has been letting our cattle-thieves go for two years . . . The courts, or rather the juries, into whose hands we have put the law, are not dealing the law. (284)

The Judge assumes that, *as a rule*, the black people who are lynched in the South have had their due process and were found guilty, while ironically in Johnson County democracy has been violated because the citizens have elected to office those who represent their viewpoint. The situation can only be redeemed when an elite group of corporate cattlemen send out their hired gunmen to lynch the so-called rustlers without a trial. But then Wister's idea of democracy presupposes that "All America is divided into two classes, – the quality and the equality," since "through the Declaration of Independence . . . we Americans acknowledged the *eternal inequality* of man." The real meaning of the Declaration was that "every man should thenceforth have equal liberty to find his own level," which gives rise to "true aristocracy": "Let the best man win! That is America's word. That is true democracy. And true democracy and true aristocracy are one and the same thing" (101). In practice, if we follow the example of *The Virginian*, the true aristocracy of a true democracy is the agency of those who rule by force. Such a true democracy is what a later generation would call fascism.

Judge Henry stresses to Molly that lynch law is only a stopgap until "civilization can reach us" (284). As Slotkin notes, "Wister distinguishes 'civilization' from 'government' by arguing that certain forms of democracy produce a degenerate form of politics: one in which mongrels and failures, the 'equality,' are enabled to assert against the 'quality' their claims for power and a redistribution of wealth" (1992: 181). Still, Wyoming in 1892 was not a frontier wilderness; and the corporate cattlemen of the Wyoming Stock-Growers' Association (WSGA) were not pioneers but representatives of eastern and European capital. Though the Judge disavows any comparison between the southern lynching of black people and the lynching of so-called rustlers in Wyoming, he also draws attention to their obvious connection. Why would Wister choose a lynching as the central event in his novel? At the time it would have been impossible to produce such a representation that did not have a racial connotation.

Slotkin has discussed the history of American cultural discourse in which the figure of "savage war" or "race war" has been applied repeatedly to social conflicts that arise out of the contradictions in the social system, with the effect of displacing democratic traditions "from a frame in which progress and right order are presumed to emerge from the widest imaginable diffusion of property and political power to one in which progress depends on the exclusion/ extermination of a congenitally regressive type of humanity and on the aggrandizement of a privileged race or people" (1992: 21). Thomas Jefferson imagined that class conflict in this country could be avoided through the exploitation of a boundless frontier by a nation of yeoman farmers who would themselves be the arch-defenders of property and the class system. Yet he also subscribed to a theory of racial inequality concerning black slaves and Indians and presumed that any conflict between unequal races would lead to a war of extermination (Slotkin 1985: 73–6). For this reason, he hoped to avoid such wars through, in Slotkin's words, "an enlight-ened program of teaching the Indians Christianity and agronomy" (70). Though he criticized the moral influence of slavery on the slaveowners, he regarded wars against the Indians as necessary and dreaded the emancipation of black slaves for fear it would, in his own words, "produce convulsions which will probably never end but in the extermination of the one or the other race" (Jefferson 1984: 264; see also 264–70, 288–9). Throughout *The Fatal Environment*, Slotkin (1985) has documented in disturbing detail the American use of the figure of race war in the nineteenth century as the justification of direct social domination of one party or social class by another through force. During the era of the Johnson County War, most of the victims of the WSGA were shot in the back; but lynching makes a better metaphor for frontier justice because of its link with violence against black people. Lynching racializes the victim; and the conditions of a race war suspend the normal requirements of civilization, including justice in a court of law.

Owen Wister traveled to Wyoming in the summer of 1885 upon the recommendation of a specialist in nervous disorders, the notorious Dr. S. Wier Mitchell, whose "rest cure" Charlotte Perkins Gilman imaginatively documented in "The Yellow Wallpaper." As Jane Kuenz observes, unlike his prescription for maladjusted women, Dr. Mitchell sent the young Wister, who wanted to study music instead of finishing law school, out west to experience manly physical exertion and freedom (2001: 110). He stayed first at the ranch of Major Frank Wolcott, one of the leaders of the 1892 invasion (Shulman 1998: xv). Within a few months, Wister was acting as man-ager of the cattle company owned by his two former classmates at Harvard, Frederic O. de Billier and Hubert E. Teschemacher, both of whom participated in the invasion (White 1968: 126–8; Smith 1966: 185–7). He returned to Wyoming in the summers of 1887, 1888, and 1891, before the invasion, associating exclusively with the members of the Cheyenne Club, the organizational center of the WSGA (Wister 1998: xxxv). As Slotkin stresses, he enjoyed prac-ticing a "democracy of style" with men who "had proved them-selves fit in what Wister (like [Theodore] Roosevelt) saw as the Darwinian competition of western life" (1992: 170).

On October 12, 1889, he rode in the smoking car of a train with one of the men who had been accused of lynching Jim Averell and

Ella Watson on the Sweetwater River (and these are the names that Michael Cimino later appropriated for his central characters in *Heaven's Gate*). Helena Smith calls that hanging "probably the most revolting crime in the entire annals of the West" (1966: 121); but Wister had only this to say in his diary: "He seemed a good solid citizen, and I hope he'll get off. Sheriff Donell said, 'All the good folks say it was a good job; it's only the wayward classes that complain'" (Wister 1958: 91). After the lynching, one of the lynch party, Albert J. Bothwell, got what he apparently wanted when he took possession of the two victims' property (Smith 1966: 134). Though Watson may have taken stolen cattle in return for sexual favors, the evidence suggests that she was murdered for her land (Hufsmith 1993; Meschter 1996: 23–33). According to Helena Smith, only "the flimsiest sort of hearsay" links Averell to cattle-stealing, but "substantial testimony" indicates his opposition to the corporate cattlemen over land affairs (1966: 121). She quotes the editor of the Casper *Weekly Mail* to the effect that Averell "favored the settling up of the Sweetwater with small ranches and the making of homes for hundreds of families, instead of having it owned or controlled by one or two" (132). According to a contemporary source, Averell, a surveyor, determined that Bothwell was holding some land illegally and contested it in court, which decided in his favor (Flagg 1969: 31). On April 7, 1889, three months before his hanging, Averell wrote a letter to the Casper *Mail*, which contained words (emphasized below) that Michael Cimino later incorporated into his screenplay for *Heaven's Gate*. Averell distinguished between "the settlers who have come here to live and make Wyoming their homes and the land grabber who is only camped here as speculator in land under the desert land act." The latter, he concluded, opposes anything *"that would settle and improve the country or make it anything but a cow pasture for eastern speculators"* (quoted in Meschter 1996: 103, emphasis added). According to Smith, Averell's letter was "well-written . . . too well-written" (1966: 132); and he has sometimes been described as a graduate of Yale, Cornell, or Oxford (Kittrell 1954: xxxvii), though there is no convincing evidence of that (Meschter 1996: x, 5–23). This is the flimsy basis of Cimino's recreation of Averell as Jim Averill, a wealthy easterner, with a southern accent, who graduated from Harvard. In *The Virginian*, Wister refers to the hanging of Cattle Kate lightheartedly in the context of a joke (1998: 13).

When I read *The Virginian* as a boy, I found it almost repulsive, though I did not have the historical knowledge or critical consciousness that would have allowed me to recognize its ideology. One explanation of my response can be seen in Don Ranvaud's comments on *The Virginian* in the *BFI Companion to the Western*: "Wister's story . . . is a radical break with the 'codes of the West', a transgression of Western mythology" (Buscombe 1988: 308). How can Wister's novel transgress the code and myth it supposedly founded? The answer might be that by the fifties Western movies and many of the fictions they were based on had so transformed the "code of the West" that Wister's novel read like a violation of its own rule. The same can be said of the 1946 film version with Joel McCrea, which came out four years after the release of William Wellman's *The Ox-Bow Incident*, the classic Hollywood condemnation of Western lynch law. Earlier versions of *The Virginian*, like the 1929 film with Gary Cooper, may have made more sense in their context. The earliest version, Cecil B. DeMille's 1914 film, remained very close to the stage play that Wister co-authored with Kirk La Shelle a year or so after publishing the novel. As Richard Hutson notes, "DeMille's early-career conservatism would roughly coincide with Wister's; consequently, this first screen version of Wister's story captured . . . something of Wister's own sense of the meaning of the actions of the novel" (2003: 133). The play had already made the connection between the lynching of Steve and the Johnson County War more explicit than the novel had by referring to a list of suspected cattle thieves whom the cattlemen intend to lynch (Wister and La Shelle 1958: 31–2, 50–4). Certainly, if *The Virginian* violated my childhood understanding of the Western code, it was because that code had been based on the classic Westerns from 1939 to the early sixties. These were movies in which men of property or their representatives were mostly scoundrels, tyrants, or cowards; and the Western hero was a man – and occasionally a woman – who challenged the authority of wealth rather than executing its will.

The West Went to Hollywood

Still, though this study will argue for the negative influence of *The Virginian* on the classic and postmodern Western, that relationship is not one of simple cause and effect; and the recent scholarship on early Hollywood and the emergence of the Western clarifies the context in which Wister's tale can be seen as one of several possibilities for the film genre. Almost simultaneous with the publication of *The Virginian*, the earliest cinematic Westerns, such as the Edison Company's *The Great Train Robbery* (1903), were actually considered to be crime films. The word "Western" emerged as a genre term between 1907 and 1911 (Neale 2000: 43–6). A related genre, the "labor-capital" film, had emerged by 1910; and before World War I, the majority of these films were pro-labor rather than conservative (Ross 1998: 56–7, 116, 213). In 1912, David Horsely, who owned the Nestor Motion Picture Company, and Frank V. Tousey, who was a dime-fiction publisher, formed an alliance "to produce stories that would be featured simultaneously on nickelodeon screens and in the publisher's leading national dime-fiction western newspaper, the *Wild West Weekly*" (Smith 2003: 108). As Michael Denning has shown, the nineteenth-century dime novels portraying Western heroes like Deadwood Dick and Jesse James were "less stories of the Wild West than stories of Labor and Capital"; and these had as much influence on the early Westerns as Wister's novel (1987: 163). Horsely wanted a cinema that would support working-class causes and later worked with the Brotherhood of Railway Trainmen to found the Motive Motion Picture Company, which would make pro-labor films. His earlier project with Tousey nonetheless failed (Smith 2003: 108).

Native American producer and director James Young Deer went west in 1911 as the head of West Coast productions for the French-owned Pathé company, but his positive portrayals of Native Americans in the movies were short-lived (Smith 2003: 71–103). When Thomas H. Ince began to make movies in the Santa Monica mountains of Los Angeles for the New York Motion Picture Company after 1911, he used Westerns "to serve American nationalism" and "distanced the genre from dime novels and other cheap amusements" (106, 125). By 1912, Gilbert M. Anderson, who had formed Essanay with George K. Spoor, had abandoned stories with Indians and Mexicans as central protagonists in response to the criticism of journalists and exhibitors (38–41, 58–9). Though Anderson's early Westerns had appealed to predominantly working-class audiences by featuring Western bad-men characters in the tradition of the dime novels, after the establishment of the National Board of Censorship by the Edison Trust manufacturers in 1909, he conformed to more middle-class standards and "domesticated the western outlaw" through the creation of Broncho Billy, in collaboration with Western writer Peter B. Kyne (139–41, 144). In these films, Broncho Billy was never wealthy nor ever owned significant property, but he was also never allowed to appear transparently working-class or "to reflect a working-class ideology" (149).

D. W. Griffith and William S. Hart both sympathized with the situation of blue-collar labor, though they failed to carry that critical consciousness across the racial divide. Because of Griffith's own near-poverty for many years, he felt, in the words of Lillian Gish, "deeply sympathetic to the sufferings of the poor, to the injustices inflicted upon them" (Ross 1998: 37–8). Nonetheless, as a director of Westerns, Griffith's early films, from *In Old California* (1910) to *The Battle of Elderbush Gulch* (1913), anticipate his racist masterpiece *The Birth of a Nation* (1915), which is itself a type of Western and perhaps the most appropriate companion piece to Wister's *The Virginian*. In both works, the turning point involves the lynching, respectively, of a rustler and a black man accused of rape – one act leading to the Virginian's final showdown with Trampas in Wister's novel and the other to an overt race war between the Ku Klux Klan and the community of former slaves under the influence of carpet-baggers in Griffith's film. Furthermore, the romantic subplots of both films involve the vindication in a northern woman's eyes of a white southerner's commitment to a form of social justice that transcends written law. Admittedly, the near-rape of Lillian Gish's character by a black politician is a more dramatic vindication than Molly's final submission to the Virginian's masculine charm, but these plots lay the groundwork for a kind of Western story and hero that would be dominant in A features until 1939 and would even survive after that, though in ways that were problematic and contradictory.

In his Westerns, William S. Hart followed Anderson in featuring "western bad-men characters to exploit such figures' popularity with working-class audiences" (Smith 2003: 137; see Ross 1998: 131). Like Anderson, he also wanted to reach "a large cross-section of the moviegoing public, particularly middle-class patrons." Hart's writers drew on earlier Westerns and stage plays, including *The Virginian*, but "modified them to reflect the dominant notions of Anglo-Saxon manhood and Progressive-era moral reform" (Smith 2003: 157–8). The contradiction in Hart's films lay between the commitment of his bandit characters to the greater social good, on the one hand, and their transcendence of the law for which their careers as outlaws has prepared them, on the other. In *The Toll Gate* (1920), Hart clearly suggests that the outlawry of his character Black Deering represents the misguided application of his moral transcendence as a white man. At the beginning of the film, Deering tries to persuade his gang that it's time to stop working as outlaws unless they want to get hanged. However, the gang is persuaded to rob one last train by Tom Jordan, who betrays them to the authorities. The US cavalrymen who apprehend Deering allow him to escape when they realize that he is the same man who once warned them of an imminent Indian attack and thus saved the lives of women and children. Deering hunts down Jordan, who has become the leader of a gang of Mexicans. After burning down Jordan's saloon, which the local sheriff describes as an act that might have done the town a favor, Deering is chased by both the sheriff's posse and Jordan's gang. When he loses his horse, he runs on foot until he sees a child drowning in a spring and saves him. The child and his mother live alone, and Deering takes the place of the father who mysteriously disappeared a year earlier. In this *Shane*-like sequence, Deering's true nature is brought out by the woman and the child. At one point, after Deering realizes that the missing husband is none other than Jordan, he contemplates raping the mother in revenge; but her innocent trust and confidence in his true nature dissuades him from such a heinous act. The duality of Deering's personality is conveyed by the black clothes and mask he wears whenever he engages in outlawry. In the titles, his masked image appears whenever his dark side is dominant. When he decides not to rape the mother, he seems to undergo a religious conversion (Ill. 5), and his masked image vanishes from the movie. Finally, he turns himself over to the sheriff, who comments, "They may call you Black Deering, but by God you're white." When Deering learns that the sheriff has to fight Jordan's gang in order to save his posse, he asks to join him in order "to die like a white man." Finally, he confronts Jordan and says that he will kill him for two reasons, one that Jordan knows and one he will never know (presumably his desertion of his wife

ILLUSTRATION 5 Black Deering's conversion. *The Toll Gate* (1920). William S. Hart Productions. *Producer:* William S. Hart. *Director:* Lambert Hillyer

and child). Once again, this violence is justified by Deering's transcendence of ordinary law, and in the end the sheriff lets him go free as long as he agrees to stay on the Mexican side of the border. When Deering gives up the woman as the "toll" he must pay for his crimes, the sheriff comments, "You can't tell how white a man is by the color of his coat."

After Hart's decline, the most popular Westerns were either national epics, like James Cruze's *The Covered Wagon* (1923) and John Ford's *The Iron Horse* (1924), or series Westerns. The silent epics celebrated rather than criticized the national identity, illustrating "Hollywood's interest in pageantry, patriotism, and the reputed glories of the Old West" (Etulain 2001: viii). The silent series Western, as Peter Stanfield argues, had an intended audience that valued "the exhibition of performance" (2002: 41). This kind of Western "sought to be inclusive in its cross-generation and -gender address," but by promoting "the performance of spectacle rather than narrative causality and psychological realism, it displayed a class-consciousness that marginalized its appeal to a middle-class audience" (45). The movies of Tom Mix, which owed a lot to the work of Anderson and Hart, reflected "a movement away from the moral fervor of Woodrow Wilson and toward the more relaxed, less reformist impulses of Warren G. Harding and Calvin Coolidge" (Etulain 2001: 16–17). In other words, such movies appealed to working-class audiences but did not convey to them any critical class-consciousness that could articulate social antagonisms rather than neutralize them.

After the success of Victor Fleming's talking version of *The Virginian* in 1929, Hollywood produced a series of epic Westerns with sound, including Raoul Walsh's attempt to make a star out of the unknown John Wayne in *The Big Trail* (1930). Wayne's character combines the frontier innocence of Natty Bumpo with the moral absolutism of the Virginian. As Scott Simmon points out, one of his lines is a quotation from Andrew Jackson: "One man with courage makes a majority" (2003: 135). Like Judge Henry and the Virginian, his character sets democracy aside in the interests of a transcendent law with which he identifies both in terms of his masculinity and his race. The failure of this and other 1930–1 Western epics derives, according to Stanfield, from their inability "to produce a credible romance intrigue" (2001: 24). Since these prestige Westerns were expensive to produce and made little money, and since the studios had already reduced their commitment to series Westerns, the Poverty Row studios and eventually Republic Pictures took over the production of series Westerns in the thirties (Stanfield 2002: 77–9).

Stanfield has argued effectively that, after the onset of the Depression, "series Westerns . . . addressed themselves to the issues of class struggle and division, and . . . this critically disparaged and apparently simplistic genre can in fact be approached as an important site at which audiences could contest the dominant interpretation given to the socio-economic transitions of capitalism" (2001: 78). Yet Stanfield fails to note the contradictory nature of the series Western that offered a popular defense of Franklin Roosevelt's New Deal – for example, when Gene Autry described himself as "a kind of New Deal Cowboy" (quoted, 90). As Giuliana Muscio stresses, the New Deal was fundamentally "a 'conservative' program," with the primary aim of neutralizing the social antagonisms that had erupted as a result of the Depression (1997: 3–5). It attempted to synthesize "two cultural and ideological positions that had previously been entirely separate within the history of American thought – populism and the 'frontier spirit.'" If the frontier spirit of rugged individualism represented the conservative side of the equation, populism, according to Muscio, was the subversive side, with its "deep-rooted advocacy for redistribution of power and wealth" and "its continuous challenge to capitalism," as recent historians have stressed (9). Though the cowboy heroes of the Republic Westerns engaged in the struggle to redistribute wealth in the spirit of populism, they were also frequently agents of the government or at least pursued goals consistent with the goals of the New Deal. They reconciled frontier individualism and populist social consciousness by transforming the cowboy into "the agent through which the banal, the mundane, the everyday are subject to 'magical' transformation" (Stanfield 2002: 139). Stanfield associates the socially "mediating role given to the cowboy" with the heroes of the dime novels (2001: 91, 110); but while there are parallels between series Western heroes and the heroes of dime novels, the more significant of the latter group, like Deadwood Dick and Jesse James, were, in their most interesting narratives, fighting the power of capital rather than trying to mediate and neutralize the contradictions of a democratic culture in which capitalism is dominant (Denning 1987: 159). Furthermore, not all series Westerns were critical of capitalism. For example, John Wayne in Republic's *Westward Ho* (1935) is a Virginian-like vigilante leader whose tough- ness and unscrupulous commitment to taking the law into his own hands anticipates Wayne's performance as Thomas Dunson in *Red River.*

Still, before 1939 the series Westerns were far more radical than the A-Westerns of the thirties. Gary Cooper's Wild Bill Hickok in Cecil B. DeMille's *The Plainsman* (1936) is a reincarnation of the Virginian with more firepower, less interest in eastern women, and a brutally racist view of Indians that the movie endorses. King Vidor's *The Texas Rangers* (1936) is a throwback to Broncho Billy in telling the story of some comical good–bad men who become entirely good in undertaking the defense of private property. Films like these would continue to be made throughout the history of the Western; but another kind of A-Western emerged in 1939 that incorporated some elements of the B-Western while redefining the influence of Wister's *Virginian.* In any case, the series Western did not articulate class struggle as a form of social antagonism generated by the capitalist system itself. Rather, by "freeing itself of linear historical logic" – whether this takes the form of fusing the past and the present, as in the Autry films, or of re-creating the past as a direct address to the present as in some of the early Republic films of John Wayne – "the B-Western can obsessively retell a disconnected two-era fable in which the nineteenth century resolves the economic and ethical problems of modern urban life" (Simmon 2003: 154). Overall, B-Westerns had the function of neutralizing the contradictions of capital, though not without exposing them first, which attracted writers associated with the Hollywood left (Buhle and Wagner 2002: 135–8) and African-American singer-actor Herb Jeffries, who starred in a group of serial Westerns aimed at black audiences (Leyda 2002).

Marx Goes West

As the recent scholarship on the pre-1939 Western suggests, the code of the West is conflicted and contradictory, which is precisely why it works so well as a form of mass culture. Robert Ray writes on a "certain tendency" in Hollywood movies to seek the formal reconciliation of contradictory mythologies while maintaining a clear "avoidance of choice" in political terms (1985: 25–69). The thematic conventions of Hollywood movies rest on "an industrywide consensus defining commercially acceptable filmmaking. This consensus's underlying premise dictated the conversion of all political, sociological, and economic dilemmas into personal melodramas." In particular, such movies raise and offer solutions to "problems associated with the troubling incompatibility of traditional American myths" (57). From this perspective, Ray invokes the movie *Shane* as "an ideal recapitulation of Classic Hollywood's thematic paradigm" and calls it "a 'screen memory' of Classic Hollywood" (70). For Freud, a screen memory is a recollection of childhood that seems meaningless on the surface but harbors within its figurative structure, which is the effect of condensation and displacement, a history that has been forgotten but the knowledge of which is both decisive and threatening to the ego (1964: 43–53). For Ray, *Shane* is a screen memory of the film history that precedes it; it makes visible "narrative structures that were fundamental to Classic Hollywood as a whole" (1985: 71). These narrative structures are so pervasive that one can describe many of the genre movies of Hollywood's classical era as "thinly camouflaged westerns" (75).

I do not disagree with these remarks as far as they go, but they do not fully address the forgotten history that underlies the Western movie. Ray restricts his concerns to the Hollywood tradition as if that tradition were self-contained and only refers to history negatively through its disavowal of any particular external reference. Certainly, the relation of mass-cultural movies to real history is negative and involves distantiation and disavowal, especially when it claims to be mere entertainment. However, where there is disavowal, there is also articulation; and a genuine screen memory harbors within itself signs of the history it has blocked from view. Though Hollywood's screen memories may tend toward the formulaic, as several scholars have argued (Cawelti 1976: 85; Schatz 1981: 36), the formula itself is contextualized differently in each individual work and interacts genealogically with the different social contexts to which it responds over time.

The criticism has often been made that the Western movie privileges the individual and individual action over society and social responsibility (Gibbons 1996). While I would not dismiss this view out of hand, I would stress that we do not live in a world in which it is possible or desirable to leave individuals or the concept of the individual out of the account. Within the capitalist cultural system, individuality can be and has been a material location for cultural resistance. Can anyone imagine that Karl Marx himself would have become a critic of the capitalist system if he had not decided initially to go it alone, to separate himself from the dominant system of values peculiar to his own class and social situation? No one turns against the dominant political economy and cultural system because they find an alternative form of collective existence, a real utopia somewhere beneath the surface of the earth, as some recent Hollywood films would suggest. Any transformation of social consciousness necessarily involves some turning inward and alienation from the socius as it currently exists. In a crucial section of the *Grundrisse*, Marx suggests that capitalism is a "moving contradiction" that undermines itself through the "free development of individualities." This results from "the general reduction of the necessary labour of society to a minimum, which then corresponds to the artistic, scientific etc. development of the individuals in the time set free, and with the means created, for all of them." Capitalist production aims at reducing the amount of necessary labor time (the amount of living labor required for the reproduction of labor capacity itself, the reproduction of the worker) and increasing surplus labor time (the living labor in excess of necessary labor for which the worker receives no payment). The latter produces surplus value and profit. In the attempt to reduce necessary labor time ever more, the capitalist must feed some of the surplus value derived from the production process back into that process as fixed capital or machinery. In theory, this reduction of necessary labor, through the increase of fixed capital, tends toward universal unemployment and the impoverization of the general population of capitalist society; but capitalism also needs consumers and an ever-expanding market for its goods. Over time, the survival of capitalism depends on the gradual transformation of surplus value into social capital and the creation of a situation in which "general social knowledge has become a *direct force of production*" (Marx 1973: 706). This transforms the relation of the worker to the production process itself:

> He steps to the side of the production process instead of being its chief actor. In this transformation, it is neither the direct human labour he himself performs nor the time during which he works, but rather the appropriation of his own general productive power, his understanding of nature and his mastery over it by virtue of his presence as a social body – it is, in a word, the development of the social individual which appears as the great foundation-stone of production and of wealth. (705)

At the risk of oversimplifying, I will summarize Marx's argument in this way. Capitalism starts from the assumption that every worker is an individual who owns nothing more than his own labor power and who must sell that labor power in order to survive. Eventually, through the process I have just described, the survival of capitalism depends on the invention of the social individual who is equal to more than the value of his labor power. The "general productive power" of the "social individual" is *not* the private property of the individual worker, which distinguishes it from "labor power" that can be exchanged by the worker for objectified or dead labor in the form of money that can be further exchanged for such use values as food, clothing, shelter, and so forth. The general productive power of the social individual belongs to the whole of society and cannot be measured in terms of necessary labor time. Capitalism can no longer survive through the reproduction of labor capacity in the form of the individual worker; it must reproduce and expand general knowledge as the primary force of social production. It must therefore expand culture and the free time necessary for cultural production. This guarantees not only the expansion of general knowledge but the production of the consumers of cultural goods, which are the dominant commodities in such a system. In others words, in the effort to reduce necessary labor time, capital creates more free or disposable time as the form of general wealth – the *common*, to use the term of Michael Hardt and Antonio Negri (2004: xv–xvi, 196–202). Free time makes possible the production of social desires and the expansion of material needs that give ground to what Marx called communism, "not a stable state which is to be established, an *ideal* to which reality will have to adjust itself," but rather "the *real* movement which abolishes the present state of things" (Marx and Engels 1947: 26). According to Negri, communism is "the negation of all measure, the affirmation of the most exasperated plurality – creativity" (1984: 33). Communism is the desire for free time, or rather for the time in which to practice freedom and to develop true individuality. Capital creates this antagonism out of itself and then attempts to constrain it – to transform free time into a kind of work. It does this through the modern culture industry, which aims to transform free time and leisure into forces that serve the interests of capital and thus contribute to the reproduction of the class system. Free time becomes work when it consolidates the social command of capital.

Individuality, therefore, can be a point of resistance to capital and ultimately the basis of communism as a form of both negative and positive desire. Those "personal melodramas" that harbor unresolved "political, sociological, and economic dilemmas" articulate desires that can be turned against the social command of capital and made to reveal the hidden histories of class struggle that mass culture normally works to disavow. It may be true that the industrywide consensus in Hollywood requires in its movies the conversion of all sociopolitical conflict of interests into personal melodrama, but such a conversion also suggests that Hollywood is required to process and articulate contradictions and dilemmas in some form. When Marx spoke of the "free development of individualities" as the "moving contradiction" of capitalism, he described a world in which human desire had been awakened to its own subversive relation to any absolute system of values, including economic values, through its access to free or disposable time. It is a world that produces individualities and incommensurable personalities that come back to challenge and transform the social ground of their own origin. With one hand, capitalism attempts to impose on the world and its peoples an absolute system of values as a justification of the class system and its corresponding distribution of wealth; and with the other, it fosters individualism and desire as a function of the culture of consumption that inevitably subverts the authority of its system of values.

Works of mass culture like the Hollywood Western provide individuals who are the products of capital's contradictions with a melodramatic scenario that can enable them to give ethical definition to their own desires. This happens because such works derive their emotional intensity and intellectual force from another history that they harbor, a history that is conveyed to the spectator indirectly, not as a coherent narrative but as a structure of feeling. In discussing the childhood screen memories of Leonardo da Vinci, Freud compared such memories to

> the body of legends, traditions and interpretations found in a nation's early history. In spite of all the distortions and misunderstanding, they still represent the reality of the past: they are what a people forms out of the experience of its early days and under the dominance of motives that were once powerful and still operate to-day; and if it were only possible, by a knowledge of all the forces at work, to undo these distortions, there would be no difficulty in disclosing the historical truth lying behind the legendary material. (1964: 34)

It is probably never possible to undo all the distortions that go into the body of fictions and myths that constitute a nation's cultural traditions, including the traditions that have been transformed into the commodities of mass culture by the culture industry. Furthermore, one cannot say of the works of mass culture that they simply reflect the collective experience of a people in the way that we think of traditional folklore or popular culture reflecting such experience. As works of mass culture, movies require huge investments of capital; and there can be little doubt that the producers, directors, actors, writers, and other creative workers who facilitate this process must pass through a screening, however implicit and unrecognized, that protects the interests of capital and its need to reproduce and legitimate the class system. Yet, at the same time, the profit motive that drives the culture industry also makes inevitable that it will subvert itself by fostering individuality of response in the spectator and by supporting creative visions and narratives that articulate potentially subversive social desires.

In a sense, capital will do anything to connect with an audience, which includes producing images of its own negation. One should not imagine that these cultural images can have much revolutionary effect on their own, however. Any effect they have must be mediated by the overall cultural history of society. They produce structures of feeling that configure with the system of such structures, a system that is linked to the dominant ideologies, myths, and values of the total culture or hegemony (Burgoyne 1997: 6). Ultimately, these "emergent" or "alternative" structures, to use the language of Raymond Williams, are ambivalent in their relation to the "dominant" structures (1977: 121–7). On the one hand, the institutions of mass culture try to manage and contain emergent or alternative cultural forms; on the other, they *produce* or *reinforce* them as the expressions of social antagonism.

In the field of labor history, Leon Fink has noted the reluctance of historians to cope with the impact of twentieth-century mass culture on the formation of working-class consciousness:

> Why, in principle, is it easier for us to assess the world of the New York journeyman mechanic in 1830 than that of the Schenectady electrical worker or the Detroit wildcat striker of the 1940s? Can it be in part that the cultural apparatus [of the nineteenth century] at our disposal – with its tight-knit communities, ethnic neighborhoods, moral codes, and skilled-worker republicanism – no longer fits but, except for notions of mass embourgeoisement and depoliticization, we have little to put in its place. (1994: 189)

In a related argument, Roy Rosenzweig challenges the notion that the impact of mass culture on the formation of class-consciousness in the twentieth century is entirely negative and can be reduced to the overworked formula that dominant culture serves only to "divert workers from seeking more fundamental changes." According to this historian,

> workers who had spent their time in the movie theater in the 1920s might find their way to the union hall in the 1930s and 1940s, as they sought to achieve what the movies promised but the larger society failed to deliver and as they became increasingly able to make common cause with workers from different ethnic and religious groups. (1983: 227–8)

Perhaps, with reference to the second half of the twentieth century, one can no longer use a term as coherent in meaning as "working class" to describe the formations of class consciousness that emerge, in part, through interactions with mass culture. The class positions that find support in mass culture are not unified by cultural or socioeconomic identity but by their general antagonism toward the current distribution of wealth and the social institutions that enforce it.

The Hollywood and Hollywood-inspired Western movie functions as a screen memory of the social antagonisms that play a central though disavowed role in American history. The Johnson County War is a historical event that expresses such antagonism, though it is only part of a larger social process. That event cannot be separated from the period of working-class unrest and struggle in the United States during the last three decades of the nineteenth century that has been called by some labor historians the Great Upheaval. For example, there was a cowboy strike in Texas in 1883, which Ruth Allen (1941) identified at one time as the only such strike in history. Yet there is evidence of another strike in Wyoming in 1886. This strike is documented by Jack Flagg (1969: 15), who participated in it, then was blacklisted by the corporate cattlemen of the WSGA, and eventually shot at by the regulators in the Johnson County War. Helena Smith believes that this Wyoming strike was precipitated by the Knights of Labor, though she has no proof. Her assumption seems to be that, in the context, the Wyoming cowboys were undoubtedly encouraged to strike by the labor struggles they were hearing about in other parts of the West (1966: 33). The year 1886 was also that of the Great Southwest Railroad Strike led by the Knights of Labor (Allen 1942). As Allen observed, "It has not been fully appreciated that the most dramatic, the most direct action in the American labor movement [in the 1880s] took place in the mines and on the railroads of the West among workers who had ridden the range and followed the cattle trails" (1941: 34).

Every Western movie, like every work of mass culture, is overdetermined by political, sociological, and economic forces; but the dominant Western, from 1939 to the present, owes a particular debt to the Johnson County War in the same sense that it owes a particular – though not exclusive – debt to the Western novel that was inspired by the event, Wister's *The Virginian*. In the rest of this study, I am not going to narrate the complete history of the Johnson County War, which has already been done by Helena Smith, but rather read the movies that are the most significant cultural screen memories of that event and others like it. The movies I focus on could be said to crystallize tendencies that are much more widespread in the Western and in the movies that Ray calls "disguised westerns" (1985: 75, 145). As critics from Will Wright (1975: 29– 32) to Richard Slotkin (1992: 278–9) have pointed out, the year 1939 initiated the "renaissance" or "golden age" of the Western, which, taking into account pauses during World War II and the gradual slowdown in the production of Western movies starting in the sixties, continued until the early seventies. Since then, there have been repeated efforts to revive the Western; and all of them, in one way or another, give representation to the social antagonisms that one associates in American history with class struggle, race war, and gender division. At stake in all these antagonisms is the question of wealth and its relation to force and power.

CHAPTER 3

CROSSING THE BORDER

Jefferson's Double-Cross

George Marshall's 1939 Marlene Dietrich vehicle, *Destry Rides Again*, is one of the strangest Westerns ever made, with its mixture of classical Western formula and screwball comedy. Yet if you set it beside a movie like *Stagecoach*, you can see a polarity within the Western myth concerning the construction of masculinity and the relations between gender and class. John Wayne's Ringo Kid is not the "macho" figure that Wayne would perfect in his later career, but he is such a masculine hero in formation. By contrast, in *Destry Rides Again*, James Stewart's Tom Destry actively resists and criticizes the dominant paradigm of masculinity until the film's last act, when he conforms to it; and even then, before he succeeds at that act, his efforts are subverted by the women of the town, who, under Dietrich's leadership, transform themselves into a collective force that wipes out a gang of virtual land grabbers without the use of guns (although Destry has to kill the villain after Dietrich's Frenchy takes the bullet meant for him).

Nothing in *Stagecoach* states directly that the war between the Kid and the Plummers involves property, and yet conflict over property is the underlying issue here. The Plummer brothers have killed Ringo's father and brother, have framed him for killing their foreman, and are now ruling over the town of Lordsburg. The reference to "foreman" suggests that the Plummers are cattlemen; and the sheriff of Tonto, Curly, refers to the fact that he and Ringo's father used to "punch cattle" together. Other statements imply that the Plummers control the legal authorities in Lordsburg. The town's name, despite its New Mexican provenance, may seem ironic given the fact that the Plummers do not resemble lords by any criteria; but there may be an unconscious allusion here to the history of the western cattle boom of the 1880s. In Wyoming, during that period, some of the dominant representatives of capital were in fact close to being lords, since many of the big cattle corporations on the open range were owned by Scottish and British corporations. As Helena Smith notes, "To the cowboys, oblivious to distinctions of rank, the importations were all 'lords'" (1966: 11). Horace Plunkett, born into Anglo-Irish aristocracy, headed the Frontier Land and Cattle Company and brought in "a plethora of partners, shareholders, office holders, who were all Eton chums, County Meath neighbors, and the like"; like others, he assumed that "any scion of the gentry was qualified to operate a cattle 'ranche'" (104). Wister had argued in the mid-nineties that the English nobleman was a natural cowboy, "a born horseman, a perfect athlete," and "fundamentally kin with the drifting vagabonds who swore and galloped by his side" (1998: 331). Jack Flagg, who was identified as a "rustler" by the corporate cattlemen during the Johnson County War (Smith 1966: 94, 97–107), took a different view in the roundup of 1884: "Englishmen in knee breeches, accompanied by their general managers, buggy bosses and valets, rode around with an air of lordliness which was ridiculous" (Flagg 1969: 8). Many of the original "cattle barons" were neither American citizens nor models of "Western" masculinity. The ones from the UK mostly pulled out of the industry in the late 1880s (the men who, according to Wister, were forced "to leave the country or be ruined" by the homesteaders); but when the WSGA organized the invasion of Johnson County, the leaders among the cattlemen included two Harvard graduates from Boston and Wall Street, respectively, a union officer from Kentucky, and an Englishman.

However, the invasion also included 25 "young professional gunmen from Texas" (Smith 1966: xii). This is not the first time gunmen had been used to settle labor disputes in the Old West. During the Great Southwest Railroad Strike, the railroad hired a gunman who was ranked with "John Wesley Hardin of the '40 notches'." This led to a gun battle that constitutes what Allen calls "one of those tragic events which mark the history of labor struggles" (1942: 78–9). The Plummers resemble gunmen more than cattlemen, but both guns and capital were critical to the reality that lay behind the Western myth.

Ringo's father and brother would have come into conflict with the Plummers over the ownership of land or cattle. Curiously, Ringo still owns a ranch "across the border," which suggests that one has to leave the country in order to have access to land without coming into conflict with capital or its instruments of violence. As in Wister's *Virginian*, the dominant ideology suggests that only those have a right to wealth who already have it or who subordinate their interests to those who already have it in the manner of the Virginian himself. Yet *Stagecoach*, in contrast with *The Virginian*, also makes it clear that Ringo will not have a natural right to property or the way of life it promises until he avenges the death of his father and brother. Though Ringo is hardly a kid, his sobriquet will be justified until he proves himself to be a man. The class system in *Stagecoach* correlates with gender hierarchy: the feminine is identified with lack of power and physical force, and those elements at the bottom or on the margins of society are either feminine or subject to feminization. At the very outset in Tonto, Doc Boone (Thomas Mitchell), the town drunk, and Dallas (Claire Trevor), the prostitute, are brought together when they are driven out of town by the ladies of the Law and Order League. It is perhaps sheer coincidence, but nonetheless ironic, that the name given to this women's club is the name of a vigilante organization that emerged during the Great Southwest Strike against Jay Gould's railroad empire in 1886. As these antistrike leagues spread from Missouri to Texas, they represented the interests of the corporations. They mimicked the "secret passwords, grips, and recognition signs" of the Knights of Labor, which led the strike; and after the strike's defeat, "the Kansas league took on the task of maintaining social control in the state's urban areas, focusing at once on the eradication of lower-class drinking and gambling dens and on the elimination of alleged 'socialists and red flags' from labor organizations" (Fink 1983: 122).

In the movie, this group does not represent effective female power, since the law and order they defend hypocritically victimizes men and women without resources, while it lacks any power to prevent the violence of cattlemen like the Plummers. Similarly, the other passengers on the stagecoach have been feminized in the sense that they are excluded from the dominant configuration of power. Curly (George Bancroft) is the sheriff and represents the law; yet he wants to put the Kid in jail to protect him from the real "bad" men who remain free. The stage driver, Buck, is a clown played by Andy Devine; and, given the ethnocentrism of this genre, he is married into a disempowered group, the Mexican Americans. The whiskey drummer, Peacock (Donald Meek), is a sweet, ineffectual saint, who lets Doc drink all of his samples and cringes in horror at the thought of encountering Indians; but he has a family somewhere and, as a Christian, identifies himself with the situation of women, including Dallas. Lucy Mallory (Louise Platt) is genteel and pregnant (and, like a true lady, doesn't allow her pregnancy to be visible in any way!), but she is constantly dependent on the attention of others and must conform to social norms even when she recognizes their injustice toward Dallas who nurses her through her delivery. Hatfield (John Carradine), the southern dandy, is deadly with a gun but has been feminized by the defeat of his "civilization" in the Civil War, a "civilization" for which he longs nostalgically. Finally, Gatewood, the banker, though he espouses the ideology of capital (he says, the government should reduce taxes and not interfere with business, and the country needs a businessman for president), is actually a submissive husband who steals from his own bank in the effort to escape his wife. As Edward Buscombe notes, Gatewood's outburst could have been read by the 1939 audience as the response of the financial establishment of the thirties to the so-called "communist" aspects of Roosevelt's New Deal (1992: 31).

In an important interpretation, Tag Gallagher remarks that, in *Stagecoach*, "Each character . . . represents a culture or a class in microcosm" (1986: 153–9). John Ford said that his movie could be usefully compared with Maupassant's "Boule de Suif," and Buscombe comments that what the two stories have in common is an "acute class consciousness" (1992: 36). The most powerful illustration of this consciousness is the dinner scene at the first way station, which Gallagher brilliantly analyses (1986: 153–9). When Ringo asks Dallas to take a seat at the end of the table where Lucy Mallory is seated, he fails to realize the class difference that immediately makes this situation untenable. Hatfield suggests that Lucy would be cooler at the other end of the table; and when they move, Gatewood joins them. The use of subjective shots emphasizes "Dallas's passive victimhood and Lucy's active aggression," and the objective shots convey in spatial terms the class structure that determines the relationships between these characters (153). Ironically, near the end of the sequence, as the camera tracks left behind Dallas and the Kid toward Hatfield and Lucy, the image almost creates the impression of Lucy's regret over what she has just done, though it may only be her pregnancy and disorientation that disrupts her composure. By implication, every member of the group is the victim of class, even if they completely identify with that hierarchy.

The characters in the aggregate represent the class system as both a destructive force and a feminizing social structure that can be redeemed, within the logic of this Western, only through the restoration of masculine power and violence. Ringo has been virtually castrated by the dominant power of the Plummers and the legal system that backs them up; but in his final confrontation with them, he redeems not only himself and the "fallen" woman Dallas but the social order as well. In giving the Kid his gun back, Curly chooses right over legality; and Doc stands up to Luke Plummer even before the Kid does and redeems his own masculine identity. Dallas can now be the strong, passionate woman she really is and, like Lucy, have children of her own. The other characters may not change, but their worth is reevaluated in a world in which the Ringo Kid has become the dominant figure of masculinity and personal autonomy. Ringo and Dallas cross the border into a better world that may or may not be Mexico (just as the location of the main action may or may not be Arizona and New Mexico). As Michael Coyne has argued, this ending is "as anti-American . . . as any major Western reached before the Vietnam era, far more so than the 'unAmerican' closure of *High Noon*, which John Wayne found repugnant in the 1950s" (Coyne 1997: 22). Still, as Doc and Curly walk off together, the implication is that the border to be crossed is internal rather than external to civilization.

At the end of *Stagecoach*, the class system is not so much defeated as it is transformed through fantasy. By crossing the border, the Kid and Dallas have liberated property from capital and the physical force that backs it up, so that land becomes mere use value that can never be exchanged or accumulated as superfluous wealth. Since Gatewood exposes the underlying social possibility that capital derives from theft, he presumably goes to prison; and since the Plummers show that the excessive accumulation of private property depends on violence, they get the extralegal death penalty. The other characters supposedly remain who they are, but their social class can no longer be the basis of their exploitation or privilege. Even Lucy, the last vestige of antebellum Southern womanhood, must undergo a change once she realizes that in going west she has crossed the border of her own cultural identity. Or at least that would be true if society were to follow the direction of Ringo and Dallas. In this scenario, class struggle and social contradiction are reduced to a conflict between gender identities; and the conflict is resolved through the simple assertion of natural masculine authority and power against their perversion by the Plummers, an act that virtually sets the world aright. Though Ringo, like the Virginian, takes the law into his own hands, he does not do it in the interests of property and in the service of dominant class power. His outlawry is a mode of self-valorization without any appeal to transcendent forces beyond human desire. Furthermore, despite the film's questionable gender politics, it analyzes gender as a form of the division of labor, and resistance to gender-based oppression – even in the case of disempowered men – as class struggle.

Destry Rides Again is less brilliant as pure cinema and more conservative in its view of the class system, but it nonetheless complicates the relation between gender and class that emerges in Westerns like *Stagecoach*. It is more conservative because Thomas Jefferson Destry is no outlaw like Ringo, but rather embodies a concept of law and order that clearly transcends and rules over the class struggles that it mediates. To this extent, he conforms to the model of *The Virginian* and his avatars in the films of William S. Hart and others. As Slotkin summarizes, the historical Thomas Jefferson feared the new forces of capital that tended to dominate in the eastern cities and to create "separate and antagonistic classes of the very rich and the very poor." For this reason, he believed in the promise of an unlimited frontier that would support "the character and the ideology of the 'yeoman farmer' – a free individual, living on his own land, independent of others for the necessaries of life yet depending on his fellow citizens (and society in general) for protection, law, and civilized amenities" (1985: 70). Bottleneck represents the subversion or double-cross of Jefferson's promise by those social forces that have transformed the unlimited frontier into a bottleneck that prohibits the fair distribution of wealth. In Tom Destry, the founding father has returned to enforce both the spirit and letter of the law he helped to create.

The villain in this movie is the gambler Kent (Brian Donlevy), who has been using a rigged poker game to grab all the land and cattle around the town of Bottleneck. He then charges cattlemen a fee to drive their herds across this land, a trail they apparently cannot go around, hence another reason for the name of the town. Kent signifies the role of the speculator and of land speculation in the history of the United States, though admittedly this history has been distorted almost beyond recognition. Like the speculator, Kent does no real work and produces nothing, while the entire basis of his authority and power over the community depends on the understanding that ownership is, in Limerick's words, "a purely conceptual act." As she concludes, "To the speculator, profit bore no relation to actual physical labor and derived instead from a manipulation of the legal principles set up to convey and protect property" (1987: 69). The cheating gambler may be a perfect figure for the land speculator, who frequently used "dummy entrymen" to grab land under falsified claims (62). In Wyoming, according to eyewitness Jack Flagg, the big cattlemen

> brought friends from the east and had them file on all the finest land, some of whom never saw the land again after it was filed upon. In fact, land was filed on in Johnson county at the Cheyenne land office by men who had never seen it. I know whereof I speak, because I am living on and have a patent for a piece of that land. (1969: 13)

In *Destry Rides Again*, Tom Destry respects the law to such an extent that he supports Kent's seizure of a rancher's property because of a legal document that entitles him to it. Eventually, though,

Destry is able to prove that the document was obtained illegally in a rigged poker game and that the former sheriff was murdered when he confronted Kent with the crime. The film implies that men like Kent are a deviation from the norm of capitalism and that, though they may temporarily appropriate and distort the law to their advantage, the law will eventually assert itself and set things right. To this extent, Destry's relation to Kent is consistent with the New Deal's "antimonopoly strategy." In response to populist demagogues in 1937, "[President] Roosevelt proposed economic measures with neopopulist and antimonopolistic themes, including the so-called tax on wealth, and encouraging the development of unions" (Muscio 1997: 25). Ironically, with respect to Hollywood, this initiative led to the US Justice Department's case against the major studios, known as the Paramount Case, which originated in 1936 and culminated in the 1948 Supreme Court ruling that brought about the dismantling of the old studio system with its vertical integration, including control of first-run theaters and the practice of block booking (143–95). In other words, for Destry as for Roosevelt, it is the law and not physical force that determines the right to private property. Furthermore, the law is on the side of families and legitimate social relationships rather on the side of gamblers, prostitutes, and monopolists.

Dietrich's character introduces a wrinkle into this neat, hegemonic scenario. Frenchy is a showgirl and probably a prostitute, but she differs entirely from Claire Trevor's Dallas in *Stagecoach*. Dallas's parents were massacred by Indians, and she had to resort to prostitution in order to survive on her own. Frenchy, by contrast, was a New Orleans showgirl; and though her history may have forced her into selling herself, she has embraced necessity, including her alliance with Kent, and literally celebrates her refusal of the bourgeois norm of feminine identity. Her nemesis among the town's "ladies" is Lily Belle Callahan (Una Merkel), who insists that her Russian husband use the surname of her former husband, Mr. Callahan. Throughout this film, Boris Callahan, whose real name is that of the Dostoyevskian misanthrope Stavrogin, struggles to regain his lost masculinity; but in a poker game with Frenchy, he suffers the ultimate humiliation of losing his pants. As a result, Lily Belle and Frenchy get into a knock-down-drag-out fight over who has the right to own this symbol of masculinity. Destry intervenes with a mop and broom and nearly gets annihilated by Frenchy. The allegorical implications are obvious. The class system, which privileges those who use force and deception to accumulate wealth and power, has emasculated the common man and subverted "natural" gender hierarchy so that the women rule over the men, with the exception of the one "real" man at the top. Frenchy virtually dominates every man except for Kent, who controls her and will use force against her if necessary.

Since class conflicts have been translated into gender conflicts, Destry challenges both the dominant masculine paradigm and the gender hierarchy that capitalist social practices produce if they are not restrained by a "higher" law. He refuses to wear the phallic guns and insists that the law must be deployed through reason and not force. At the same time, he not only wears pants but has an extra pair he can lend to Boris as a reward for joining the side of the law. He criticizes and disciplines the hypermasculine cattleman, Jack Tyndall (Jack Carson), who plainly believes that might makes right, an ideology that would have been endorsed by the Wyoming corporate cattlemen. Though Tyndall's sister Janice is clearly the socially appropriate object of Destry's desire, she is far less interesting to him than Frenchy is. On the contrary, in order to undermine the dominant version of masculinity that Kent represents, Destry must steal the affections of the woman who serves Kent's interest. Consequently, the film ends with a series of reversals. First, Tom gives up on reason and straps on his guns to enforce the law through violence. At the same time, surrendering to her passion for Tom, Frenchy betrays Kent and saves Tom's life by sacrificing her own. Her last act is to wipe the makeup off her face so that Tom can kiss her. Even before that, however, Frenchy has been transformed from the antithesis of the proper bourgeois woman to the leader of the town's women as they become a collective force for social change. Ultimately, the whole movie has anticipated this event since, as Buhle and Wagner argue, *Destry* represents "a kind of collective subjectivity . . . first in the raucous laughter of the crowd, next in the action taken by the men, and then reasserted uproariously by the women whose action makes it a social story" (2002: 140).

When Destry is ready to give up on the Jeffersonian vision, Frenchy and the women of the community become a new kind of subject that can bypass the men and redeem the community by revealing its power to defeat the forces of speculation through

ILLUSTRATION 6 Social identity as artifice. *Destry Rides Again* (1939). Universal Studios. *Producer:* Joe Pasternak. *Director:* George Marshall

collective action and without excessive violence. The last images in the movie show a harmonious countryside, which signifies the return to the class harmony of Jeffersonian order, and the reassertion of masculine authority as Boris Callahan takes his proper name back and assumes the masculine role of patriarch with his wife, Lily Belle. In 1939, to those who had lived through the Great Depression and sometimes witnessed the violence of banks and corporations against ordinary men and women, such a conclusion must have had an inevitable significance.

Earlier in the film, when Destry suggests that Frenchy may not be such a bad person underneath all the makeup, she wipes her makeup off and looks at herself in a mirror, at which point there is a dissolve from Dietrich's mirror image to the image, from exactly the same angle, of Janice Tyndall looking at herself in another mirror (Ill. 6). Though Janice's face looks as if it is without makeup, she turns to the other women in the room to comment on the effectiveness of the makeup product she has used. This suggests that the conventional woman's "conventionality" is the result of artifice just as much as Frenchy's more rebellious and explicitly erotic look is. When Frenchy wipes off her makeup at the end of the movie, she is not aligning herself with the conventional woman but with a social individual that has not yet achieved a true existence, the person that Frenchy becomes by anticipation when she leads the women of the town against Kent and his men. Therefore, the restoration of Jeffersonian order through Frenchy's death turns out to be another double-cross.

The Virginian Crossed Out

According to Slotkin, the new wave of Westerns that appeared in 1939 "drew on both Beardian progressivism and Popular Front populism" (1992: 286). From the progressivist viewpoint, a movie like Michael Curtiz's *Dodge City* celebrated the technology of the railroad and promoted the Beardian view that, after the closing of the Frontier with its cheap land, industrialization became "a more than adequate substitute . . . because it promised a continuous and inexhaustible increase of resources for each succeeding generation and for every nation irrespective of its size" (283). By contrast, one finds a more populist viewpoint in a movie like Henry King's *Jesse James*, which "sees the railroad itself as corrupt and its building as a criminal invasion of an agrarian community" (296). In contrast with these explicitly historical and ideological films, the cinematic stylings of *Stagecoach* and the vaudeville humor of *Destry Rides Again* produce, through aesthetic distantiation, a structural critique of the class system and the historical conflicts over property that were critical to the history of the West as well as to the history of the Great Depression (Lenihan 1985: 92–3). These films focus on class as a structure that produces specific forms of the political subject that cannot be reduced to expressions of a moral program. This is what distinguishes them from the silent Westerns, the epics, and the serial Westerns of the thirties.

Furthermore, the blending of class conflict with a more general crisis of gender identity enabled these movies to sink their roots deep in the cultural unconscious. As Slotkin observes, *Stagecoach* pointedly exploits the stereotypes of B-formula movies while constructing a mythographic space for the Western through the use of Monument Valley as the background, the "visual oddity" of which gives the movie "authenticity" and enables it to represent "the alien quality of the frontier" (1992: 304–5; see Simmon 2003: 169–90).

In this movie, Ford chose a vision radically different from that of the progressive epic like Cecil B. DeMille's 1939 *Union Pacific* or from Ford's own earlier silent epic *The Iron Horse*. Similarly, the slapstick humor of *Destry* de-realizes the West as a historical referent and authenticates its "alien quality" as the screen memory of a modern alienated individual. The opening tracking shot of Bottleneck with the credits shows the West in almost the opposite way of *Stagecoach*. As opposed to the expansiveness of Monument Valley, guns are blazing and drunken men are staggering around in the town's enclosed space, a form of space that dominates the movie through the extensive use of tight shots. Still, whether spectators confront the enclosed world of Bottleneck or the expansive death-like landscape of Monument Valley, they find an alienated image of their own desire. Either desire comes up against a world that has been emptied of value and reduced to the status of a dead thing, or it finds itself enclosed within the prison-house of social norms against which it riots and rebels to no effect.

Based on the popularity of these movies and the images they promote, one can infer that the Great Depression had a transformative effect on the forms of gendered social identity (Denning 1998: 30). In these films, as in many of the romantic social comedies of the late thirties, men are unable to act on their own; and the ones who can, like the political bosses portrayed by Edward Arnold in Frank Capra's *Mr. Smith Goes to Washington* (1939) and *Meet John Doe* (1941), are morally repulsive in their embodiment of crude, acquisitive capitalism that relies more on force and extortion than on intelligence. The new man, like James Stewart's Jefferson Smith, struggles as much to be like a woman as to be like a man; he tries to be a nurturer and focuses on the needs of children and community as central to the health of the body politic. In a curious way, this redefinition of masculinity is also linked to a nostalgic longing for a Jeffersonian vision of America, a desire for which James Stewart becomes the iconic reference after playing both Jefferson Smith and Thomas Jefferson Destry in 1939. In *Meet John Doe*, Gary Cooper plays a more complex version of the same figure as the unemployed drifter who lies about his identity in order to get off the breadline. Unlike Stewart's Jeff Smith and Tom Destry, this character is flawed and lacks idealism so that he must struggle ambivalently toward a political response to the manipulative forces of capital that want to use his sudden popularity with the masses and his access to mass communications as the instrument of their power and social domination.

The year before the release of *Meet John Doe*, Cooper played a similar character in the once overrated but now underrated William Wyler film, *The Westerner* (1940). In a fusion of comic and dramatic styles, Cooper plays a Western loner who manages to escape lynching through the use of his wits by telling tall tales. Critics like John Hawkridge in *The BFI Companion* have faulted the film for its emphasis on dialogue over action and interior shots in the studio over exterior shots on location (Buscombe 1988: 310). However, this emphasis on dialogue enables Cooper to create a different kind of Western hero; and the supposedly lackluster exterior shots in this movie have the effect of bringing the Western into the present, since, through Gregg Toland's cinematography, they resemble the stark yet familiar Depression-era landscapes more than the mythographic Western space that John Ford created (Ills. 7–8). More explicitly than the 1939 films, this movie alludes to the Johnson County War and similar Western range wars; but it also links class struggle from the past to the conflicts of the Depression, by substituting the image of the farmer for the cowboy and small rancher. The exterior shots focus on fields of corn that seem foreign to the mythography of Texas but echo representations of those sections of the middle United States, including the Texas panhandle and Oklahoma, that were hit hardest during the Depression. After the cattlemen under the leadership of

ILLUSTRATION 7 Monument Valley as mythographic space. *Stagecoach* (1939). Walter Wanger Productions. *Producer:* Walter Wanger. *Director:* John Ford

ILLUSTRATION 8 Allusion to Depression-era photographs of the Dust Bowl. *The Westerner* (1940). Samuel Goldwyn. *Producer:* Samuel Goldwyn. *Director:* William Wyler

Judge Roy Bean (Walter Brennan) burn down the cornfields and farmhouses of the homesteaders, the burnt-out landscape echoes the imagery of the Dust Bowl; but this time human agency rather than the force of nature bears the responsibility.

In this movie, Cooper is more the unemployed drifter he becomes in *Meet John Doe* than the Western gunfighter, and his alliance with Jane Ellen Matthews (Doris Davenport) is based more on his identification with her subaltern class position than the need to prove his masculinity. In this case, it is the woman who commits herself to property and the man who must identify with and support her social desires, though, as the movie suggests, the feminine relation to property is based on use value and not the abstract value of accumulated wealth. Through the character of Judge Roy Bean, who fantasizes endlessly about his idol Lillie Langtry, the film makes fun of masculine idealizations of women and suggests that Cole's bond with the woman as class subject offers more social promise. When Jane Ellen forces Cole to choose sides between the cattlemen and the homesteaders, he naturally aligns himself with her and, through her, with the "equality," to use Wister's phrase; but at the same time he redeems the people by remasculinizing the subaltern.

Jeffrey Brown (1995) argues that Cooper functioned as an icon of gender ambivalence in his early career. As his breakthrough role in the 1929 *Virginian* demonstrates, the star's image "was constructed as a masculine ideal fetishized by hypermasculine roles and explicitly feminized by cinematic conventions of filming. His ability to reconcile masculine and feminine traits within a single persona demonstrates Hollywood's narcissistic subtext underlying heterosexual masculine norms" (213). Brown has relatively little to say about the next phase of Cooper's career after his 1936 success in Capra's *Mr. Deeds Goes to Town*. Though he continued to make films in which he played "hypermasculine" roles, he also played more vulnerable, feminized men, despite their reluctant capacity for violence, not only in *The Westerner*, but in *Meet John Doe*, *Sergeant York* (1941), and *Along Came Jones* (1945). *High Noon* (1952) represented the fusion of both aspects of the artist's screen persona, as he played a strong man who is vulnerable and at war with his own feminine side, which finds external representation in the woman who finally saves him, a Quaker played by Grace Kelly. Cooper's next high-profile role after *High Noon* was that of the Quaker pacifist in William Wyler's *Friendly*

Persuasion, a man who must face the decision to use violence against his conscience and principles. In other words, he becomes the Grace Kelly character from *High Noon*, which shows to what extent these characters are two sides of the same coin, allegorical figures of human "will" and social "grace" or forgiveness. Both films were written by blacklisted radicals, Carl Foremen and Michael Wilson, respectively. Cooper's ability to combine traditionally masculine and feminine traits necessarily lent itself to the representation of a new form of masculinity, even as his image also worked to disavow the historical significance of that transformation in the socioeconomic upheavals of the Great Depression.

The Westerner could be read as the anti-*Virginian*, with Gary Cooper reversing his earlier role. Cole Harden is nearly lynched for horse-stealing like the Virginian's friend, Steve; but he manages to talk his way out of it. In a male-centered genre that, according to Jane Tompkins, rejects "language as false or at best ineffectual" (1992: 51), *The Westerner* is a movie in which the characters talk more than they act (the one way in which it resembles Wister's novel), although the talk is accompanied by facial expressions and physical gestures that border on the Chaplinesque. Cole's relation to Judge Bean is so homoerotic that he literally wakes up in bed next to him after a night of drinking and nurturing the Judge's Lillie Langtry fantasies. Though Cole finally has to shoot it out with the Judge, it pains him to kill the man who resembles a rattlesnake he was once fond of. Unlike the Virginian, who allies himself with a paternalistic cattle baron, Cole joins forces with a woman who struggles against the male-dominated frontier and demands her right to property – her share of the land as the national patrimony – in a culture that links the ownership of property to masculinity. After her father has been killed and the male homesteaders flee the area, Jane Ellen decides to stay and fight for her land, though she has no resources for such a fight except for the love and loyalty of Cole Harden. Instead of normalizing the patriarchal capitalist in the manner of Judge Henry, Brennan's portrait of Judge Roy Bean suggests that the frontier patriarch is pathological and that his quest for power and control disavows a failed masculinity. Though he is supposed to be the leader of the big cattlemen in this area of Texas, Bean lives in rundown, shanty-like dwellings, since for him wealth is only an abstraction and a pathological obsession.

In all these movies, the woman signifies the least empowered class position; and for that reason, the transformation of her situation requires the transformation of the whole social system. Frenchy has used her sexuality to avoid poverty and to align herself with social wealth derived from the use of force; but she has alienated herself from the community at large, particularly the community of other women. Yet she is able to use her marginal position to convert the social class of conventional women into a revolutionary force, something that these women could not have done on their own because their "properness" entails a submission to the authority of property and the social relations of capital. Dallas also has had to sell her only property, her body, in order to survive; and once again this has alienated her from the larger community, especially women. Yet she has the power to transform the Kid's rage and desire for vengeance into a desire to cross the border of culture and start a new life with a new relation to property, which involves accepting a woman like Dallas as irreducible to property and to the social conventions that make her such. Jane Ellen, in *The Westerner*, is the most conventional and least interesting of these women; and yet, in a curious way, she represents the end-result of the Great Depression, which undermined the foundation of masculine patriarchal authority in property and wealth. She is able to win the loyalty of Cole, who clearly has no desire to settle down and shuck corn. His only wealth is free time, of which he is so possessive that he spends much of the film avoiding capture not only by Bean's lynch mob but by Mary Ellen's desire for land and a conventional life, which means a life committed to work. In the end, though, his passion for her convinces him to subordinate his desire to her social and material interests. He can no longer go it alone and wander in quest of something unnamable, the big ocean on the other side of the frontier. She implicitly teaches him that masculinity can survive a social alliance with the opposite gender and the compromise of its autonomy in the interest of economic justice when it is clearly understood that the value of wealth lies in its use and not in its accumulation as abstract value. There is more than one way to cross the frontier.

As Slotkin stresses, "in Wister's novel the primary sign of social and moral superiority is not nobility but *virility*; and on this score the Virginian is pre-eminent" (1992: 176). Ironically, the Virginian proves his virility by lynching his best friend in the interest of the paternalistic property owner who will then incorporate his foreman into the dominant class. He also conquers the woman in his life, Molly Wood, whose "better birth and schooling . . . had once been weapons to keep him at his distance, or bring her off victorious in their encounters." She finally gives way "before the onset of the natural man himself. She knew her cow-boy lover, with all that he lacked, to be more than ever she could be, with all that she had. He was her worshipper still, but her master, too" (Wister 1998: 292). As Tompkins notes, "Molly's surrender represents not simply the defeat of a female by a male but also the defeat of the genteel tradition – identified with women, religion, and culture – by a rugged man of the outdoors" (1992: 142). In other words, the Virginian's victory over Molly represents the defeat of the feminine cultural capital of the East, which Wister's mother virtually embodied, by an untutored "Western" masculinity that derives from the lower classes (132–7). Still, Molly threatens not to marry the Virginian if he faces Trampas in a gunfight, an act that sets up another Western convention repeated in *High Noon* and *Shane*. According to Tompkins, these gunfights are ultimately "a revolt against the rule of women" and "stage a moment in the psychosocial development of the male that requires that he demonstrate his independence from and superiority to women, specifically to his mother" (143–4). Although Tompkins may read Wister's psychological motivation correctly, she generalizes that reading to the whole genre in a way that idealizes the culturally privileged woman and reduces a complex and historically variable set of relations to monological truth. When the Virginian conforms to a paradigm of masculinity that is clearly linked to private property and wealth, Molly, despite her initial resistance, celebrates this act that will guarantee her economic and cultural privileges in the future. By contrast, the masculinities of Ringo, Destry, and Cole are bound to a more subversive relation to property and to an alliance with the subaltern woman without cultural capital. Furthermore, Ringo and Cole are not agents of the state or of any social authority in the manner of B-Western heroes but social nomads whose violence becomes a metaphor for self-valorization against the labor market and capitalist hegemony.

   The Westerner, although not accurately portraying the historical Judge Roy Bean, nonetheless represents a class struggle that had its basis in actual history. At one point, Cole tries to mediate between the two sides of the range war by explaining both the cattlemen's fear of fences that keep their stock away from water and the farmers' need of fences to keep cattle out of their crops. This debate actually derives from the history of the cattle boom in Texas and Wyoming in the 1880s. In a scholarly book originally published in 1929, Ernest Staples Osgood explains the conflict between the homesteaders and the cattlemen in similar terms, although he points out that it was the cattlemen who illegally started putting up fences on the public domain in an attempt to prevent overcrowding of the open range (1957: 189–94). Still, while recognizing the cattlemen's violent tactics and abuse of power, Osgood more or less endorses their interpretation of the conflict over land: "Land laws, made wholly for the farmer who was expected to displace the range cattleman, invited fraud. The farmer found them impossible of honest application, and the latter regarded them as the product of middle-western and eastern ignorance" (207). Even if Wyoming and Texas were never meant to be a farmer's paradise, though, the real issue in the range wars was not over the appropriate use of the land but over who has the right to claim ownership of the open range. According to Osgood, in the late 1880s, tensions developed in Wyoming over the

> process of shifting from the public domain as a physical basis of the [cattle] industry, to the privately owned pasture and hay lands . . . It was obvious that the stockman could not acquire within the law, land enough to carry on the business as it had developed on the open range. It was equally obvious that the country as a whole would not consent to a change in the land laws that would suit the demands of the range country. The alienation of large, compact blocks of government land was completely at variance with the traditional land policy of the Republic. If this were permitted, the people of the United States stood a good chance of seeing the last of their estate slip into the hands of a few powerful companies, many of them controlled by foreign interests. (215)

Recent American historiography suggests that Osgood idealized "the traditional land policy of the Republic" (see Countryman 1996: 91–108). Still, the conflict between the cattlemen and the home-steaders was over whether any class has the right to appropriate the wealth of a nation to itself. As Limerick stresses, western expansion involved "an array of efforts to wrap the concept of property around unwieldy objects" (1987: 71). Furthermore, without restraint or regulation of "access to the public grazing lands, the federal government in effect subsidized private cattle raisers and loggers with unlimited access to national resources" (82). Though *The Westerner* and movies like it may misrepresent the historical facts, they convey a fundamental truth about the violent origins of capitalist wealth. Furthermore, masculinity and sexual difference as a whole are implicated in this social process. According to the dominant fiction that supports the property system, the sign of masculinity is wealth, even if that wealth has been appropriated through acts of violence. The alternative to that view is a reconceptualization of masculinity and gender division along the lines of a different understanding of property. This different understanding privileges use value over exchange value and the production of *common* wealth over the accumulation of abstract wealth.

CHAPTER 4

REVOLUTIONARY HYSTERIA

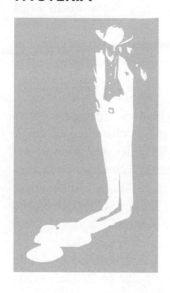

The Hysterical Fascist Killer

At the end of 1946, *Duel in the Sun* came to the screen with a vision of the West that was spectacularly iconoclastic in relation to the tradition that preceded it. As Laura Mulvey has pointed out, by placing a woman at the center of its narrative, it disrupted one of the critical elements of the Western's mythography (1989: 35), though it was not without precedents in Westerns like *Destry* and Wesley Ruggles's *Arizona* (1940), starring Jean Arthur as a self-made pioneer woman. Even more important in my judgment, it exploded the dominant paradigms of Western manhood – since the male characters in this movie constitute a parade of failed masculinities – while it also explored the relations between gender, race, and class. In the opening sequence of *Duel*, Pearl (Jennifer Jones) is presented as the product of an interracial marriage between a white man of Spanish descent from the South and a Native American woman. Her father is referred to as a "renegade creole squaw man," and the mother is the stereotypically eroticized version of the racial other.

While Pearl's mother dances inside the cabaret and functions as a sexual magnet, Pearl dances outside and attracts the remark, "Like mother, like daughter." After the father kills the mother and her lover, he recommends his own death sentence at his trial, using the argument that he has already killed "a person much superior to either of them," namely, himself. The first failed masculinity in the movie is one that has transgressed the law that separates the races. Ironically, Scott Chavez (Herbert Marshall) then sends his racially mixed daughter from this borderland or, to use the more contemporary term, "cultural contact zone" (Nobles 1997: xii), to the all-white enclave of conventional Western space, the "Paris of the Pecos" in Texas. There she encounters Senator McCanles (Lionel Barrymore), a crippled and belligerently racist patriarch who constantly points out and mocks her racial identity; Laura Belle McCanles (Lillian Gish), an aging southern belle who tries to transform Pearl into a lady; Jesse McCanles (Joseph Cotton), the pacifistic son with a law degree who secretly loves Pearl and wants to redeem her through education; and Lewt McCanles (Gregory Peck), the brutal, lawless, and sexually aggressive son who virtually rapes Pearl and completely identifies with his father's property and power.

Robin Wood points out that these characters embody a series of ideological contradictions that center on the character of Pearl: contradictions between fathers (Senator McCanles and Pearl's real father), between mothers (Pearl's Native American mother and Laura Belle), and between lovers (Lewt and Jesse). In Wood's diagram of these relations, the Senator and Lewt, the explicit racists, fall on the same side as Pearl's mother, the side of "wilderness" in the classical Western paradigm, while Chavez, Laura Belle, and Jesse, who ignore racial boundaries either in theory or practice, fall on the side of "civilization" (1995: 192). Yet the whole point of Wood's reading is that *Duel in the Sun* destroys the ideological system that posits the dichotomy between wilderness and civilization – destroys and "leaves it a heap of rubble" (195). Chavez, after all, condemns his own transgression of racial division; Laura Belle, despite her tenderness and affection, tries to impose on Pearl her puritanical social identity without recognizing its ethnocentrism; and Jesse, despite his feeble and belated proclamation of love for Pearl, happily latches onto a pure white alternative, the daughter of a railroad magnate. By contrast, the Senator, Lewt, and Pearl's mother are creatures of demand who are not afraid to cross any line if it serves their immediate purpose and gratification. The conflict here is not between wilderness and civilization, but between brutal demand that exploits others for immediate gratification and repressed desire that always postpones pleasure in the interest of transcendent goals.

According to Mulvey, in this movie the woman is not just "the signifier of sexuality"; rather, her "female presence as centre allows the story to be actually, *overtly*, about sexuality" (1989: 35). Given that movies like *Destry* and the conservative *Arizona* could also be said to posit a "female presence as center," this statement needs clarification. The film explicitly links sexual desire with the desire for autonomy and suggests the impossibility of free sexuality in a social order founded on class, property, and racial exclusion. Wood astutely argues that the movie centers on the "disruptive influence" and "revolutionary implications" of Pearl's hysteria. Indeed, this influence "pervades every aspect of the film, determines its style, produces its storms, its lurid sunsets, the intolerable heat of its sun, and finally precludes any possibility of that satisfying and pacifying sense of resolution that is supposed to be a permanent and necessary feature of traditional narrative." Wood also notes that, in this context, "Hysteria must be seen as a form of active, if impotent, protest; if it lacks revolutionary *effect*, it has revolutionary *meaning*" (1995: 189). One can appropriate a term like "hysteria" only with great caution, since, as Martha Noel Evans comments, "hysteria has persistently been defined in the vocabulary of specialists as indefinable" (1991: 2). Without getting bogged down in the long history of this term, let me offer a speculative reading of Pearl's hysteria as an expression of revolutionary desire.

By comparison with the other characters in this movie, including her father, Pearl is the class subject, the subaltern, who is not supposed to have a voice in the dominant symbolic system. Gayatri Spivak (1988) has suggested that the subaltern cannot speak; but this movie shows that when the subaltern does speak, her discourse is hysterical and extremely dangerous. Hysteria is the discourse of a desire that the dominant system cannot code and refuses to recognize, but it is also the expression of the hysterical subject's capture by that dominant discourse and her or his attempt to transcend it through the production of symptoms. By symptom in this case, I simply mean that someone like Pearl, despite the ambivalence she feels about her own desire, refuses to let go of it and finds ways of reasserting it after each setback. Freud considered "a person hysterical in whom an occasion for sexual excitement elicited feelings that were preponderantly or exclusively unpleasurable" (1963: 44). In Pearl's case, her desire finds an appropriate object in Jesse because he can never reciprocate; and it finds a release in Lewt because he punishes her for feeling it. Chavez, Jesse, and Laura Belle all talk to Pearl, but they never listen to her. The Senator and Lewt talk at Pearl, either to degrade or to manipulate her; but they become infuriated by any attempt on her part to express her own desire. Pearl clearly shares her mother's sexuality, and in the movie's first scene we see her imitating her mother's dance; but after her mother's death, Pearl seems to erase that presence from her memory and to accept her father's interpretation of family history as law. Yet the mother continues to live through Pearl's sexuality, which cannot be defined as the desire for sexual pleasure and gratification but rather for the survival of desire itself beyond the ambivalence she feels about sexual pleasure. In fact, Pearl only turns to sexual gratification with Lewt when she realizes that Jesse will never respond to her desire as the desire of an autonomous being, a judgment that only reinforces her internal sense of abjection. In the final showdown with Lewt, after she has fatally wounded him, she finds an authentic response to her passion for the first time and can freely express her desire at the moment of dying. It is not that Lewt has suddenly been transformed into the better man he always should have been. Lewt is a brutal egoist to the end, but in death he can finally accept Pearl's desire without forcing it to conform to his own. Though it may be something of a cliché, in this movie only death eradicates the class division that represses feminine sexuality and any desire that does not conform to the dominant social system, to white masculine privilege and the inequitable distribution of wealth as social autonomy.

Pearl signifies subaltern desire that finds expression through hysterical discourse and performance. Though she does not overtly challenge the dominance of the Senator's social position, she always remains the signifier of its antithesis. This movie came out at the moment when the United States was celebrating its victory over fascism; yet ironically, and probably unconsciously, it explores in symbolic terms the tendency toward fascism in the dominant social order of the United States. Early in the movie, the Senator argues with his son Jesse over the construction of the railroad across their land. Historically, as a Texas cattleman, the Senator will surely benefit from the coming of the railroad that gives him direct access to eastern markets and the northern plains; but he nonetheless opposes it because it will bring immigrants to the region who could use their votes to raise taxes and redistribute the wealth that the Senator has accumulated (Osgood 1957: 90–1). In the most spectacular scene in the movie, the Senator sends out the call to all of his cowhands to join forces with him in blocking the railroad construction crews from crossing onto his property. This whole sequence is wildly unrealistic. Though cattlemen in Texas and Wyoming began to expand their landholdings in the 1880s, they still relied heavily on the free open range until the 1890s, long after most of the railroads had been built (Osgood 1957: 216–58). In reality, the Senator could never have owned so much land or have employed so many men. Yet what we see in this scene is the allegorical representation of the possibility of American fascism and the fantasy of a working class mobilized for capital (Ill. 9). The authoritarian leader, the Senator, calls on the cowboys to fight the railroad, which in the future will not only bring to the region immigrants who may compete with the

ILLUSTRATION 9 Convergence of the McCanles cowboys, the epic image of a social fantasy. *Duel in the Sun* (1946). Selznick International Pictures. *Producer:* David O. Selznick. *Director:* King Vidor

cowboys for jobs, but is being constructed with Chinese labor that embodies the threat of racial difference to the white working class. When the Senator proclaims that his law lies in the weapons of his men, Jesse turns against him with the argument that he would "rather be on the side of the victims than of the murderers." The camera cuts from the Senator's reaction to Jesse's remark to the image of several Chinese railroad workers. Then the Senator warns Jesse that he and his men will fire on the "coolies" as soon as Jesse cuts the wire of the fence across their property. Fortunately, the US Cavalry arrives to face off the McCanles army of cowboys; and the Senator surrenders with the admission that he cannot fire on the flag he once fought for.

This whole sequence could be read as a fantasy that disavows the social context in which the film was made. With reference to the past, it presupposes that the relation between cowboys and big cattlemen was one of harmony without any hint of class conflict, when the reality included cowboy strikes and conflicts like the Johnson County War, in which the small ranchers were usually former cowboys. However, it does correctly show the sorts of racial divisions that undermined the class struggles in Hollywood in the forties. The strike of the Conference of Studio Unions (CSU) in 1945 created problems for the production of *Duel in the Sun*. Even as producer David O. Selznick and his director, King Vidor, were creating images that attempted to displace or neutralize class struggle, they were confronted by a class conflict that eventually drew their stars into its vortex. As Gerald Horne notes, quoting from the *People's Daily World* at the time of the strike,

> "The all-star cast . . . refused to work when mass picketing began" at RKO, where it was being filmed. "Jennifer Jones, leading lady in the $4,000,000 spectacle, walked out when she saw the pickets. Lillian Gish walked past the studio waving to the pickets when she saw the line. Other players – Gregory Peck, Lionel Barrymore, Walter Huston, Charles Bickford . . . did not show up at all." (2001: 168–9)

Yet ironically the neutralization of class by race marked the strike movement itself. As Horne stresses, CSU "often resorted to racist iconography in its literature" and "did not do much to oppose discrimination, even though strong efforts could have helped it."

He continues,

> The NAACP and CSU could have united in protest against the Selznick production of *Duel in the Sun*. This mogul, who was responsible for *Gone With the Wind*, was not an NAACP favorite ... When the movie was released, Roy Wilkins of the NAACP called it "colossal trash." Members objected both to the role played by Butterfly McQueen and to the stereotyped portrayals of Native Americans. (227)

Though the film is surely not a direct response to these events, it nonetheless represents a condensation of its social context, with all the attendant contradictions, including the contradiction of a class formation that defeats itself by refusing to recognize class identity across racial lines. McCanles's cowboys are about as two-dimensional as Ford's Indians in *Stagecoach*, but they nonetheless allegorically signify a working class that has surrendered its autonomy in the name of racial supremacy.

If the Senator backs down from the full realization of his own fascist tendencies, he has created in Lewt their perfect manifestation. Just as the European fascists depended on the support of their capitalists and more or less protected their interests, so Lewt embodies a fascist thuggery that uses violence ruthlessly against any force that would challenge the Senator's power. The Senator backs down from a race war that he wants, but Lewt does not back down from damaging the railroad and everything it stands for in this context, including the transformation of the white enclave of capitalist power into a democratic melting pot. Nor does he hesitate to kill his own brother when the opportunity arises (unsuccessfully, as it turns out).

Though Pearl shows no awareness of these conflicts, she signifies the same threat to the dominant social system – the threat of social desire from the location of racial, gender, and class subordination. As her name would suggest, Pearl is rare and valuable because her desire is rare and valuable and because no side of the social system can incorporate it without transforming itself in a revolutionary way. The Senator wants to get rid of her, but Lewt has a passion for her as the other he would like to dominate and control through sheer force. As I said before, the explicit racists, Lewt and the Senator, share common ground with Pearl's racially marked mother because in effect they have constructed the racial other as the projection of their own repressed desires. Lewt loves Pearl as the realization of his sexual being, but he also hates her for being more than an extension or projection of himself; he hates her for desiring something more than sexual gratification, for desiring love or, more accurately, something unnamable that lies in the promise of love more than in the actuality of it. Similarly, Jesse loves Pearl as the image of his own repressed erotic feelings; but neither he nor his mother can finally bear the vision of a sexuality that remains insubordinate to the dominant social interests with which they are both ultimately allied. Though he would modify the social system in order to avoid a race war, he ultimately fears class insubordination as much as his father does: only he would use education and enlightened democracy rather than physical force to subdue the "dangerous" classes. In this way, the differences between the father-identified Lewt and the mother-identified Jesse reflect the contradiction in the American ideology that Slotkin (1992: 29–62) locates in the difference between Theodore Roosevelt's racialism and Frederick Jackson Turner's commitment to Jeffersonian democracy through education.

Clearly, Jesse is the Tom Destry of this movie, but he nonetheless represents the failure of masculinity founded on the Jeffersonian myth not only because of his "general ineffectuality," as Wood points out (1995: 194), but because of his alignment with gender, racial, and class privilege that shapes the paternalism of his relation to Pearl. However limited in perspective, the earlier movies I discussed articulate an alliance between genders that produces a revolutionary class subject; but there is no alliance here, probably because of the explicit introduction of racial hierarchy into the set of social relations that support the capitalist mode of production. Though the movie makes no explicit reference to the Johnson County War, its indirect exposition of the possibility of fascism in the American class system finds its most substantive evidence in that conflict; and the ugly portrait of the "Western" man as fascist carries one to the polar opposite of Wister's celebration of paternalistic authority on the plains.

The late Michael Rogin has pointed out that *Duel in the Sun* is "the illegitimate parent of the civil rights movies that followed it" (1996: 169). It combines "racialized sexual hysteria with liberal political attitudes" and employs the hegemonic technique of racial cross-dressing, which, as Rogin stresses, only affirms the dominant racial hierarchy (25). As he remarks, "Selznick put brownface on the gentile girl, Jones, for whom he was leaving his Jewish wife" (169). By conflating socioeconomic difference with racial difference, the film articulates a political conflict that neutralizes the images of class struggle and sublates them into a sort of ultimate struggle between the extremes of class society: the subaltern, racially marked female, on the one hand, and the fascist white male, on the other. By having them kill each other in the famous duel, the movie virtually legitimates the dominant class society that is made to appear as a compromise between the extremes of fascist violence and unruly subaltern desires. Nonetheless, something survives this "resolution" and that is the hysteria of the movie itself that takes the form of its almost surrealistic coloring and visual excessiveness. *Duel in the Sun* produces a visual hemorrhaging of the dominant Western movie as the hysterical desire for social change that it encodes bleeds onto the screen in the form of impossible images of the West itself. Rather than the usual appeal to nature and the natural man as the essence of the frontier, this movie suggests that the West is strictly a product of the imagination, an expression of the cultural unconscious.

Rogin also points to the significance of casting Lillian Gish as Laura Belle and Butterfly McQueen as the black servant, Vashti (1996: 169). In *The Birth of a Nation*, Gish played the heroine whose impending rape by a black politician inspires the famous ride to the rescue of the Ku Klux Klan, while McQueen played the nearly hysterical black maid Prissy in the most famous Selznick production, *Gone with the Wind* (1939). In effect, *Duel in the Sun* subverts the structure of *Birth of a Nation* in two ways. First, in terms of racial identity, the heroine is not white but brown, and is not saved from rape by a white man but kills the white man who raped her in order to save another white man. Second, in terms of plot, the ride of the Senator and his army of cowboys against the railroad and its Chinese laborers replicates "the ride of Ku Klux Klan against black political and sexual revolution" in *Birth*; but this time the tide of white vigilantism is turned back (Rogin 1996: 14). As for *Gone with the Wind*, Pearl may be the antithesis of Scarlett O'Hara, who has been reduced to the feeble and ineffective Laura Belle; but Vashti is no great improvement over Prissy. The one character played by an actual woman of color in the movie is allowed to survive because she has been "*taught* to be stupid . . . by the film's apparently faultless embodiment of the finest feminine virtues" – Laura Belle (Wood 1995: 194). In effect, the white signifier of racial difference, Jennifer Jones in brownface, must die in order to resolve the contradiction between racial exclusion and democratic inclusion within the American ideology. The real woman of color, McQueen's Vashti, will live as the embodiment and naturalization of racial hierarchy within a segregated American society.

Nonetheless, I don't want to dismiss Jennifer Jones's incorporation of the racial signifier too easily. While Rogin correctly insists on a negative reading of the mass-cultural practice of racial cross-dressing, it is also important to see it as the site of contradiction. In the opening sequence of *Duel in the Sun*, for example, Pearl emerges from the Mexican border that was also the location of Orson Welles's *Touch of Evil* (1958), which, according to Denning (1998: 400–1), was Welles's "most powerful portrait of domestic fascism." Several Hollywood filmmakers who were part of the Popular Front had previously directed movies that used Mexico to explore the possibilities of social democracy, including William Dieterle's *Juarez* (1939) and Elia Kazan's *Viva Zapata* (1952). Paul Muni's Juarez, Marlon Brando's Zapata, and Charlton Heston's Vargas are all acts of racial cross-dressing that nonetheless challenge the normalization of the racist class system by the American ideology; and Kazan produced at least two other significant racial cross-dressing movies, *Gentlemen's Agreement* on anti-Semitism in 1947 and *Pinky* on racial passing in 1949. To see these films as the symptoms of a social contradiction means that they simultaneously affirm and critique the racial hierarchy that they represent. This contradiction is one that may well characterize the alliance between the white liberal establishment and African Americans during the Civil Rights Movement. Still, such racial cross-dressing may express another kind of social hysteria that allows these films to articulate a critique that the dominant system of social representations forbids in any direct form.

Notorious Ladies

Writing about *Duel in the Sun* and Raoul Walsh's *Pursued* (1947), the first of which was based on a novel and the second an original screenplay by Niven Busch, Stanley Corkin argues that these films "focus on the absent mother as a cause for psychic pain: The death of the central character's mother is a precondition of the plot" (2004: 66). He attributes these themes to "the cult of motherhood" that emerged in the postwar years in the attempt to consolidate the family by redefining the status of women who had played such a critical role in the domestic war effort (66–7). For the most part, Corkin reads these films in completely negative terms: they are "instrumental in developing the network of attitudes that resulted in the economic marginalization of women" (81). Though Corkin is onto something in recognizing the shift of the genre toward feminization (which I would trace back to the Depression), he wants to reduce this process to the expression of a Cold War logic (55, 59) that doesn't account for the possibility of a counterhegemonic perspective in the mode of its reception. Part of the problem arises from his inattention to the details of these cinematic texts. In *Duel*, Pearl's contradictory relation to her own desire does arise from the murder of her mother by her father, since it is precisely the subordination of feminine desire that drives the plot of the film. Pearl's tragedy, the same as her mother's in a sense, is that she can only liberate her desire through an act that brings about her own death. Similarly, in *Pursued*, the traumatic origin of Jeb Rand (Robert Mitchum), a memory he struggles to recover throughout the film, has to do with the eruption of masculine violence in the attempt to control feminine desire, when his father was murdered by the Callums for having an affair with Ma Callum (Judith Anderson).

Before considering the reinvention of masculinity in movies from the late forties to the early sixties in the next two chapters, I want to jump ahead to look at other "feminocentric" (though not necessarily feminist) Western movies. My point is that the hysterical discourse of *Duel in the Sun* remains a subtext of or countertext to the dominant Western movie tradition, even up to the present time. Surely the most famous feminocentric Western after *Duel*, and one that was critically though not commercially successful, is *Johnny Guitar*, which was released in 1954, the year after the release of *Shane*. Though this movie is relatively low-budget, unlike the lavish and highly profitable *Duel in the Sun* (Wright 1975: 37), it nonetheless employs a self-conscious style to de-*realize* the Western as history, which ironically enables it to take a stance both toward the contemporary context from which it emerges and toward the past that the Western tends to disavow. According to John Kreidl, Nicholas Ray thought that this movie was "the first color film to use color to its potential"; but, in my view, *Duel* had already made such an "Expressionistic use of color" (1977: 50). In the opening scenes, the saloon-owner Vienna (Joan Crawford) wears a pistol and dresses like a man to emphasize that she has compromised her femininity in order to become autonomous and empowered through the "masculine" ownership of property. Her nemesis is another woman who wears a gun, Emma Small, played frenetically by Mercedes McCambridge. Emma is the most explicitly hysterical figure in this film, but I do not think she is the only one. Jennifer Peterson calls Emma a "misogynous caricature" (1998: 322); and while that is true, it does not follow that the film postulates a gender norm, more or less embodied in the character of Vienna, to which Emma falls short. Peterson defines hysteria, quoting Stephen Heath, as a "*failed* masquerade" (330), which implies that a successful masquerade is not hysterical. However, if gender is a masquerade, Vienna's gender ambivalence suggests that neither of the two categories in the gender binary works perfectly for her.

Both Emma and Vienna are associated with property, though their relations to it are very different. Emma is a big cattle rancher who wants to block the arrival of the railroad that will bring farmers and fences. She and John McGivers (Ward Bond) are at war with Vienna, who owns property that the railroad will make valuable. Vienna wants to use this wealth in order to create a town. In this movie, something like the Johnson County War and the lynching of Cattle Kate has been fused with the more contemporary fifties McCarthyism that director Ray and screenwriter Philip Yordan strongly opposed (Kreidl 1977: 48–9). Casting Ward Bond as the male leader of the cattlemen suggests some mischievous irony on Ray's part, since Bond was a notorious reactionary and former president of the Motion Picture Alliance for the Preservation of American Ideals, which in the late forties had "openly invited the House Committee on Un-American Activities [HUAC] to come back to California and take up where the Dies Committee had left off" (Wills 1998: 195–8). Yordan referred to him as "one of the members of the fascist party in Hollywood" (quoted in Kreidl 1977: 48). At the same time, Sterling Hayden, who plays Johnny Guitar, had named names before HUAC (Navasky 1991: 100–1, 129–30, 151, 280), an act he regretted for the rest of his career (Rogin 1987: 254). According to Ray, Crawford had "refused to inform," and there were tensions between the cast members during the shoot (quoted in Kreidl 1977: 49).

Johnny Guitar is a hysterical text because for many reasons, including Ray's desire to continue making movies, it cannot explicitly state its political aim. Like *Duel in the Sun*, it offers a parade of failed masculinities; but, even more emphatically than the earlier movie, it suggests that hysteria may be the only revolutionary response to its social context. According to Peter Biskind, Johnny Guitar initially arrives on the scene as the "feminized ex-outlaw who now prefers a guitar to a gun and has nothing on his mind but marriage to Vienna"; but he becomes increasingly more masculine during the course of the movie while Vienna becomes more feminine, even cooking breakfast for Johnny near the end, though she still has to use a gun "to purge herself of her masculinized double Emma" (1983: 303). One could argue that the cases of both Vienna and Johnny represent forms of "revolutionary hysteria," as Wood defines it – perhaps not an active protest against class and gender that produces a "revolutionary *effect*," but a masquerade that both fails in specific instances but also generally succeeds in producing a "revolutionary *meaning*."

Given the radical nature of Pearl's desire, one imagines that she could have used her sexuality as the means of accumulating wealth and property in order to make herself autonomous in the manner of Vienna. By the same token, in Vienna's story Johnny can be seen as a reformed Lewt, turned proletarian, who must learn to subordinate his desire to the desire of his lover and to use his talent for killing in a more socially productive way. Yet, in a sense, the endings of these two movies are the same in their containment of revolutionary hysteria. In *Duel in the Sun*, the crippled and impotent Senator's wealth has produced the fascist Lewt who murders in the interest of capital and must be killed so that Jesse, the good son, can resolve the class struggle in a more nonviolent way. In *Johnny Guitar*, the property system has produced Emma Small, the fascist woman who wants to be a man in order either to disavow her erotic feelings for the Dancing Kid (Scott Brady) or to express her homoerotic feelings for Vienna. Emma is sexually impotent, like Senator McCanles, and "small" in more than one sense, which drives her to pursue power and to destroy any force that would challenge that process (see Perkins 1995: 228). For this reason, Emma is a psychological monster in the tradition of both McCanles and Judge Roy Bean in *The Westerner*, though what makes her portrait "misogynous" is that these earlier characters are humanized by the fact that they are or have been loved, whereas Emma is a walking negation of that very possibility. McGivers represents the capitalist class that follows Emma and then deserts her at the critical moment when it becomes clear that her violence is turning against her. At the same time, the system has also produced Vienna, the subaltern who must sell her own body in order to earn the wealth that will give her a chance at freedom. Though Vienna needs property, her goal is not to accumulate wealth as an end in itself but to share it with the men who work for her and to create a new community with the homesteaders who will come on the railroad. However, even Vienna cannot overcome the contradiction between her desire *to be a woman for a man* (namely, for Johnny) and *to achieve autonomy through property*. Her contradiction is artificially resolved when her property, the saloon, burns to the ground and when she kills Emma. In effect, the feminine desire awakened by Johnny (the fire) purges her of contradiction and she becomes a woman for a man. In the gunfight, she purges herself of gender ambivalence and regenerates the community, though only through the containment of the more revolutionary forms of hysteria.

In a critical scene, Emma and McGivers try to lynch Vienna for a crime they know she did not commit because it will guarantee their dominance and control over the territory and its economic value. I do not have to tell the reader how this echoes *The Virginian* and the events that led to the Johnson County War. In effect, the movie implies that the Cold War and the communist witchhunt that followed from it were attempts to reassert the dominance of capital, not against the threat of Soviet-style communism, but against the social desires that emerged from the Great Depression, which often took the form, even in Hollywood, of militant unionism. Throughout *Class Struggle in Hollywood*, Gerald Horne details the emergence of strong unions in Hollywood in the late thirties and during World War II. He cites the view of blacklisted screenwriter Abraham Polonsky that "blacklisting was 'mainly an attack on the major unions'; the 'blacklist . . . went on among them before it hit' the writers, directors, and actors" (2001: 5). If the historical common sense has been that anti-unionism was driven by anti-communism, Horne's study suggests that it was the opposite: anti-unionism drove anti-communism. In other words, the Cold War with its stigmatization of any radical thought as inherently un-American and hostile to democracy was a disavowal of the contradictions of capitalism itself and of its own tendency toward fascism or authoritarian control of the means of production and its distribution of wealth through the use of state violence. Just as Emma uses physical violence and mob rule to disavow her sexual desires, the capitalist state used the Red hysteria to disavow its own entanglement in the postwar global totalitarianism. Ray may not have made this decision consciously, but he chose to explore these issues in a Western because the Western had become the medium through which the history of class struggle in the United States could be articulated in a symbolic form that distorts and disavows the historical actuality.

In a sense, nearly all Westerns tell the same story; and that story finds one of its most clear historical expressions in the Johnson County War. Yet *Johnny Guitar* and *Duel in the Sun* are among the strangest Westerns ever made (Kreidl 1977: 43) because they reveal the mechanisms of the Western as a symbolic process that distorts reality as a way of responding to historical actuality. The same can be said about Fritz Lang's *Rancho Notorious* (1952) and Samuel Fuller's *Forty Guns* (1957). The former has been read by Robin Wood as "a Brechtian parable about patriarchal capitalist culture" (1988: 85), and the latter is no less Brechtian in detaching the audience from a naive identification with the characters that requires no critical thought. *Johnny Guitar* articulates character as, to use a Brechtian formula, a coherence of contradictions (Brecht 1978: 196). Pamela Robertson argues that the movie can be reduced to a form of camp that subverts its own "narrative strategies of containment" (1996: 104). I would prefer the word "Brechtian" to camp because I don't think the film is making fun of itself as much as Robertson thinks. If, as she claims, *Johnny Guitar* is a "fundamentally incoherent text" (105), it would be a coherence of incoherence, since, as Peterson stresses, "this incoherence is what allows for the programming of so many diverse readings" (1998: 332).

In this light, one can also look at a post-Cold-War feminocentric Western that might seem to have erased all signs of class struggle.

Sam Raimi's 1995 movie, *The Quick and the Dead*, shares a number of structural and stylistic similarities with *Johnny Guitar* and *Duel in the Sun*, including a striking use of color and matting techniques. Like Ray's movie, this one involves an alliance between a former gunfighter, Cort (Russell Crowe), and the avenging Lady (Sharon Stone). The Lady, Ellen, rides into a town called Redemption to avenge the death of her father, the former marshal, against the boss of the town, Herod (Gene Hackman). In this movie, there is no capitalist class; there is only the fascist leader who appropriates wealth through direct force. This figure alludes perhaps to the post-Cold-War phenomenon of kleptocracy in formerly "communist" states that have turned to capitalism. The plot of the movie is organized around a gunfighting contest that the Lady enters with the hope of getting a chance to kill Herod. Cort used to ride with Herod but has turned to religion and runs a mission for orphan children until Herod's men kidnap him, burn the mission, and force him to participate in the contest. Cort says that he has renounced violence; but when he is faced with death, he uses a gun to defend himself. Like Johnny Guitar, he struggles against his own masculine brutality and can only redeem himself by putting his violent nature into the service of the Lady. Most of the ordinary townspeople seem to be Mexican Americans who hire a black gunfighter to kill Herod; but the latter easily guns down the black man and announces to the people that he will have to raise their taxes to prevent any further acts of resistance to his authority. *Johnny Guitar* effaces the racial subtext of *Duel in the Sun*, though there is a trace of it in the attempted lynching of Vienna. In *The Quick and the Dead*, the class division undergoes a racial inflection since all the white people (and one black man, Woody Strode as the undertaker) seem to profit in one way or another from the fascist rule of Herod while the Mexican Americans are directly exploited. Still, the religious imagery suggests that the "white" Lady has come to Redemption to redeem herself and everyone else from Herod's misrule. If Cort is a Christ figure who was born again in the transformation from outlaw to missionary, he undergoes a second rebirth through the tutelage of the Lady, who teaches him to combine the role of gunfighter and missionary in the interests of social justice. At the end of the film, he uses his skills as a gunman to force Herod into a fair confrontation with the Lady. She wins the final duel not because she is faster

ILLUSTRATION 10 The Lady (foreground) as dialectical antithesis of Herod (background). *The Quick and the Dead* (1995). Tristar Pictures. *Producers:* Joshua Donen, Allen Shapiro, and Patrick Markey. *Director:* Sam Raimi

but because she represents the collective will of the community, including all races and genders.

The Quick and the Dead alludes as much to the Westerns of Sergio Leone, particularly *Once Upon a Time in the West* (1969), as to *Duel in the Sun* and *Johnny Guitar*. Yet all of these movies owe a debt to Orson Welles, who didn't make any Westerns but who continually explored the potential for the emergence of fascism within democratic, capitalist culture, particularly in *Citizen Kane* (1941) and *Touch of Evil* (see Denning 1998: 362–402). *The Quick and the Dead*, in particular, makes extensive use of compositions in depth that recall the style of *Citizen Kane* (Ill. 10). Herod is never developed to the same extent as Kane, but he recalls Kane in his isolation from the community that he tends to feminize. As Denning notes, though Kane had originally championed the workingman in his newspapers, he "always thought of 'the people' as female"; and the movie itself "recodes politics in sexual terms, as Kane's public life is displaced by his private life" (1998: 393–4). As a populist leader, Kane wins over the love of the people but then talks about them, in the words of his friend Jed Leland, "as though you owned them . . . as though they belong to you." He comes to believe that the people think "what I tell them to think." As with the people, he also comes to think he owns his lover, Susan Alexander; but in the end she says triumphantly, "everything was his idea, except my leaving him." Herod had a wife whom he killed because she was unfaithful to him. Though he makes no effort to win the people's love, he nonetheless feminizes them and then imagines that they will never fight back, "since women can't shoot for shit." However, just as his wife escaped his control, the Lady proves that she can shoot and brings him down.

In all of these movies, sexual failure gives way to authoritarian politics. In *Duel in the Sun*, the Senator in a wheelchair brings up his son to be a killer; in *Johnny Guitar*, the hysterical Emma leads a mob on a lynching party against someone they all know to be innocent; and in *The Quick and the Dead*, Herod takes over a community through force and then kills his own son (the emblematic firstborn) to prove his masculinity. In the end, the fascist creates his nemesis: the woman as subaltern who, as it turns out, can not only shoot but can command the loyalty of the subaltern man and destroy the fascist dream of gender and racial superiority. Raimi's style is perhaps even more influenced by *Touch of Evil*'s stark, almost clichéd dialogue and its unreal images of evil and good. Furthermore, it is surely no coincidence that the narrator's voice at the beginning of *Duel* is that of Orson Welles or that Joseph Cotton's Jesse McCanles is a two-dimensional reproduction of his earlier character, Jed Leland in *Citizen Kane*.

Stylistically, these feminocentric Westerns anticipate an overtly surreal Western like Jim Jarmusch's *Dead Man* (1995) more than a straightforwardly feminist Western like Maggie Greenwald's *The Ballad of Little Jo* (1993). They explore the subversive relationship of feminine, subaltern desire to masculine-identified forms of property. The alliances between men and women that emerged in the classical Westerns of 1939–40 are no longer really possible. In the new postwar environment, which would eventually give birth to a new wave of feminism, the condition for an alliance between man and woman is the feminization of the man, like Johnny Guitar, or the masculinization of the woman, like Pearl, Vienna, and the Lady. Ringo, Destry, and Cole try to articulate new forms of masculinity, but they never really challenge the gender hierarchy; and their women – Dallas, Frenchy, and Jane Ellen – may be strong, but they also seek the support and authority of a strong man. In the later films, the strong man borders on being a fascist; and the woman's resistance to social oppression takes the form of hysterical discourse that leads either to death or the reinvention of gender. Pearl kills

Lewt and dies in his arms, Vienna kills Emma and runs off with Johnny, and the Lady (who, as she says, is already dead) kills Herod and leaves Cort to run the town as marshal. Though Vienna and Johnny may get married and grow rich with the railroad, theirs will be no conventional marriage, since Vienna must always wear the pants to which her business acumen and revolutionary desire entitle her.

As these films suggest, in postmodern US culture, as well as in the global culture that has responded to it, gender has been polarized by the crisis of the class system. Still, unlike the brutal Lewt, the masculinized Emma, or the corrupt Herod, the most compelling and successful image of the authoritarian subject is the one that taught American filmgoers how to stop worrying and learn to love the Cold War. Fascism would not be so dangerous were it not so utterly seductive.

CHAPTER 5

BAD FATHERS MAKE GOOD SONS

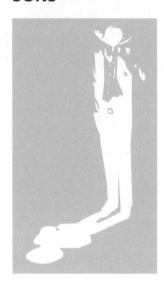

Shoot the Father

A few weeks before the release of *Duel in the Sun* at the end of 1946, John Ford's *My Darling Clementine* also came to the screen. If *Duel* initiated a "minor" tradition or countertradition *within* the dominant Western, *Clementine* consolidated the classical Western movie and set the tone for what would follow, at least until the early sixties, when the Western underwent another shift in its mythography. The differences between this retelling of the Wyatt Earp story and the Westerns of 1939–40 are subtle, especially by comparison with the near-breakdown of the Western system in *Duel*; but *Clementine* more or less reverses the crisis in masculine social identity and defuses the social critique of the class system that was emerging in mass culture before the US entry into World War II. Tag Gallagher maps out the allegorical significance of this movie in rather stark terms:

> Wyatt Earp (the U.S.) gives up marshalling in Dodge City (World War I), but takes up arms again to combat the Clantons (World

War II) to make the world safe. Victory is horrible, and Wyatt must return to the wilderness, to his father (confession; reconstruction), leaving innocence, hope, and civilization (Clementine) behind, "lost and gone forever," a distant memory (the long road) in Tombstone (the world of 1946). (1986: 225)

Though one hardly imagines that any spectator walked out of a theater in 1946 with this message clearly imprinted on the brain, it has to be conceded that the emotional force of such a movie derives from the way it internalizes its historical context and projects an image of the national subject that resonates with collective social experience. Henry Fonda's Wyatt Earp offers a first glimpse of the national subject that was to come out of the war experience, a first sketch of the masculinist Cold Warrior with all of its contradictions. As McBride and Wilmington put it, this is Ford's "most whole-heartedly militarist Western" (1975: 85–6). The Clantons emotionally signify the threat of fascism, reduced in this context to a family of thugs who appropriate wealth through acts of violence. The class conflict here is barely visible. The Earps are cattlemen, and apparently so are the Clantons; but the Earps presumably have earned their portion of wealth while the Clantons steal theirs. In this role, Henry Fonda casts off the revolutionary potential of characters like Frank James and Tom Joad, though he brings some of their "boyish" charm to the role of Earp.

Unlike the Ringo Kid and Tom Destry, there is no chance that Wyatt will be attracted to any woman who is not the utter realization of what is proper, indeed of property itself. Clementine Carter (Cathy Downs) has been the fiancée of Doc Holliday (Victor Mature), whom she has come out west to find. But Doc no longer respects property or proper relationships: he is the last vestige of the outlaw hero, a version of Jesse or Frank James, though he is not motivated by critical class-consciousness in any form. Rejecting Clementine and everything she stands for, Doc chooses as his lover the barroom singer Chihuahua (Linda Darnell). We can deduce from Wyatt's remarks and Chihuahua's general appearance that she is supposed to be a mixture of Apache and Mexican, though this is another cross-dressing performance that resonates with Jennifer Jones's Pearl. Wyatt clearly has no use for Chihuahua, and Clementine dismisses the latter's passionate competition for Doc's love with the remark to Wyatt: "I think it's just a common case of hysteria, Marshal." Hysterical discourse has no revolutionary force in the postwar Fordian Western until *The Man Who Shot Liberty Valance*. By the same token, Doc is no liberal and recalls Pearl's father since his choice of Chihuahua reflects his own self-negation. Like Pearl, Chihuahua dies in the end; and her death is directly linked to Doc's decision to enter the gunfight that will bring about his own death. Though Doc has manners and some remnant of class distinction, he despises all of these social conventions because he lives in the face of death, "the undiscovered country," to use the phrase from Shakespeare that Doc recites – a force he can neither own nor govern and that calls into question the values of civilization as he understands them. Tombstone is the appropriate name for Doc's town, while his disease is the illness of a democratic culture that can produce a force like the Clantons.

Walter Brennan's Old Man Clanton lacks any of the comic qualities of his earlier character, Judge Roy Bean; but he does resemble the Judge in one sense: the wealth he appropriates through violence adds up to nothing. The Clantons accumulate wealth as something dead, something to be accumulated for its own sake. They don't live in comfort, and even their pleasures are stolen. But after the theft of his cattle and the murder of his brother, Wyatt becomes more like the Clantons, as we see in his first face-to-face encounter with the old man. The alternation between close-ups of Walter Brennan and Henry Fonda is chilling and represents one of the finest moments in Fordian cinema (Ills. 11–12). After becoming

ILLUSTRATIONS 11–12 Symbolic father against symbolic son. *My Darling Clementine* (1946). Twentieth Century Fox. *Producers:* Darryl F. Zanuck and Samuel G. Engel. *Director:* John Ford *(shot/reverse shot sequence)*

marshal, Wyatt, like the Clantons, stops doing any real work and spends most of his time gambling, eating, going to shows, or sitting on the porch in front of the hotel. Between the beginning of the film, when Wyatt and his brothers labor on the cattle drive, and the end, when they face the Clantons in a gunfight, they do nothing except exhibit their possession of free time, which is warranted by their reputations as lawmen. If it wasn't for the Clantons, Wyatt would spend all his time hobnobbing with Doc or chasing after Clementine.

This moderately subversive tendency contradicts Wyatt's otherwise conservative signification in this narrative (McBride and Wilmington 1975: 89). His brothers follow his beck and call without question, and the townspeople defer to the man who introduced himself to the community by *literally* kicking a drunken Indian out of town. Later he tells Chihuahua that if she doesn't fall into line he will send her back to the Apache reservation where she belongs. Furthermore, if the Clantons and Doc Holliday are godless, Wyatt and his brothers are equally uncomfortable with religion. Wyatt lies to Clementine when she assumes that he is about to go to church; and though he escorts her and dances with her at the church social, he hardly demonstrates any piety. Like other Western heroes, Wyatt's relation to the community is ambivalent; and when a few townspeople offer to help him at the O.K. Corral, he responds that "this is strictly a family affair."

In the end, Wyatt's victory against the Clantons is horrible because of "his alliance of implacable vengeance with legal and moral justification . . . He stays in Tombstone only four days, with motives initially opportunistic and only belatedly communal" (Gallagher 1986: 226). One has to question if Wyatt's motives are ever communal, since as soon as the Clantons are dead he leaves town. Unlike the earlier end-of-the-Depression Westerns, there is no alliance between the marginalized male and the subaltern female. Chihuahua, the subaltern woman, dies; and Clementine, who is no more subaltern than Molly Wood in *The Virginian*, is left behind. In this context, there is no mixing of masculine and feminine; and the formation of the community implies the clear-cut necessity of a separation of masculine and feminine values, and ultimately, in the post-World-War-II context, of state interests and communal social desires. Wyatt's ride down the long road from Tombstone to

California is strictly symbolic. He represents the necessity of masculine brutality as the condition of feminine social relationships. By the same token, the woman who represents those relationships in this allegory is no longer the bearer of any subversive desire but the embodiment of private property itself, the foundation of the community as a naturalized (and therefore invisible) class system. When Wyatt says that he loves that name "Clementine," he expresses the pleasure of ownership. This national subject introjects the death principle as the primary means of defending democracy against its antithesis and ironically becomes the mirror image of the thing he sets out to destroy.

Don't Shoot the Father

The contradiction within the national subject becomes the content of Howard Hawks's *Red River*, though Hawks neutralizes the problem by giving the story a comic edge. This movie almost single-handedly invented the myth of John Wayne – his construction as a signifier of the national identity. Hawks filmed *Red River* in 1946, but it wasn't released until 1948. The year 1947, of course, was that of the Hollywood Ten; but from the time that HUAC, chaired by Martin Dies, first went to California in 1939, to the issuance of subpoenas to suspected Hollywood communists by the committee's new chair, J. Parnell Thomas, in 1947, John Wayne took no public political position. As Garry Wills comments, "The same careerism that kept him from wearing a uniform [in World War II] kept him from taking a stand . . . He became 'outspoken' only after the Waldorf conference had ended the [ideological] war and the industry was voicing *only* one side" (1998: 197). By the Waldorf conference, Wills refers to the meeting of 50 top Hollywood executives at the Waldorf-Astoria Hotel in New York two days after the US Congress voted to cite the Hollywood Ten for contempt of Congress. The studio heads announced that the Ten would be suspended without pay and that the studios would no longer employ Communists or subversives if they knew of them (Navasky 1991: 83). The next year John Wayne achieved superstardom and became a political activist in the Motion Picture Alliance for the Preservation of American Ideals (MPAPAI), succeeding right-wing Ward Bond as its president. His role after Hollywood surrendered to authoritarian politics was, in Wills's phrase, to "shoot the wounded" (1998: 197). In *Naming Names*, Victor S. Navasky documents Bond's personal efforts to make sure that Hollywood lived up to its anticommunist promises, including his personal phone calls to executives warning of and checking on potential communists (1991: 107, 149). It seems unlikely that Wayne was ever so enthusiastic and probably just went along with the dominant crowd of bullies during the era when Ronald Reagan became the head of the Screen Actors Guild and was secretly handing over names of suspected communists in the organization to the FBI as early as 1947 (430).

Red River is part of that context, even though it could not consciously anticipate what was to come. Not only Wayne but Borden Chase, the author of the story and the screenwriter for *Red River*, was active in the MPAPAI. According to Hawks's biographer Todd McCarthy, though Hawks and the people he associated with (Wayne, Gary Cooper, Victor Fleming, Hoagy Carmichael, and Walter Brennan, among others) were ultraconservative, the director himself "had little more patience for the rhetoric and bullying of the right than he did for the left," and carefully avoided ever becoming active in right-wing causes (1997: 448–9). However that may be, what makes *Red River* such a powerful movie is not only its articulation of the dominant American ideology of that era but its disclosure of that ideology's contradictions, particularly as they are played out in the relation between Wayne's patriarchal Thomas Dunson and his adopted son, Montgomery Clift's Matthew Garth. Initially, Wayne had his doubts about Clift and thought he was "a little queer," but he came to appreciate his acting, as did Hawks as soon as he started shooting the film (414, 421, 423–4). In my judgment, Dunson in *Red River* is one of Wayne's two best performances, the other being Ethan Edwards in Ford's *The Searchers*; and in both cases Wayne's foil is a younger man who calls into question his patriarchal authority. This allows or perhaps forces Wayne to play against his own ideological signification and thus to expose its limits and contradictions. Ironically, the movie that invented John Wayne as a signifier was also the first movie to call into question or critique what he signified.

Thomas Dunson starts his career by breaking out of a wagon train and leaving behind the woman he loves to seek land in Texas. This woman is presumably killed by Indians, and her place is then taken by the young boy, Matthew Garth, who shows up with a cow to complement Dunson's bull. Dunson, in the tradition of Faulkner's Thomas Sutpen, demonstrates the origin of private property when he seizes the land from its Spanish proprietor with the comment that Don Diego took it away from the Indians and now Dunson is taking it away from him. To seal this act, Dunson shoots down Diego's hired gunman. Thus the film lays down two basic premises from which the rest of the action follows: first, the full realization of masculinity requires its identification with private property as well as both a separation from the feminine and the elimination of any racial others who get in the way; and second, private property itself derives from theft that has been legitimated by force. As Robert Sklar noted some time ago, "*Red River* is a film about cows, horses, gun play, brave women, daring men – and capitalism" (1996: 153). Fifteen years later, after Matt returns from the Civil War, Dunson announces that he is broke and will drive his cattle north to Missouri where the markets are. Apparently, the possession of property doesn't guarantee the production of wealth derived from that property, and the rest of the movie is about how wealth is created and who has a right to it. As he prepares for the cattle drive north, Dunson shows that his methods haven't altered that much from when he seized the land by force. Like the Wyoming cattlemen several decades later, this Texas rancher has a rather loose notion of what constitutes private property when it comes to cattle. He gives his men orders to brand all the cattle they come across with his brand, regardless of other brands they may bear. When Matt questions this practice, Dunson makes no apologies.

According to Osgood, the Texas cattle owners who drove their cattle north in 1866 were "usually small cotton and corn farmers as well as stock growers" who came back from the Civil War to claim "possession of their long neglected stock, which roamed at large beyond the fenced-in fields." These early roundups were called "cow-hunts." Sometimes the cattle were taken north by drovers "who 'put up' a herd, taking the cattle on credit and giving a list of brands and amounts due to the owners" (1957: 28–30). Though Dunson is an owner with his own herd, he also takes the cattle of others and agrees to pay them a flat rate upon his return. But he doesn't wait for permission before he starts *putting up* other men's cattle. In the movie, there is no suggestion that Dunson does any farming; and he hardly represents the average Texas cattleman of that era but rather is a composite of cattle-kings like Charles Goodnight of the Goodnight-Loving Trail and John S. Chisum (not to be confused with Jesse Chisum of the Chisum Trail), "the undisputed King of the Pecos," who was often accused of buying cattle whose "brands reflected no connection with the name and address of the sellers" (Drago 1970: 45, 49). One can assume that if Dunson takes cattle that are branded, he is certainly going to take every maverick he can find. According to Helena Smith, in Wyoming in the 1880s, the WSGA passed laws that virtually made all mavericks (unbranded cattle, usually calves that had been orphaned or had left the mother) the property of the Association (1966: 57–61). The popular belief was that "every cattleman of any prominence from the Rio Grande to the Canadian line" had got his start with "a long rope and a running iron" (53). She also offers ample evidence that the cattle barons of Wyoming violated the property rights of small ranchers with an impunity they could not tolerate whenever it was the other way around (71–5). In this context, Dunson's image suggests that the right to wealth derives from personal authority and power. Those who are willing to take it have a right to it.

Dunson's authoritarian personality finally gets the better of him on the cattle drive. John Belton has called the movie a "reworking of *Mutiny on the Bounty*," which "rewrites the conflict between ruthless authority and democratic defiance in the language of the Western" (Buscombe 1988: 292). The difference, however, is that *Red River* is largely the love story between two men, and this element helps to mollify the contradictions between Dunson's fascist attempt to rule by terror and Matthew Garth's more democratic effort to govern by consensus (see Biskind 1983: 278–84). Corkin argues that the conflict between Dunson and Garth is ultimately nothing more than a clash over "management theory," which he bases on a reading of this film and *My Darling Clementine* as works that "adapt the terms of frontier mythology to postwar international relations" (2004: 47–9). Though this thesis has a good deal of merit, which I will come back to later, there is a tendency toward reduction in Corkin's reading of these Westerns that ignores or downplays those elements that point toward contradiction rather than the pure expression of nationalist ideology. In the case of *Red River*, it ignores the fundamental crisis that the whole film centers on once we get beyond the prehistory of the founding of Dunson's Red River D Ranch. At the end of the film's first sequence, Dunson explains to sidekick Nadine Groot (Walter Brennan) and the boy Matt Garth his vision of the future ranch that he will make out of the land he has just seized from the Mexicans. Through a series of cuts and dissolves with Dunson's narration as voiceover, the film carries us 15 years into the future, right after the Civil War, and finally dissolves into an image of the older Dunson. Though he now has the ranch and thousands of head of cattle just as he predicted he would, he comments bitterly that "there isn't a head worth a plug three-cent piece." This sequence begins with Dunson in a medium shot, but the camera tracks back to reveal Matt and Groot looking down on Dunson's crouched form, while Matt takes over the center of the frame. This shift is what the rest of the movie is about: whose vision will occupy the center, Matt's or Dunson's?

While Dunson has been creating his herd, Matt has been away fighting in the Civil War (presumably on the side of the South). In effect, Matt has been engaged in communal action while Dunson has been accumulating property in the quest for personal wealth (which recalls Wayne's own history in the forties). When Dunson stands up, his enormous stature makes Matt look small and feminine by comparison, a feminization that is reinforced by Dunson's observation of the woman's bracelet that Matt wears, the bracelet that Dunson gave to the woman he loved and then took off the Indian who apparently had killed her. It suggests that Matt's character represents some sort of reunification of the masculine and the feminine. Groot is also a feminized character with a woman's first name. Since Groot apparently has no property of his own apart from what Dunson chooses to give him, his character suggests that only the purest form of masculinity has the right to wealth. At the end of this scene, Dunson retakes the center when he mounts his horse after Matt has demonstrated the fact that he may be a little faster with a gun. After Dunson leaves, in a two shot of Matt and Groot the camera is set up at an angle that makes Matt look slightly taller than Groot, though in the earlier shot he was of slighter stature. Then Matt comments to Groot that he has seen Dunson afraid for the first time, and though Groot resists the idea, he admits that there is a problem and moves toward Matt's position for the rest of the movie.

For all of his power, Dunson has not yet proven that his seizure of property actually produces wealth. There is something missing from his character, something that calls into question his version of the masculine and of the national subject.

A contradiction emerges on the cattle drive when Matt finally turns against Dunson's tactics as they gradually become more and more authoritarian. After he has killed several men unnecessarily and driven off others, Dunson decides that he is going to hang the deserters – who are, in effect, strikers against his management of the drive – as a deterrent against any further defections. Up to this point, Matt has stood beside Dunson whether he thought he was right or wrong, but when the latter's actions become tantamount to a lynching, Matt withdraws his support, a decision quite different from that of the Virginian. Every word of dialogue in this scene is critical. When the deserters are brought in on horseback, Dunson is sitting like a king on his throne and tells the men to get down because he doesn't want to look up at them. They should be crawling, he says, emphasizing that they are inferior life forms as far as he is concerned. As Suzanne Liandrat-Guigues notes, Dunson submerges himself in the "here and now of his actions" to such an extent that he cannot see beyond the immediate situation toward their future consequences, something which Matt can do. His relentless commitment to action threatens "a regression towards the subhuman" that, I would add, historically has taken the form of a projection of the "subhuman" onto the other that contradicts or opposes the principle of capitalist command (2000: 42). To Dunson's accusation that these men are deserters and thieves, they reply that the law may see it differently. Dunson announces that he *is* the law.

One of the deserters, Teeler (Paul Fix), responds with an argument. He suggests that all the men on the drive want to get the herd to the market, but Dunson wants to do things his way and only his way. Though several reports suggest that there is better route to the market through Abilene, Dunson won't trust anyone but himself and is willing to kill men who don't submit to his dictatorship. Teeler stresses that the herd doesn't belong exclusively to Dunson but to all the cattlemen in the state. In the context, it seems clear that even the trail hands are cattlemen to the extent that their lives and labor have been invested in this industry. Teeler admits he signed a pledge to finish the drive but not with the man whom Dunson has become. The challenge is ultimately to Dunson's right to wealth and power. Teeler's words suggest that the right to wealth cannot be based exclusively on force. Ultimately, this right is determined by the consensus of the community as to the worth and value of the individual who facilitates wealth production through the exercise of leadership. In other words, despite social inequity and the legal status of private property, real wealth is a communal production; and no man can legitimately accumulate wealth without winning the support of the community and without justifying the use of human labor. Furthermore, Teeler's words call into question the effectiveness of Dunson's leadership since he has not been able to transform the ownership of property into real wealth, and his technique of managing the cattle drive has failed. He cannot sustain the loyalty of his labor force except through terror (which is the technique of fascism), and he wants to treat men as if their labor were abstract property – as if the production of wealth had nothing to do with their creative autonomy. After hearing Teeler's argument, Dunson announces that he is going to hang the deserters, which has the effect of validating everything Teeler has said. At that point, Matt turns against this symbolic father of the community.

Matt Garth is able to take the herd away from Dunson because without hesitation the community of cowhands supports his leadership. In fact, though Matt tells Dunson that he will not allow him to hang the deserters, he never actually draws his gun against the man who raised him, and it is Cherry Valance (John Ireland) and the other cowhands who actually fire on Dunson to prevent his killing his adopted son. At the end of the film, the spectator realizes that Matt has no intention of ever drawing his gun against the father figure. When Matt says he will stop Dunson from lynching the men, he doesn't mean that he will shoot him but that he will lend his support to the revolt. Matt knows the community well enough to gamble that they will follow his leadership and fire on Dunson without actually hurting him. Though Matt is unquestionably in charge of the cattle drive from this point forward, he bases his leadership on social trust and collaboration. He takes the risk of trusting the word of others that there is a railroad in Abilene, Kansas, which will enable them to avoid the increased distance and danger of the cattle drive to Missouri. Corkin points out that the "shift [from Dunson to Garth] is very much in the spirit of reform and is not a revolution" (2004: 48). However, Corkin seems to presuppose that revolution can only be understood as a total transformation of the mode of production and leaves out of account the dynamics of class struggle as an ongoing crisis within capitalism itself.

Matt Garth is not a theorist like Frederick Taylor, and his purpose involves more than organizing the work process in order to increase production and reduce the overall cost of necessary labor. As the narrative of the film makes clear, he recognizes that despite Dunson's legal ownership of the cattle (which is problematic) and of the labor of the cowhands, the real ownership of the means of production is necessarily social. Dunson's managerial technique is dictatorship and rule by force, whereas Matt's method is not simply rationalization in the manner of Taylorization but a response to the genuine desires and needs of the men who accept his leadership. He is able to lead by consensus because he shares power with the men he leads and allows them to participate in the decision making.

In one of the most compelling shots in the film, right after Matt has deposed Dunson and taken over the cattle drive, the spectator sees Wayne in a wide shot from the rear, standing on the ground but leaning against his horse in the far right of the frame. Clearly, the king has been deposed and pushed to the margins. The last shot in this sequence is of Dunson from the same angle, but now standing on his own away from the horse, still on the edge of the frame, watching the cattle drive move away from him in the distance (Ill. 13). Ironically, this visual emphasis on Wayne's natural force and biological fitness calls into question the Wisterian ideology that racial superiority determines the right to wealth.

Red River expresses a kind of nostalgia for the founding father of capital, even though it repeatedly calls into question the validity of his authority and claim to power. First, Dunson leaves a woman behind and gets her killed. Then, he kills one man (and later, it appears, six others) in seizing the land, an act that would be justified by the ideology of American exceptionalism, according to which "Dunson's claim *should* prevail" because "he plans to use the land, in capitalist terms, productively" (Corkin 2004: 43). Nonetheless, in capitalist terms, Dunson's production of cattle – as well as his seizure of cattle that do not belong to him – will produce only the

ILLUSTRATION 13 Father of capital deposed. *Red River* (1948). Monterey
Productions. *Producer and director:* Howard Hawks

economic value of subsistence if he can't find a market. He has, in
effect, overproduced and created an economic crisis, not only for
himself but for the cowhands who work for him and the other
ranchers in the region. The drive north to reach a railroad connection to the eastern markets is the only possible solution; and when
Matt learns about it, he remarks to Groot, "We could make it." To
which Groot instantly responds, "We?" From the outset, Matt understands the cattle drive as a communal action, something Dunson
never figures out. Finally, after Matt leads a revolt against Dunson's
authority, he meets a woman, Tess Millay (Joanne Dru), who is
nothing like the woman Dunson left behind. She is independent
and not exactly concerned with conforming to the conventional
image of the proper woman, since she appears to be either a
gambler or a dance-hall girl who travels in the company of less-
than-proper society. Though Matt leaves her behind in the manner
of Dunson, he has already chosen a woman who refuses to be left
behind. At first, she tries to kill Dunson herself to protect Matt;
then she agrees to marry Dunson if he will agree not to kill Matt.
But her real purpose is to travel with Dunson and warn Matt of his
coming.

Dunson's final showdown with Matt is one of the most preposterous conclusions in the history of the Western, and yet it works. As Liandrat-Guigues argues in defense of the ending, "To make one of them disappear would have been a normalising way (a Hollywood 'happy ending') of allowing us to think that only one was in the right." The present ending, though less historical, is "a more Hawksian one" (2000: 43). In other words, the ending holds in some kind of imaginary resolution the contradiction at the heart of American democracy between the tendency toward authoritarian political figures who would monopolize the use of violence (both nationally and internationally) and the democratic quest for communal solutions to social problems, between radical individualism and collective interests. As Liandrat-Guigues concludes, "The outcome of Hawks' film assures a return to clarity and to the redeeming laugh" (45). The ending comforts by suggesting that the American contradiction could never lead to the violence of European fascism, on the one hand, or of Soviet communism, on the other. As always, the US is the exception. Matt refuses to pull his gun on Dunson until their conflict devolves into a fist fight that is abruptly interrupted when Tess pulls another man's gun and fires, before telling the two men to stop it since it is obvious that Dunson isn't going to kill anybody and that these two men love each other. After this intervention of the feminine, everyone is reconciled and the Red River D becomes the Red River D and M.

According to Corkin, both *Red River* and *My Darling Clementine* implicitly support "the postwar global strategy of 'Empire by Invitation'" (2004. 34) in which US foreign policy basically worked on the principle that, in the words of Thomas J. McCormick, "the rest of the world would win more than it would lose by acquiescing in American hegemony: greater security and material rewards in exchange for diminished autonomy" (1995: 3). From this perspective, Earp embodies the United States as a global policeman protecting the interests of capital. However, I disagree with Corkin's view that the Clantons can be seen in a positive light as the resistance of Arizona's "smaller ranchers" against the "large Texas cattle concerns that expanded to establish ranches in Arizona, driving smaller ranchers out of the market" (2004: 40–1). This interpretation, though it may be accurate in terms of the real history of Arizona in the 1880s (see Simmon 2003: 262, and Brown 1991: 66–8), mistakes the historical significance of Western mythography for history itself. Rather than have Wyatt conform to the image of the Virginian – no longer as socially palatable in 1946 as it was in 1929 – Ford and his writers simply reverse the historical reality. At the beginning of movie, the Earps are represented as pioneers driving a small herd west to start a new ranch in California. In fact, as Simmon observes, the opening shots of the cattle drive follow other classic Westerns in alluding to "the independent laborer" (2003: 262). The Clantons represent the greed and brutality of capital accumulation that is not mollified by law, morality, or even pleasure.

In fact, they embody what Hannah Arendt called the mob in *The Origins of Totalitarianism*: "the residue of all classes" (1973: 107), "not only the refuse but also the by-product of bourgeois society" (155). The mob expresses openly the Hobbesian philosophy that "if man is actually driven by nothing but his individual interests, desire for power must be the fundamental passion of man" (139). Accordingly, the acquisition of wealth by force, as in the case of Dunson, justifies itself and the means used to attain it. As Arendt stresses, all of this is expressed by Hobbes's philosophy, which "foresees and justifies the social outcasts' organization into a gang of murderers as a logical outcome of the bourgeoisie's moral philosophy" (142). The only way of preventing total anarchy in such a situation is to construct a "political structure of so 'unlimited a Power' that it can protect growing property by constantly growing more powerful" (143). Thus, the "fictional" Clantons would be the inevitable by-product of the capitalist system that produces the need for a supercop, the ultimate lawman like Wyatt Earp, who himself challenges the boundaries of the law and remains an ambivalent figure within the community he defends because his real authority is not based on law but on power. For Arendt, this dialectic represents the threat of fascism or totalitarianism, the moment when the ultimate lawman is also the leader of the mob.

Ironically, *Red River* suggests one possibility of redemption from the vicious cycles of endless accumulation of capital and power – the recognition of the humanity of each individual and of the social basis of political authority. When Dunson attempts to lynch the men who refuse to accept his ownership of their labor, he implicitly denies their humanity and presupposes that power and power alone gives him the right to dominate others. He identifies himself as the law because he sees law as nothing more than an expression of power. Matt and the cowhands revolt and show him that without their support his power adds up to nothing. They could kill him, but they don't because that would be to assert power for its own sake once again. For them, the law is a matter of pragmatic social consensus and not the expression of power relations. In the end, Dunson himself seems to accept this situation and the principles of democracy on which it is based. But the question remains as to why our society needs this myth of the father, why men cannot rule themselves without nostalgia for the strong man whose brute force enables him to create wealth out of nothing.

Ironically, Dunson's counterpart in *My Darling Clementine* is Walter Brennan's Old Man Clanton. Though it may seem perverse to identify Clanton as Wyatt's father figure, it follows from the fact that the former is the only man in the film consistently identified as a father, while Wyatt is repeatedly identified as a son along with his brothers and his friend Doc. Paternity here is symbolic but nonetheless articulates the dialectical relationship between fathers and sons in the Western. Fathers are associated with the primitive accumulation of capital, a process that generates the son as the opposition and antithesis of the father. Both Clanton and Dunson demonstrate that primitive accumulation involves out-and-out theft, but there is no nostalgia for the father in Ford's film. Furthermore, the symbolic sons, both Wyatt Earp and Matt Garth, prove themselves to the community not only by defeating the authoritarian father but by mastering or eliminating the racial other. Wyatt's first act in Tombstone is to kick a drunken Indian out of town, while Matt (in addition to defending slavery by fighting for the South in the Civil War) calls for the total extermination of the Indians attacking the wagon train of gamblers and women with the argument that otherwise they will come back to hit the herd. Both films express the same contradiction: on the one hand, they reject the Wisterian ethos of class superiority that is justified by biological difference and the accumulation of wealth through force; and, on the other, they insist on attributing power to a privileged race, the white race, while denying humanity and wealth to the racial other. As I said before, this contradiction rears its head in most Westerns, even if only implicitly, though the most powerful and complex articulation of it occurs in John Ford's masterpiece.

Forget the Father

The Searchers gives no explicit representation to the history of class struggle. It is, after all, more an Indian Western than a gunfighter Western, the former being a subgenre that is not the main focus of this book, though it cannot be left out of the account because it is always in the background. *The Searchers* is both an Indian Western and a gunfighter Western because it foregrounds the isolated loner who occupies a marginal relation to a community of which he is, in some sense, the defender, though in this case he defends it not against the greed and violence of the primitive capitalist, such as Ryker in *Shane*, but against the racial other who threatens the very principles of family and property on which the so-called civilized community is founded. Or rather, I should say, the racial other challenges the concept of family as a form of private property.

In his critique of the representations of Native Americans in Western movies, Armando José Prats describes the myth of conquest that underlies these constructions as one in which "perspective articulates and validates the racio-culturally defined region that I would like to call *the spaces of the Same* . . . The land belongs not to him who inhabits it but to him who beholds it" (2002: 78). Yet John Wayne's Ethan Edwards is initially part of that which is beheld by the true conquerors of the wilderness, the small ranchers, the property owners, people like his brother Aaron and his family who come out of the interior space of the ranch house, which in the film's opening shot is a space of shadow, to witness Ethan's emergence out of the desert. As Buscombe and other critics note, the object of Ethan's desire, the thing that brings him out of the empty, phallic world of self-enclosed masculinity, is Martha, his brother's wife. Buscombe remarks that "All Ethan's actions are in the shadow of his illicit desire" (2000: 9). Visually, Ethan's actions are always in the glaring light of the desert landscape, while the objects that are constituted by his desires lie in the shadows of an interior space. It is as if private property and the family unit that is bound to it are themselves the shadows cast by a desire that must necessarily be seen as illicit from the perspective of those institutions it founds, those objects it constitutes. The spaces of the same, to use Prats's language, are those enclosed spaces that disavow the radical heterogeneity of the open space of desire; and yet there could be no enclosed space, no private property, without the space of wild desire. This is the force that binds Ethan to the wilderness, the desert, and to those human beings who live in that space, the Indians.

As numerous critics have pointed out, John Ford's choice of Monument Valley as the shooting location of the film does not reproduce an accurate image of the Texas cattle ranges in 1868, the time and place indicated after the credits. On the contrary, the image of Aaron's ranch in the middle of a desert and relative waste-land strongly suggests that property and labor in and of themselves do not produce superfluous wealth beyond subsistence, even if that subsistence is comfortable. The significance of superfluous wealth, as Marx understood it, is autonomy, the freedom to employ time in the manner of one's choosing, according to one's desire (1973: 634). Aaron Edwards appears to have little interest in superfluous wealth or in the possibility of using Ethan's labor power, as he indicates when he questions Ethan about why he has come back, since Ethan wanted to clear out before the war and didn't come back for three years after it ended. Ethan responds defensively that he can pay his way, at which point he produces $180 in freshly minted gold coins. As Jonathan Freedman has argued, "the entire course of the film's plot is generated by the newly minted Union gold coins that Ethan has stolen before the film begins and that he proceeds to put into circulation for its duration" (2000: 590). Peter Lehman, after making a similar assertion, offers the disclaimer that such things "are suggested as possibilities" (1990: 391; see also 2004: 248), though I would agree with Freedman that these possibilities are "more likely than not" (2000: 597).

Any ambiguity about the legal status of Ethan's gold coins may point to the fact that the origins of capital must necessarily reside in a mystery that serves to legitimate another fantasy, the myth that capital grows itself, generates value out of itself through the mere utilization of living labor. In one and the same gesture, the film suggests that the origin of capital is theft, at least metaphorically, and disavows this origin through the production of a myth. Ethan is that myth, the image of the primitive capitalist whose accumulation of wealth under conspicuously mysterious circumstances makes possible the circulation of capital and the exploitation of labor, but only on the condition that any memory of the origin of wealth is forgotten even as primitive accumulation itself is repeated through the appropriation of surplus value – the value of labor that can be translated into superfluous wealth. Marxists, and Marx before them, frequently make the point that, within the framework of the capitalist labor market, the exchange between the capitalist and the worker is not unfair because it has not been produced by an act of coercion. Exploitation lies in the relations of production that force the worker to sell his or her labor power in order to live. However, the economic power that enables the capitalist to exploit labor and enforce the class system derives from an act of capital accumulation that historically originated in violent if not overtly illegal activity.

Aaron and Martha have produced subsistence through their labor and have little else to show for it, except for the family and those comforts of human relationship that lie in the shadowy realm of their domestic world. The latter could be termed *affective wealth*. In his quest for superfluous wealth without labor, Ethan has lost something of incommensurable value that brings him back to Aaron's ranch. Ethan has come back not because he wants to work the land, since he no longer needs to work in order to live (at least for the moment), but because Aaron has the one thing he wants, the one object his money cannot buy – Martha. A man who could expropriate the wealth of others through theft or speculation could more than likely take his brother's wife if given the opportunity; and though it seems unlikely that Martha would allow such a violation of her marriage, Ethan's secret desire, as Buscombe notes, "violates the sanctity of his brother's home" (2000: 9). In this rigidly patriarchal world, the feminine embodies the principle of wealth beyond subsistence and beyond the market, of a force in the laboring process itself that cannot be reduced to labor power as an abstraction. Aaron has presumably worked the land, though we see no signs of it, in order to construct the physical space, such as it is, in which the family can emerge and grow; but it is Martha who bears children and creates the emotional and cultural environment that virtually transforms the wasteland of this wilderness into a garden, to use the vocabulary of Henry Nash Smith (1970: 174–83). She creates the possibility of happiness, or affective wealth, that money in and of itself cannot buy. Ethan can use his gun to appropriate wealth and destroy anyone who gets in his way or tries to take it from him, but he cannot create anything. He embodies the principle that the right to wealth derives from force, but he also exhibits the futility of abstract wealth, the ethical and emotional poverty to which it leads.

Buscombe expresses the common view that "Scar, the Comanche chief whom Ethan pursues, is in some sense Ethan's unconscious, his id if you like. In raping Martha, Scar has acted out in brutal fashion the illicit sexual desire which Ethan harboured in his heart" (2000: 21; see Eckstein 1998). To some extent, Ethan is reminiscent of Shane who also appears to love the wife of another man, though Shane is not afraid of labor and sacrifices his life to defend the Starrett family from another version of the primitive capitalist, Ryker. The latter is a man not unlike Ethan; and one can imagine that, should Ethan accumulate enough wealth and power over the next two decades after 1868, he will become the sort of man who will respond to a new generation of homesteaders and the class conflicts that culminated in the Johnson County War in the same way he responds to the Indians. Therefore, Scar's attack on the Edwards family, their property, and the icon of value beyond subsistence or the market – Martha – represents more than Ethan's sexual desire but rather his economic desire to expropriate and consume the wealth of his brother, which would include his brother's wife, and to destroy everything that gets in the way of that expropriation, including the brother himself.

Scar's raid drives home another point that concerns Ethan. Aaron and Martha have labored to produce their home and family life, but the material condition of that production was the expropriation of the wealth of Native Americans (Colonnese 2004: 337). I emphasize the expropriation of wealth as opposed to property because whether Native Americans assimilated European concepts of market culture, which would include the legal concept of private property, as the "Five Civilized Tribes" did, or whether they developed a more nomadic relation to the land as the Great Plains Indians like the Comanches did in the nineteenth century (Hine and Faragher 2000: 138–9, 181), the fundamental issue lay in the fact "that Indians possessed the land and that Euro-Americans wanted it" (Limerick 1987: 190). According to recent historians, after Native Americans were driven to the Great Plains by colonizing pressure from the East, they underwent a change from communal egalitarian societies to societies in which "there were wealthy men with many horses and poor men with few" (Hine and Faragher 2000: 8–9, 39).

With respect to the "obsessive white worry about Comanche raiders kidnapping white women for sexual purposes," so visible in *The Searchers*, James F. Brooks notes that "the larger reason for Comanche kidnapping was the need for slave labor, especially female labor, in the horse, cattle, and bison robe business" (2004: 271). In some sense, then, the Plains Wars were actually a struggle not only over the distribution of wealth but over the control of labor as a means of production. Since Ethan fought for the South in the Civil War, which was also in part a struggle over the control of labor as a means of production, he has already demonstrated a view of labor that is more or less identical with that of Indian leaders like Scar whom he supposedly hates.

Aaron may not be a wage slave in the conventional sense of selling his labor power to someone else; but by investing his labor power in the production of goods for the market, which presumably is the goal of his ranching enterprise, he becomes a slave to that market. He must work in order to live at a subsistence level. Both the Indians in the movie and Ethan have something that Aaron has surrendered, which is autonomy in relation to the market. Though they are not beyond expropriating the wealth produced by labor (slave labor in the case of the Indians, wage labor and slave labor in the case of Ethan), they have no desire to sell their labor for subsistence. By raiding Aaron's farm and destroying the products of his labor, the Indians attack those social relations that are threatening their autonomy. By raping and killing Martha and the other children, along with Aaron, they destroy the value beyond market value that seemingly justifies slavery to the market. By taking Debbie to raise as an Indian, they repossess, in some sense, the irreducible value of a way of life that has been stolen from them and legitimate their right to wealth through the use of violence. Furthermore, though Ethan and most critics have assumed that the captive Debbie (Natalie Wood) becomes one of Scar's wives, the historical reality is that such an event would be unlikely among Plains Indian groups, since, in the event that a child was captured and adopted, the adoption entailed "a parent–child incest taboo." This prohibition also had "an economic function of profit for the household" through the market for brides (Brooks 2004: 281–2). Though Ford may or may not have known this fact, he nonetheless constructs a situation in which Debbie represents superfluous wealth beyond labor. Ethan's pursuit and hatred of the Indians, therefore, is a pursuit and hatred of the implications of his own desire, both economic and sexual; and in this context, it is difficult to see how to separate the two.

Ethan is able to know and understand the Indians because they are a projection of his own identity. They are not only the image of his desire, but they embody the originary violence or trauma that underlies the so-called civilization that displaces them. Later Scar reveals to Ethan the motive behind the apparently motiveless violence of the Indian attack on the Edwards ranch, which is the murder of Scar's sons by white men. Furthermore, the film has already revealed by that point the brutality that underlies the foundation of "civilization" in the massacre of the Indian village by the US Cavalry, the results of which Ethan and the adopted son of Martha and Aaron, Martin Pawley (Jeffrey Hunter), witness. In his long search for Debbie, Ethan comes to signify the link between racial identity and economic autonomy precisely through his fanatical hatred of Indians, which amounts to a disavowal of his transgressive desire both for his brother's wife and for wealth without labor, which means ultimately wealth derived from the labor of others, including, even if only indirectly, the labor of Aaron and Martha. Ethan's quest is to destroy the traces of this originary violence by projecting it onto the Indians and then destroying the memory of it by destroying those who bear its signification. In the end, Ethan's construction of whiteness through the appropriation of Indianness brings about the dissolution of his own identity, his own displacement from the dominant narrative of the nation (see Prats 2002: 281). As the founding father, Ethan has employed the violence he would identify as "savage" in order to create the racio-cultural space of the same, which incorporates the concepts of private property, the family, and the nation.

Ethan exemplifies what Prats calls the Double Other, the one who *"realizes the heroic ideal of his culture and embodies its most exalted being by becoming his culture's very idea of savage Otherness"* (2002: 182–3). In its foundation, the space of the same is ambivalent or othered. The wealth that lies beyond subsistence requires the expropriation of the other, whether that other refers to the Native Americans or to the class of those who must sell their labor in order to live. Ethan's appropriation of the space between the dispossessed Native Americans and the exploited wage slaves of the market culture derealizes both positions and articulates a fantasy of the nation that erases the expropriation of land and the exploitation of labor on which it is founded. The space of the same is the fantasy of the nation's miraculous birth out of nothing. It is in this sense that we can speak of what Henry Nash Smith called the "virgin land" (1970; see Worland and Countryman 1998).

Freedman points to another figure that Ethan must erase in order to legitimate the nation and the social system he founds. Futterman, the man Ethan pays for information about Debbie and the man he shoots in the back for trying to rob him, can be read as a composite of Jewish stereotypes (2000: 591). Even if one questions the man's literal Jewishness within the framework of the film (Baughman 2000: 605–9), Futterman nonetheless conforms to a stereotype that has racial connotations, and the actor's appearance by contrast with that of John Wayne suggests a racial difference. As Freedman stresses, "the function of the stereotypical Jew [is] to embody a negative response to the market so that gentile participation in it can proceed relatively unexamined" (2000: 592). Once again, like the Indians, this racial other congeals in his representation a negative aspect of Ethan's own desire, including Ethan's desire to appropriate wealth without labor. When Futterman tries to rob Ethan, he engages in the very act that has made Ethan into the symbolic father of the nation and validates the principle that force determines the right to wealth. Futterman asserts his own right to it and loses out to Ethan. Furthermore, in Freedman's reading, Futterman expresses another aspect of Ethan's desire, the element of it that his racism works at disavowing: "The threat frequently encoded by the Jew is a crossing of racial divides that is first cultural and then sexual, of the promiscuous interminglings of human beings across cultures, ratified and accomplished through the act of trade, that ultimately becomes understood as the tabooed and attractive possibility of miscegenation" (593). Futterman is literally a caricature of Ethan's own sexual and economic desire. His "shady" economic transactions have "sexual implications," since the object he trades to Ethan is Debbie's dress (591). Supposedly, Futterman got the dress from an Indian, but there is the strong suggestion that Futterman has somehow participated in the sexual violation of Debbie since he has exploited her alienation from white culture, symbolized by the dress, for purposes of profit. In a sense, by reducing Debbie to the status of a commodity that can be exchanged for profit on the market, Futterman has symbolically killed her and destroyed the value beyond value that she derived from her mother. Therefore, it is not surprising that Ethan anticipates Futterman's actions and sets him up to be killed when he attacks Ethan's camp. Ethan must kill Futterman in order to disavow his own economic desire as well as his implicit intention to do to Debbie in reality what Futterman has done symbolically.

Through Futterman, economic exchange is associated with miscegenation. In Ethan's case, the wealth he has accumulated in the form of gold coins enables him to wander and search for Debbie while Jorgensen engages in the hard labor of raising his cattle for the market. Presumably, Ethan will compensate Jorgensen and still make a profit without having to do any work. The source of his wealth derives from his ability to become what he imagines the Indian to be – to assert force and appropriate wealth without selling himself or sacrificing his autonomy. In this respect, the Indian has become a social fantasy of the hegemonic culture, a fantasy already alive in the nineteenth century (see Abbott and Smith 1991: 227–8). Consequently, one could argue that symbolically Ethan's wealth is already the product of miscegenation, since it involves the symbolic crossing of racial divides and the expropriation of the other, who is necessarily racialized. From this perspective, savage or race war is de facto a form of class war. After all, if one accepts the general principle that the true attribute of wealth is free time and autonomy, then from the beginning the struggles between Native Americans and the colonizers, as well as between the capitalist class and wage labor, have been over the distribution of wealth. The Indian Wars can be seen as the resistance of Native Americans to the class system that was being imposed on them by white culture. As Sitting Bull noted about the white race, "These people have made many rules that the rich may break but the poor may not . . . Possession is a disease with them" (Hine and Faragher 2000: 256).

Though nothing in The Searchers explicitly states that Ethan has had sexual relations across racial boundaries, there are some curious suggestions that should be noted. All of these have to do with Ethan's relation to Martin Pawley. Near the end of the film, Marty protests the plan to attack and destroy Scar's camp because it will lead to Debbie's murder by the Indians, which, according to Colonnese, misrepresents Comanche social practices (2004: 339).

Suddenly, Ethan makes his most bizarre and improbable revelation. After explaining that Debbie will be better off dead, he goes on to justify the contemplated massacre by telling Marty that the "long and wavy" scalp he saw earlier in Scar's tent when they were negotiating with the Comanches belonged to Marty's mother. After a moment's hesitation, Marty remains unimpressed and wants to risk himself for Debbie's life, but Ethan's revelation has implications Marty can't see. For one thing, how could Ethan recognize some-one's scalp unless he was on the most intimate terms with that person? Lehman has suggested the possibility that Marty is Ethan's son, which "would . . . explain his reaction to Marty's Indian-like appearance" at their first encounter when Ethan says rancorously that Marty could be mistaken for a "half-breed" (1990: 390–1). Since Marty is one-eighth Cherokee, it follows that his mother could have been part Indian, and if Ethan is his father, then misce-genation has already taken place at the foundation of the relation between the symbolic father of the nation and the only man in this film who can qualify as his son and heir. Furthermore, given Ethan's racism and general tendency toward violence, one can easily imagine that the enmity between himself and Scar goes back to this original act of violence. Ethan could be the one responsible for the murder of Scar's sons; and if not Ethan, then someone like Ethan. One could postulate a scenario in which men like Ethan took away Scar's land and the relatively free way of life associated with it, to which Scar responded by killing some of the settlers. He may have killed Marty's mother precisely because of her relation to Ethan and her betrayal of Indian culture. (Such a scenario may not have any anthropological validity, but it has allegorical validity within this Hollywood tradition.) Ethan then kills Scar's sons, which leads directly to Scar's retaliation against the Edwards family. In a sense, Ethan's involvement in the expropriation of Indian lands for white settlement is itself an act of miscegenation that is correlated with his sexual relation to a woman of Indian descent. Once again, economic desire and sexual desire, from this perspective, are the same thing.

As Freedman sums up the movie's significance, "[economic] ex-change and race mixing are correlated with one another, organized under the affective heading of shame." He cites Lehman (1990) and Pye (1995b) to the effect that both forms of exchange constitute "abhorred or tabooed behavior that Ford uses to establish contrasts with his own deeply felt investment in categories like 'land' (as opposed to capital) or whiteness (as opposed to race mixing)" (Freedman 2000: 594). But the darker implications of Ethan's identity as the expropriator of land and labor suggest that the land is not so virginal and that no location of pure legitimacy exists. In fact, the apparent innocence of the Edwards and Jorgensen families hinges on Ethan's assumption of the burden of shame for the sin of primitive accumulation; their legitimacy depends on his lawlessness, their sexual propriety on his transgressive desire. As Marx noted, "revolutions are not made with laws" (1977: 876). In his summary of the history of primitive accumulation, he noted the significance to the formation of the capitalist class of "those moments when great masses of men are suddenly and forcibly torn from their means of subsistence, and hurled onto the labor-market as free, unprotected and rightless proletarians" (876). In the European context, Marx saw the expropriation of peasant land, which means the expropriation of the peasant's right to use the land, as the founding act, but he also recognized the expropriation of Native American lands and African slave labor as central to the same process on the opposite side of the Atlantic (915). These expropriations explain the origin of American capital.

But just as the frontier white families are not innocent, neither are the Indians: "the mounted warrior of the plains . . . was in fact not an aboriginal character at all but one born from the colonial collision of cultures." For example, the Comanches came from elsewhere to dominate "the southern plains, raiding Indian and Mexican villages from the Mississippi all the way west to the Rio Grande" (Hine and Faragher 2000: 138–9). This is not to justify the brutality of American empire-building but to suggest that any idealization of the Old West as a precapitalist enclave fails to recognize the contradictions that from the beginning lay behind its formation as both a socioeconomic and mythological space. Ethan Edwards embodies the contradictions at the origin of the capitalist culture of the United States. He expresses the racism that historically justified the primitive accumulation of capital in the form of expropriated land and labor, particularly the labor of slaves, and the ongoing expropriation of the superfluous wealth that derives from the social relations of capital. At the same time, by bequeathing his wealth to Marty and finally bringing Debbie back to the enclave of the family,

ILLUSTRATION 14 A racist American gaze. *The Searchers* (1956). Warner Bros. *Producer:* Merian C. Cooper. *Director:* John Ford

he gives birth to a racially mixed community from which he must be symbolically excluded (Freedman 2000: 595).

In the film's darkest moment, Ethan turns back for one last look at the white captives being held by the US Cavalry. Every critic comments on the look on Wayne's face (Ill. 14), which has been seen as expressing both vicious hatred of and torment over the condition of the women who have supposedly experienced racial mixing (Grimsted 2004: 309–10). The confusion about the significance of the look testifies to the complexity of Ethan's racism. Before looking in that way, he says, "They ain't white anymore. They're Comanch." The unforgettable look comes in the sequence immediately after Ethan and Marty discover the dead Indian woman whom they call Look. This is the woman whom Marty had accidentally bought as his wife in a trade that he could not understand because of his ignorance of Native American languages. Because Marty keeps saying "Look, look" to her, she assumes that he wants that word to be her name. Lehman notes that Ethan first pronounces her name as "Luke" while Marty immediately calls her "Look." Lehman further argues that in the famous and embarrassing scene in which Marty kicks her down a hill, she is a denied any reverse shot that would express her reaction to this violence, though later she is taken seriously by both Marty and Ethan after she has been killed in the massacre of her village by the cavalry. Lehman calls the latter shot the missing reverse shot since we finally see her; but what we see, for only a second, is the body of a dead Indian woman, a body that can no longer express reaction or point of view (1981; 1990: 405, 411). Symbolically, Marty's naming of Look kills her by making her nothing more than the expression of Marty's look, his way of seeing her. Yet when she dies, it's as if Marty begins to realize for the first time that she was an autonomous being. Earlier in the film, Marty told Laurie (Vera Miles) that he has to follow Ethan in order to protect Debbie because he has seen Ethan's "eyes at the very word 'Comanch'." When he names Look, he doesn't consider or realize that the gaze that could kill Debbie could also kill Look; but when Ethan discovers her body, Marty expresses not only remorse but anger at the murder of someone so obviously innocent.

Though Ethan also mourns Look's death, he reveals in the next scene the depth of his ambivalence not only about the racial other but about miscegenation. His confused look at the captives, whether it is one of hate or pity, shapes what we see in this scene; and Ford may signal this distorted vision through the presence of the woman in a dark cloak holding one of the captives by the shoulders. This figure is played by the actress Mae Marsh, who starred in Griffith's *The Birth of a Nation* as the young woman who leaps to her death when pursued by a black man with a sexual interest in her. By the time of *The Searchers*, which was made not long after the Supreme Court ruled on *Brown vs. Board of Education*, Ford would have been well aware of the distorted images in the earlier film; and he surely suggests that Wayne's gaze is the gaze of one who is haunted by an outmoded racist ideology (Eckstein 2004: 8–9; Henderson 2004: 292–3, 304). A few scenes later, Ethan acts in a way that erases the ambivalence of his look. He and Marty have seen the mature Debbie in Scar's teepee, but when she comes to their camp later in order to warn them away, Ethan draws his gun on her, while Marty stands between them. It is interesting to note that Debbie is nothing like the "hysterical" captives that Ethan looks upon with such hateful torment in the earlier scene at the fort. She seems perfectly assimilated to her environment, which suggests that she has accepted her identity as an Indian.

Though there are various ways to read this sequence, it seems to me that there is a direct challenge to Ethan's dominating gaze through the development of something like the dialectic of the look. Though Marty initially recognizes from the look in Ethan's eyes that, as he says to Laurie, "he's a man that can go crazy wild" – that is, become a savage – it is only through the mediation of the character Look that Marty discovers his own participation in the racist gaze. When he sees her dead, he seems to realize, if only unconsciously, the social effects of his own way of looking, and though Ethan expresses regret, the very next scene dramatizes his inability to see racial mixing as producing anything but the monstrosity of hysteria, as he understands it. In the scene when Debbie comes to warn them, she appears initially as nothing but a black speck on the top of a distant sand dune. She is visually present, but the meaning of this presence is ambivalent, unmarked by any determinate identity. When she suddenly stands up and runs down the hill, Marty turns around and sees her first; then, as he moves toward her, he effectively blocks Ethan's gaze for a moment. Seen through Marty's eyes, Debbie appears as a white woman who has assimilated Native American culture without becoming hysterical, without exhibiting any obvious signs of brutalization. When Debbie says, "These are my people," Ethan tells Martin to stand aside, but Marty turns around to shield Debbie from Ethan's gaze and gun. Later, after Ethan and Marty escape the Indians by running into a cave, they are able to look out at the spectacle of the Indians attacking, which clearly suggests that Ethan's look has reasserted its authority; but after the attack, when Marty comes out of the cave, the visual imagery strongly suggests that he is coming out of a womb and is in the process of being reborn. The darkness of the cave recalls the darkness of the Edwards home at beginning of the film, only this domestic, feminine space in the heart of a natural rock formation suggests symbolically that the essence of such "civilization" is not peculiar to the culture of white people and doesn't require the concept of private property but exists in dialectical opposition to every masculine, phallic space, in which violence determines social identity.

With this antithetical space in the background, Marty completes his education when he confronts Ethan over the issue of property and relationships. From Ethan's will, Marty learns that Ethan has left all of his property to the younger man with the claim that he is without "any blood kin." Marty points out that Debbie is Ethan's kin and throws the will back at him, saying he doesn't want any of Ethan's property and that he "ain't forgettin' you was gettin' all set to shoot her yourself." Ethan simply responds, "She's been livin' with a Buck!" The point is not that Marty now transcends the racism of Ethan's world or the social principles of property and class on which it is founded. His response to Ethan is emotional rather than critical; and though by the end of the film he will have risked himself to save Debbie from her captivity, he abused Look and drove her away to perish at the hands of the horse soldiers. Nonetheless, Marty refuses Ethan's demonization of racial mixing and his reduction of family relationships to property. He refuses Ethan's demonizing "look" that transforms a captive like Debbie into the "hysterical" female that Ethan saw at the fort.

By the end of the film, Ethan saves Debbie by sacrificing himself on the altar of savagery when he scalps Scar, who is already dead. He also makes it possible for someone with Indian blood to become his heir. As in *Red River*, the founding father must once again come to terms with the son who opposes not only the father's authority but the origin of the social system the son inherits from the father. When Ethan picks her up in his arms, Debbie ceases to be the grown woman who has lived with a buck and becomes the little girl to whom Ethan gave his war ribbon. In one gesture, he erases both her Indianness and her sexual maturity. As Prats argues, "When Ethan . . . scalps Scar, he restores Debbie's 'whiteness' by surrendering his own. Her Indianness is not so much *reversed* as *displaced*. Ethan transfers it to himself" (2002: 63).

Yet I would put it differently. Debbie's Indianness, as well as her sexual maturity, is a part of her history, just as Marty's Cherokee "blood" is a part of his. Neither of them can erase that history, but Ethan as the founding father can at least displace it. His racism has justified the expropriation of the other, the Indian, as the condition not only of his own material privileges but of the market system that exploited the labor of his brother and Martha. In this way, Ethan has indirectly brought about the exploitation and death of the thing he loved most in the world (a fate he shares with Thomas Dunson). Ethan cannot reverse this process, but he can displace it by taking onto himself not Debbie's or Marty's Indianness but the "savagery" that is identified with Indianness, including the savagery of Ethan's own transgressive sexual desires for the racially marked woman as well as for his brother's wife. Finally, his exclusion in the final shot of the film when the door is shut on him doesn't support the view that he has become "Debbie's equal through the shared token of savagery," so that he "can recognize her as a savage and still save her" (2002: 70). In effect, Ethan has gone down with Scar, has absorbed savagery into himself. This act then makes possible the thing he has stood against throughout the film, a society that normalizes racial mixing and redistributes the wealth on both sides of the racial and class divide.

Ethan's exclusion from this society represents the exclusion of men like the Virginian's father figure Judge Henry, along with Ryker, Judge Roy Bean, Old Man Clanton, and Thomas Dunson. It is a beautiful dream, but it is also a lie, because the father we forget, the history we repress, comes back to haunt us and seduce us over and over again. The sons never really escape the sins of their fathers. Bad fathers make good sons only because, in the end, good sons become bad fathers. Martin's transcendence of race and class comes at a price: he proves himself the son of Ethan by killing Scar, just as the Virginian proved himself the son of Judge Henry by lynching Steve who had gone over to the side of "savages" like Trampas. As Brian Henderson notes (2004: 71), Marty becomes the exemplary nonwhite when he kills Scar, an act crucial to the formation of the national subject that can integrate the other into its own myth. Martin transcends race and class by postulating whiteness as the signifier of transcendence. Now he can marry a white woman, inherit Ethan's property, and become a frontier policeman in the manner of Wyatt Earp. The good son resolves all contradictions and erases the memory of the father's violence at the foundation of the nation. Thomas Dunson, Ethan Edwards, and even Old Man Clanton – the founding fathers become either famous or infamous, but in either case they reduce history to a legend of creation *ex nihilo*. Like Monument Valley, they embody the past as ruin (Hutson 2004: 98, 103–4). But just as Wyatt Earp rides off into Monument Valley at the end of *My Darling Clementine*, Marty will eventually become one of the monuments in the desert after he has brought about the ruin of his own desire for something more than the space of the same, a desire glimpsed when he first appears in the film riding his horse bareback like an Indian. The monuments teach us not to pursue the creative realization of our desires but to transcend desire toward an identification with the transcendent father of the race. They teach us to send our desires back to the desert from which they emerged.

CHAPTER 6

MEN ON THE VERGE OF A NERVOUS BREAKDOWN

The Gunfighter and the Proletariat

With characters like Thomas Dunson and Ethan Edwards, who both follow in the tradition of Faulkner's Thomas Sutpen in *Absalom, Absalom!*, or even like Wyatt Earp, who defeats Indians, gunfighters, and rustlers with surgical skill, the masculinity that had been called into question by the Great Depression was not only reinvented but reinvigorated with something in excess of anything preceding it. For these men, as for the Virginian and Judge Henry, the law is what they say it is; but the difference between these men and the Virginian is that in one way or another their values are questioned or undermined by the works in which they appear. Even Wyatt Earp, who remains the first and most uncritical articulation of the type, has to ride off in the end and leave his Clementine behind, because he can't be integrated into the community he has devastated through the violence of his family affair. Furthermore, these films all have a populist bent to them and are never overt defenses of a dominant class, though they are often implicitly defenses of a

MEN ON THE VERGE OF A NERVOUS BREAKDOWN 109

dominant race. However, between the fascist father, who subordinates the law and the political system to his will, and the revolutionary hysteria of those subversive individuals, male and female, who question gender and class hierarchies, there is another group of men whose masculinity triumphs, but only at a price – only by recognizing its limits and the moral uncertainty it tries to disavow. These are the men who go on despite their self-doubts or the doubts of others around them, and who often leave society, die, or simply fall apart, in the process of redeeming society. These men appear in Westerns that critics have identified as "psychological" and that André Bazin once labeled "superwesterns" (Bazin 1971).

As I suggested in Chapter 1, the antithesis of John Wayne's image of the Western hero is Alan Ladd's Shane. While Wayne's hypermasculinity tends to embody the authoritarian principle in American culture and the questionable origins of capital (until *The Man Who Shot Liberty Valance*, when even Wayne's character starts to fall apart), Ladd's more feminine image suggests the possibility of a new form of masculine identity that may not be exclusively masculine, or rather that is not founded on the radical exclusion of the sexual or even the racial other. In saying that Shane's character need not exclude the racial other, I recognize that in its original form it certainly does, since there are no racially marked people in Stevens's film. However, there are numerous examples of Shane figures with different racial identities that have emerged since the fifties, including the heroes of Sidney Poitier's *Buck and the Preacher* (1972) and the more recent and postmodern example of Mario Van Peebles's *Posse* (1993), both of which insert African Americans into the historical reality as well as the myth of the West (see Taylor 1998). The most recent and interesting example is the character played by Ving Rhames in the movie *Rosewood* (1997), which is not strictly a Western but has the structure of one. In his commentary on the DVD version of the film, director John Singleton points to the influence of Ford on his style; but I would suggest that he uses Rhames to create a character antithetical to the Ethan Edwards figure and inevitably alludes to the Shane tradition in doing so.

Furthermore, if John Wayne's persona tends to manifest the viewpoint of capital as a force that expropriates and accumulates wealth through violence, Alan Ladd's Shane suggests the possibility of an antithetical viewpoint. Though it is not strictly "proletarian" in the nineteenth-century sense of the word, this antagonistic subject represents the emergence of a social identity that refuses to sell itself as labor power, that refuses to work in that sense, and that holds onto its autonomy while resisting or struggling against the exploitation or domination of others. Shane is the purest expression of such an antagonistic social identity in the fifties Westerns, but there are elements of this formation in other "gunfighter" Westerns in which "professionalism in the arts of violence is the hero's defining characteristic" (Slotkin 1992: 379). In virtually every case, the gunfighter is a man in search of a relation to the larger community, though in some cases the community will not accept him and in others he must leave or reject the community in order to assert his relation to it. This figure is distinguished from a man like Ethan Edwards, however, by his alienation from the thing that constitutes his identity, the gun itself. Ethan's identity, though it may occasionally surprise us, is always integrated by the character's self-certainty, while the gunfighter I refer to is a walking embodiment of self-doubt.

For this reason, the image of such a gunfighter anticipates and helps to shape the emergence of a new form of the political subject in the capitalist culture of the late twentieth century, a culture in which the divisions between labor and capital are not as obvious as they were in the nineteenth century. Particularly in the industrial nations, the social location that opposes capital cannot be limited to one class formation but is diffused among all the different groups that must subordinate their interests to the interests of capital – wage earners, the unemployed, the underemployed, women, people of color, migrants, homosexuals, youth, the aged, and so forth. Virtually every group that struggles for a redistribution of wealth against the interests of the dominant capitalist class contributes to the formation of a social identity antagonistic to capital. Hardt and Negri still use the term "proletariat" to designate the social antithesis generated by capital but distinguish it from the industrial working class of the nineteenth and early twentieth centuries. "Today," they write, "the working class has all but disappeared from view. It has not ceased to exist, but it has been displaced from its privileged position in the capitalist economy and its hegemonic position in the class composition of the proletariat." In this sense, "The Proletariat is not what it used to be, but that does not mean it has vanished," since under that category "we understand all those exploited by and subject to capitalist domination." This is not "a homogeneous or undifferentiated unit," however. Rather, considering the "differences and stratifications" of labor today, "all these diverse forms . . . are in some way subject to capitalist discipline and capitalist relations of production. This fact of being within capital and sustaining capital is what defines the proletariat as a class" (2000: 53).

High Noon is the most powerful example before *Shane* of the kind of Western that postulates such a socially antagonistic form of the subject, though it is not the first. Even before 1946, when two antithetical traditions reached maturity with *Duel in the Sun* and *My Darling Clementine*, a Western of a different sort had already appeared, an anti-Western that was more explicitly than any other against the vision of Owen Wister in the sense that it literally inverted all the categories that Wister had affirmed in *The Virginian*. William Wellman's *The Ox-Bow Incident* (1943) may be that rare thing, a sociological Western, since it is an allegory on the horrors of mob rule as another fascist threat within American culture. As in *The Virginian*, the central event is a lynching, although in this case we learn immediately after the event that the men hanged were innocent. *Ox-Bow* never overtly engages in a class critique and attributes the greater injustice to the mob, not to a dominant class. Yet one must keep in mind the views of Hannah Arendt that I cited earlier to the effect that the mob is the "by-product of bourgeois society" and indirectly expresses the social power of class dominance. In *Ox-Bow*, the signifier of that dominance is a rich man who pretends to have been a Confederate officer in the Civil War. Class power is further sanctioned by the marginality of a black man, the cowpunchers, a disaffected son, a storekeeper, and the few others who oppose the lynching. This movie dramatizes the crisis that will emerge with increasing evidence in the culture of late capitalism, the evidence of a mass culture that virtually splits the population through its powers of interpellation, its way of hailing them, into those who identify with and those who do not identify with the viewpoint of capital.

Hardt and Negri use the example of Herman Melville's Bartleby the Scrivener to define an individual who dis-identifies with the sovereign power of capital through the politics of refusal: "*The refusal of work and authority, or really the refusal of voluntary servitude, is the beginning of liberatory politics*" (2000: 204; original emphasis). Ironically, capitalist culture generates its mass culture through the construction of markets based on the differentiation of the desires of what Hardt and Negri call the "multitude." It offers the masses images of their own revolt and their own nomadic desires in the effort to contain those disturbances within the framework of entertainment. As Hardt and Negri stress, "the Empire [their concept of a new form of global sovereignty and domination] does not create division but rather recognizes existing or potential differences, celebrates them, and manages them within a general economy of command. The triple imperative of the Empire is incorporate, differentiate, manage" (201). This concept of Empire is what I would call the subject-position of capital. The gunfighter of the fifties Western is a Bartleby the Scrivener, whose weapon articulates his refusal of work. However, like Bartleby, this refusal may come down to "*a kind of social suicide*" (204; original emphasis) unless the person who refuses can find a way of transforming that negative act into a reconceptualization of the community.

Henry King's *The Gunfighter* (1950) is the vision of such a social suicide. Though this is one of the first psychological Westerns to be recognized as such and anticipates *High Noon* with its emphasis on the unity of time and place, its psychological depth is offset by its sociological superficiality. We get no sense as to why Jimmy Ringo became a gunfighter or as to what the social system in this world is. Class is invisible, and the larger community stays outside of the barroom in which most of the drama takes place. Despite Gregory Peck's riveting performance, the movie makes little sense ultimately except as a protest against a life of violence. Nonetheless, it is a challenge to the Cold War ideology then in formation. As Slotkin notes, "The image of the gunfighter as a professional of violence, for whom formalized killing was a calling and even an art, is the invention of movies" and reflects the emerging feeling among Americans that they were "supremely powerful and utterly vulnerable" (1992: 383–4). It is not primarily "a critique of capitalist excess, but of power and world preeminence" (390). Ringo, in other words, is supposed to be a sort of Wyatt Earp figure; and though there is no suggestion that he was ever a lawman, his own statements suggest that he killed men primarily in self-defense, at least once he had earned a reputation as a gunfighter. He embodies the ambivalence of the American public toward the Cold Warrior who emerges as the agent and protector of American world dominance after World War II. On the one hand, the community celebrates and relies on these figures to create national security; on the other, they fear them and frequently turn on them as agents of the very evil they are supposed to combat. *The Gunfighter* suggests that identification with power eventually destroys human beings by destroying their ability to integrate with and participate in the community. In post-World-War-II Westerns, the individual who identifies with power is either deluded by the fantasy of omnipotence, like John Wayne's characters in *Red River* and *The Searchers*, or paranoid like Ringo; and these mental states eventually make them vulnerable to the revenge of the community that condenses its fear into the form of an idiot avenger, like the one who finally shoots Ringo in the back.

The Man Who Did Not Corrupt Hadleyville

High Noon combines the psychological depth of *The Gunfighter* with a sociological vision that is more comprehensive than that of *The Ox-Bow Incident*. It is well known that Carl Foreman, who was informally blacklisted after writing the screenplay for the film, intended it to be an allegory of the HUAC period in Hollywood when, in effect, the filmmaking community, including the cowardly moguls, sat back and allowed the destruction of lives and careers by a group of Washington bullies and quasi-fascists (Drummond 1997: 19). The film reproduces this situation more accurately than most critics have recognized. The premise of the plot relies on the telegram informing the marshal of Hadleyville, Will Kane (Gary Cooper), that, in his words, "They pardoned Frank Miller." To whom "they" refers isn't clear until Will explains to Amy (Grace Kelly), the Quaker woman he has just married, that he was instrumental in bringing about Miller's conviction for murder, for which Miller was sentenced to hang until "up north they commuted it to life." Will doesn't know how Miller got his pardon, just that people up north have brought about his release, presumably through their influence with the authorities. In a later sequence, when Kane enters the church to ask for help against Miller, Gary Cooper's face conveys feelings of having been betrayed when his friend Henderson (Thomas

Mitchell), one of the public officials of Hadleyville, turns on him and blames him for the inevitable gunfight that must take place and will ruin the reputation of the town. To justify this view, Henderson explains that "People up north are thinking about this town . . . about sending money down here to put up stores and build factories." If these different threads are put together, they imply that Frank Miller is somehow in alliance with those "people up north" who have the money to invest in this small town and who may have used Miller in the past as their hired gun.

Despite what Henderson says, it seems unlikely that the people up north would object to law enforcement in Hadleyville unless it were against a man whom they regard as their own agent. Though the movie never states this explicitly, it is implicit and consistent with Foreman's intention in the screenplay. It is also consistent with Zinnemann's probable intention, since as an Austrian Jew he understood the experience of having been betrayed by a community and by a capitalist class that handed the reins of power over to a gang of thugs (Prince 1999a: 84–5; Zinnemann 1992: 11). Presumably, the people up north make the laws and govern their execution through those they put in political office, but they also evade or bend the law when it serves their interests through the use of men like Miller (a situation that inspires Robert Altman's revision of *High Noon*, *McCabe & Mrs. Miller*). The people up north resemble the corporate cattlemen of Wyoming who resorted to violence in the Johnson County War, which was sanctioned by the state and federal authorities. Furthermore, the alliance between the law and the outlaw, when they both serve the interests of capital, is not unique to Wyoming or to the other scenes of social violence in the Old West. Even the political context of Hollywood that culminated in the witch hunt, to which the film obliquely responds, involved similar alliances.

As Gerald Horne asserts about Hollywood in the thirties and forties and for which he presents ample evidence, "Relations between mobsters and moguls were quite intimate" (Horne 2001: 120). The International Alliance of Theatrical Stage Employees (IATSE), the union which at that time forbade local strikes and maintained a friendly relationship with the studios, was taken over by gangsters in the thirties. Though the American media typically blame unions themselves for the presence of organized crime, they ignore the fact that gangsters take over unions through violence and intimidation and usually sustain their power by taking payoffs from businesses in return for labor peace (Muscio 1997: 128). The two heads of IATSE in the thirties were clearly in bed with the moguls. As one of them recalled, "the time came when we all sat together, [Nicholas] Schenk [of MGM], [Sidney] Kent [of Fox], myself and Browne and agreed to take $50,000 from each of the major producing companies and $25,000 from each of the independent companies." CSU, the more militant union that opposed IATSE, called these payoffs "bribes to ensure labor peace," while the studios claimed "they were being extorted by the mob." But extortion hardly describes a situation in which a Fox executive arranges for a union boss and his wife "to be transported to Brazil and Europe in 1938 when tax agents wanted to query the union leader about the sources of his wealth" (Horne 2001: 45–7). In 1941, the two mob-connected leaders of IATSE were convicted of extortion, while the head of 20th Century Fox received a short prison sentence in the same case. A federal judge denounced the studios "for participating in these nefarious activities with full knowledge of the facts" (24–5). The mafia gangster Johnny Roselli was convicted of extortion in 1944. The trial revealed that he was "a 'confidential investigator' for . . . the studio's leading labor negotiator" (5, 121). However, in 1947, after the studios had locked out CSU workers and a few weeks before the blacklist officially came into being, Roselli was paroled, while the jailed heads of IATSE had been released in 1945 (105). Roselli went on to marry an actress and become "a producer of some repute, working at Eagle-Lion studios 'in an advisory capacity'" (22). In 1947, Walter Winchell reported that one of the IATSE mob puppets was "back in Hollywood" and "having secret meetings with movie producers in connection with the strike [of CSU]." As the *Los Angeles Daily News* reported, the man responsible "for numerous beatings and at least half a dozen long, unhappy rides for hapless theater owners, small union officials and others who opposed him" was being treated like a celebrity by the Hollywood elite. During the CSU lockout, he even had a "conference with several big shots of the picture industry" (quoted, 25). Since CSU was founded in 1941 to "fight against the gangster interests" in the Hollywood labor movement, it isn't surprising that the moguls would turn to gangsters for help during the critical strike and lockout of 1946–7 (22). If anti-unionism drove anticommunism, as Horne's study indicates, one should not be surprised that Hollywood was more forgiving of its gangsters than it was of its Reds, not to mention the fact that the practices of gangsters weren't that different from the practices of professional anticommunists, who sometimes took payoffs from potential victims of blacklisting (McGilligan and Buhle 1997: 187, 289). This link between business and organized crime was not unique to Hollywood (Norwood 1996).

When Will Kane decides to confront Frank Miller and his gang, he symbolically confronts the raw power of capitalism with the will of the individual, hence the significance of his name. Furthermore, the movie posits individuality as the only defense against the corruption of the community by the ideology of self-interest, though at first it may appear that self-interest is the primary motive for Will's decisions. His first reaction to the news of Frank Miller's imminent arrival is to ride out of town in a hurry with his new bride, after which he quickly realizes that he has to go back and remain marshal for one more day in order to answer the threat that Miller poses. His initial explanation for going back sounds like a classical masculinist proposition: "They're making me run. I've never run from anybody before." After he returns to town, however, he qualifies his initial reasoning by commenting that if the new marshal won't be there for another day, it "seems to me I've got to stay." Then he adds that Miller and his men probably will come after him and his wife when they're alone on the prairie and, in any case, will go on pursuing them indefinitely. Self-interest, in fact, is a critical part of Kane's thinking as it should be, but the interior drama that visually unfolds in the face of Gary Cooper (Prince 1999a: 83–4; Zinnemann 1986: 62) suggests that self-interest alone will not do justice to the man's motivation. Nor is it simply an issue of proving his masculinity, as several feminist critics have remarked, though masculinity is certainly in question here, indeed in crisis. Joanna Rapf sees Kane as "a classic male, mythic hero, his persona not that different from John Wayne's" (1990: 77). Gwendolyn Foster doesn't go quite that far but definitely sees Kane as downstaged by the women (1999: 93). In this section, I will try to show that Kane and the two women, Helen Ramirez (Katy Jurado) and Amy, triangulate each other in specific ways that point toward a subject-position that exceeds that of any one of them.

At one point, Amy tells Will he doesn't have to be a hero for her, and his response is a bit strident, perhaps even hysterical, as he raises his voice to insist that he's not trying to be a hero and says, "If you think I like this, you're crazy." As Garry Wills notes, these lines echo a similar set of lines in the 1929 version of *The Virginian*, though this does not make the movie a simple restatement of Wisterian themes as Wills suggests (1998: 274). When the Virginian shoots Trampas, he is defending the interests of capital and demonizing its social antagonist. There is no Western hero who identifies more completely with the ruling class than the Virginian. In Will's case, his protest to Amy would be empty words if they were not backed up by the tremendous conflict of feelings and desires evident in Cooper's face for the rest of the film. Immediately after his protest, his voice calms as he notes that "This is my town, I've got friends here." He intends to swear in a group of deputies, and with such a "posse" behind him, he thinks, "Maybe there won't be any trouble." It was precisely this aspect of Kane's character that so revolted Howard Hawks and John Wayne, who saw instinctively how much this strategy violated their concept of masculine identity and its social alignment with the dominant class. Despite the fact that Amy believes trouble is inevitable, at this point it does not seem likely that Will expects or would even desire to face the Miller gang on his own. Furthermore, as we learn later in the film, he has never faced Miller on his own before, since in his earlier encounter he was backed up by a group of professional deputies along with volunteers from the community. Initially, Will does not expect to confront Frank Miller without community support; and it is at least arguable that, were the community completely united behind Will, the Miller gang would think twice about seeking vengeance or engaging in any other acts of violence. Finally, given the community's role in Miller's earlier conviction, it seems unlikely that he will limit his vengeance to the marshal alone, a fact that Clint Eastwood later exploits in *High Plains Drifter*, his version of *High Noon*. In effect, when Henderson and the other citizens of Hadleyville ask Kane to leave, they are aligning themselves with the power that has released Miller from prison, a force that may bring about their own destruction or at least subordination. From this perspective, one can understand the allusion to Mark Twain's "The Man Who Corrupted Hadleyburg" in the town's name, Hadleyville. Kane is trying to save the town from corruption by wealth as an objective force. The townspeople imagine that if they subordinate themselves to the will of Frank Miller, they will somehow benefit by gaining some of the wealth that lies behind his power. They fail to realize that real wealth lies in autonomy and the free development of the self in collaboration with others. That's the lesson Kane wants to teach them, whether he knows it or not.

Hardt and Negri argue that, with the decline of the political significance of the industrial working class in the late twentieth century, a more useful term for what takes its place is the "multitude." This is the force whose struggle against capital generates and is generated by the globalization process, which has replaced the centralized imperialism of an earlier period with a decentered "Empire." The multitude is the force of "productive, creative subjectivities," which are "in perpetual motion" and "form constellations of singularities and events that impose continual global reconfigurations on the system" (2000: 60). However, the multitude is not the full-blown realization of proletarian class-consciousness but its mere possibility, a possibility that is constantly being corrupted, even as it is generated, by Empire. The latter corrupts the multitude by "the pure exercise of command" that is "directed toward the destruction of the singularity of the multitude through its coercive unification and/or cruel segmentation." Corruption is anything that brings about "the rupture of the community of singular bodies and the impediment to its action" (391–2). The antithesis of corruption is the formation of the multitude into what Hardt and Negri call a *posse*, a term they use in its Latin sense, particularly in the philosophical vocabulary of Renaissance humanism. It means "having power," but it is not the power that simply derives from being part of a group, such as the nation, the race, or the gender. In meanings derived from its Renaissance sources and culminating in Spinoza, the term addresses "what a body and what a mind can do." For Hardt and Negri, this metaphysical term has become political in referring to "the power of the multitude and its telos, an embodied power of knowledge and being, always open to the possible." As they conclude, "Posse is the standpoint that best allows us to grasp the multitude as singular subjectivity: posse constitutes its mode of production and its being" (407–8).

Hardt and Negri relate this understanding of "posse" to the use of the term by contemporary rap groups, though they disdain the obvious reference to "Wild West lore" and the "American fantasy of vigilantes and outlaws" (408). But Westerns are not as homogeneous or transparent as they imagine; and, in the case of *High Noon*, as in the case of Mario Van Peebles's *Posse*, the significance of the term may be closer to their use than they realize. In an effort to speak plainly, let me say that the strength of a community does not derive from a group essence, such as that imposed by the ideology of the nation, the race, the gender, or even the class, when these terms are narrowly construed to reduce their members to an irreversible identity without reference to individual decisions or acts of the will. When Kane returns to Hadleyville, he engages in an act of resistance to the "people up north" who have used the law for their purposes without reference to the good or even the voice of the community. Will's decision makes him a proletarian subject whether he knows it or not, and his attempt to form a posse is an attempt to empower the community and to bring the law back to the service of the common good, which includes the relative autonomy of each individual. Unlike the Virginian's, his purpose is not to lynch anyone, to go outside the law solely in the interests of private property. On the contrary, as he makes clear when he addresses the community in the church, he intends to honor the law by not arresting Frank Miller's gang when he has no charges against them. Mary P. Nichols stresses that the movie explores "the two sides of American individualism": "the lonely heroism of Marshall Will Kane and the selfish and fearful withdrawal of citizens into their private lives" (1998: 591). However, the withdrawal of the citizens lies precisely in their identification with the viewpoint of power and their willingness to betray those elements of the community, such as the Mexican Helen Ramirez or Kane himself or anyone who has supported Kane in the past, to the brutal force of the Miller gang. They have in fact surrendered their "singularity," their autonomous power of mind and body, for a kind of conformity that articulates itself through the ideology of self-interest, an ideology that should never be confused with the community's real interests, since the latter can only be determined through the autonomous decisions of individuals in real dialogue with each other.

Following the logic of Hardt and Negri, the community is corrupted through its unification behind the ruling ideology of self-interest and through its segmentation according to gender, race, and class. Nichols astutely recognizes that Kane sees the law and the political process through which a "posse" has to be formed as instruments that serve "to protect the rights of individuals, their individual choices, and their private lives" (599). However, Nichols naively imagines the conflict here as one between Kane's legitimate exercise of command, his lawfulness, and Miller's blatant "lawlessness" (596). Miller's pardon and legitimate release from prison make him an agent of a legal system that supports the accumulation of power and wealth by the "people up north." The conflict here is not between the law and its antithesis but between the autonomy of the multitude, which has the right to determine its own collective good through the practice of freedom without coercion, and the power of a dominant class that has accumulated superfluous wealth and power precisely through the corruption of the community and its laws. Therefore, Kane is not protecting individuality and private life as expressions of the bourgeois ideology of self-interest. Rather, through his own example, he posits individuality as a singularity of mind and body that makes autonomous decision possible and thus makes it possible for the multitude to empower itself, not through the negation of singularity in a Hobbesian contest of all against all, but through the assertion of singularity as the ground of social empowerment through acts of association and resistance to domination.

Gary Cooper brilliantly exhibits Kane's growing fear as he realizes that the community will not back him and that he has no choice but to face Miller alone. The critical moment comes when he enters the stable and apparently contemplates running away. His former deputy sheriff Harvey Pell (Lloyd Bridges) shows up to encourage Kane to make a quick exit from town. Because Harvey wants Kane's job and resents the fact that his boss won't support his bid for it, he has deserted Kane during the crisis. When Harvey asks him if he's scared, Cooper's facial expression as he says, "I guess so," is a masterpiece of understated acting that conveys both the man's terror and his determination to go on (Ill. 15). Though characters played by John Wayne may occasionally admit to fear as the sign of their rationality, they never show it in the way Cooper does in this shot (Thomas 1995: 78). In making the film, Cooper found it "easy to comply with Zinnemann's instruction to look 'tired', as he was troubled by arthritis, back pain, and an ulcer" (Kaminsky 1980: 168–73), conditions that he undoubtedly used to effect in his portrayal of

ILLUSTRATION 15 Terror and determination. *High Noon* (1952). Stanley Kramer Productions. *Producer:* Stanley Kramer. *Director:* Fred Zinnemann

Will Kane. By contrast, Harvey exhibits no fear whatsoever and seems perfectly contented to get Kane out of town and handle things himself, though it is obvious from the context that his courage derives from his stupidity and ignorance about what he's up against.

Will Kane's inconsistencies and contradictions point to this critical fact: the proletarian subject that attempts to empower the community is not a finalized subject but a subject in formation, a subject that grows out of the desire to resist the domination of capital, including the agents of its violence. Though the voice of the dominant ideology, given material expression in the film by the theme song, calls on Kane to be a man, the desire he expresses through his actions, including his physical gestures and expressions, points toward something beyond conventional masculinity. The song also contradicts the dominant masculinist ideology when it indirectly expresses the desire for a community that is embodied by the feminine other: "Do not forsake me, oh my darlin'." As Foster notes, while the song suggests that "Will Kane's quest in *High Noon* is the stereotypical desire to please and possess the female," it ironically "foreshadows that it is the men in the film, the hero's best friends, who will forsake him, and not Amy Kane" (1999: 93). In point of fact, Will Kane, like any singularity that emerges from the multitude, can only grope toward an identity that will constitute a real alternative to the subject-positions promoted by the dominant ideology. Will's decision to marry Amy and become a storekeeper already indicates, within the framework of the Western genre, his willingness to surrender the hegemonic form of masculinity that the Western hero is supposed to typify. Will is apparently ready and willing to give up the gun for the broom, which suggests his willingness to surrender the phallus as the instrument of his masculine identity and power, and enter into the kind of relationship that Amy desires, one that is not based on the master–slave paradigm but on mutual cooperation and collaboration – the force that Grace Kelly's name signifies, social grace. After their wedding ceremony, Will pledges that he will do his best, while Amy does the same; and this whole sequence is very different from the relationship between a man and a woman that one finds *The Virginian* or its key film versions. Amy may love Will, but she does not regard him as "more than ever she could be" or as "her master," the words that Wister uses to describe Molly's final view of the Virginian. When Will decides against Amy's plan of action, which is to continue running from the Miller gang, he is not simply asserting his masculine authority and experience but responding to the very desire that Amy has awakened in him, the desire for a form of selfhood that is both autonomous and an expression of the multitude, not in the sense that it conforms to a group identity but in the sense that it is constructed as a dialogical response to the singularities that make up the community. Will doesn't want to live in a world in which you have to run in order to hide from power. He wants to relate to the community in the same way he relates to Amy.

Rapf has noted that in the original shooting script Amy explains her identity to Helen Ramirez in rather anachronistic terms: "*Back home they think I'm very strange. I'm a feminist. You know, women's rights – things like that*" (1990: 79; original emphasis). Though these lines were cut from the film, they suggest that Amy struggles toward a critical consciousness for which she does not have a proper name. Will Kane does the same thing. He asserts his autonomy and the singularity of his mind and body that have been determined by a particular history to possess specific skills and forms of knowledge, including the knowledge of how to use a gun. From the moment he turns his wagon around and heads back to town, he risks his specific relationship with Amy for a larger relationship to the social community that he feels is the necessary condition of any relationship. Without a stable community from which you don't have to run and in which you don't have to fear the excesses of power that derive from superfluous or exploitative concentrations of wealth, any true relationship is doomed to become a negative image of the dominant ideology. The ending of *High Noon* suggests that such a relationship beyond the present social system is not possible except through what Adorno called a "definite" or "determinate" negation – a construction that reproduces the dominant relationship in a way that is inwardly self-critical and exposes its own limitations and contradictions as the contradictions of the system to which it negatively responds (1992: 158–9; 1997: 36).

According to Rapf, at the end of the movie, the woman must give up her ideals in order "to kill for 'her man'," while the man never gives up his ideal (1990: 78). But this reading leaves out of account the fact that Kane makes a decision and takes action in the midst of personal doubt and profound anxiety about the value of what he is doing. It leaves out Cooper's great performance of a masculine action that is not self-certain or heroic. When Kane decides to act alone, he does surrender his ideal, which would be to act through the community, through its empowerment as a posse. However, he takes this decision in the belief that if he does what is right, he makes it possible for his ideal to survive as the ground of hope, as the future possibility of an empowered community of singularities or true individuals. I would argue that Amy takes up a gun for the same reason: not to surrender her ideal but to discover its true social significance. In the end, Kane and Amy stand together against the power of wealth and against the community that betrays them to it, but this doesn't mean they have given up on community. Their isolation negatively articulates the desire for a true community, one that can only come through social transformation.

The pivotal figure whose presence has the effect of exposing the contradictions implicit in any heroic stance, whether it is Will's decision to fight or Amy's initial stand for pacifism, is Helen Ramirez. According to Foster, after Amy goes up to Helen's hotel room because she thinks Helen may be the reason Will refuses to leave, she enters into an act of "female bonding across racial lines." Foster concludes that "Theirs is a heroic struggle that is perhaps far more interesting than that of the central hero, Will Kane" (1999: 93–4). Though I agree that both women are struggling toward liberated social identities, their bonding is far more problematic than Foster suggests. Helen effectively argues against Amy's pacifism in saying that she, Helen, would never leave a man she loves to face such a situation on his own. At one point, Amy defends herself by referring to the violent deaths of her father and brother, who presumably died in a gun battle even though they were on the right side. She insists that there has to be a better way to live. This is the utopian aspect of Amy's vision that Will implicitly accepts and, ironically, may be one of the motivations for his decision to go back to the community. Later, Helen explains that she hates the town and, by implication, the community, because, as she says, "To be a Mexican woman in a town like this." When Amy interrupts with "I understand," Helen fires back somewhat sardonically, "You do? That's good. I don't understand you." Then she proceeds to challenge Amy's pacifism with the argument that it is unrealistic and transgresses against what should be the commitment of her love. Amy wonders why Helen doesn't stay since she obviously cares about Will Kane, but the latter simply responds that Kane is not her man.

Earlier in the film, Helen was the first townsperson Kane visited after he had talked to the judge and then to his deputy Harvey. In this scene, the two characters express feeling for each other, which suggests that one of Kane's motivations for returning to town was his concern about Helen's fate at the hands of Miller. He surely knows that the townspeople will not protect her. Furthermore, Kane and Helen admit to not having seen each other in over a year, with an emotion that is given accent by their facial expressions and voice tones. They speak in Spanish, which emphasizes the intimacy of the situation. This scene suggests unresolved love, and it appears that the failure of their relationship may have to do with barriers of race and class that Kane doesn't want to challenge. This is not very heroic of him, and a more traditional movie would not have drawn attention to the possibility of such a problem. However, Kane at least exhibits an awareness of his failure to transcend the racial barrier that is missing from Amy's naive claim to understand Helen without knowing her history or experience.

It may seem odd to refer to Helen's difference as a class as well as a racial difference, especially given the fact that she seems to be one of the most prosperous people in Hadleyville. Though we don't know Helen's history, the Western genre itself allows us to infer that her money probably derives from some form of prostitution, in the manner of Vienna in *Johnny Guitar*. Furthermore, though she is clearly a successful entrepreneur, who owns the local saloon and is part-owner of a store, her use of capital is not driven solely by the profit motive. When she decides to leave the town and escape the threat of Frank Miller, she summons the local storeowner and asks if he would like to buy out her share of his store. From the exchange, it becomes clear that Helen is a silent partner who was willing to invest in this man when others probably were not, though the man may not publicly admit to her partnership because she is Mexican. She gives the man terms that are extremely favorable to his situation, and he expresses a slightly embarrassed gratitude. Clearly, when she chooses to invest her money in other human beings, Helen does not objectify them as abstract labor power but rather as autonomous persons with whom she can collaborate in the production of wealth. Of course, the storeowner is an Anglo, just as her bodyguard, who appears to be extremely loyal to her, is also Anglo. Helen has no difficulty entering into relations with those who are racially different from her; and even though she is the agent of capital, she controls it and subordinates it to the good of a community. She legitimates her wealth not through force but by asserting its social value, its ability to foster the singularities of the multitude that point toward a future beyond the necessity of capital itself. To that extent, Helen, like Will Kane, anticipates a form of the political subject that transcends racial and class divisions and transforms capital into a form of public wealth. Nonetheless, her exit on the train and failure to realize her passion for Kane represent the failure of the community to transcend itself and its corruption by racial division. She hates the town because it could be something better, a feeling that correlates with Amy's desire for a better way of living.

When Helen tells Amy that Kane is not her man but Amy's, the camera cuts to a close-up of Kane with the words of the song in the background: "I vowed it would be my life or his'n, / I'm not afraid of death, but, oh, / What will I do if you leave me." At this moment, Kane knows that he is alone and has to face Miller because he can't run away from his own desire for a real community, a posse, even if it's only a posse of one. He goes to the barber to get cleaned up after his fight with Harvey, but his disarray suggests that the man is falling apart and trying to put on at least the appearance of stability. Then he goes back to his office to discover that the only man who volunteered earlier, a man he forgot about, is backing out after hearing that Kane is alone. When the man leaves, Kane literally buries his head on the desk, almost on the verge of tears. Finally, after sending away a boy who wants to fight with him, writing his will, and releasing the local drunk, Kane is down to the bare essence of who he is. He walks out on the street and watches as Helen and Amy pass him in a wagon on the way to the train station. Then the train finally arrives, with Frank Miller getting off as Helen and Amy get on. As Miller walks into the camera, there's a cut to the most famous shot in the film. It begins with a close-up of Kane's face, which has been juxtaposed with the face of Miller. As opposed to Miller's cool professionalism as he examines his gun, Kane's face exposes a man clearly on the verge of a nervous breakdown. Then, in the famous crane shot (Ill. 16), the camera tracks back and up as Kane looks around desperately for help that isn't coming, nervously adjusts his gun belt, wipes the sweat from his

ILLUSTRATION 16 A man on the verge of a nervous breakdown. *High Noon* (1952). Stanley Kramer Productions. *Producer:* Stanley Kramer. *Director:* Fred Zinnemann

brow, and finally turns to walk away from the camera toward the encounter. When Amy hears the first shot, Helen's arguments finally take hold of her as she exits the train and runs to help the man to whom she has committed herself. This is an act of grace, a gift that has no rational motivation or expectation of reward. It is without self-interest, at least of an economic sort.

Though there's an element of cliché in all of this, the final showdown is hardly the traditional one of the Hollywood gunfighter Western. On his own, mostly through craft and by hiding from rather than directly confronting his enemies, Kane kills two of the Miller gang. Amy kills one of them by shooting him in the back, and when Frank Miller uses her as cover, she scratches at his eyes to enable Kane to shoot him. Then when the community finally appears, Kane throws down his badge and leaves town with Amy. The message is clear: unless a community empowers itself through the social collaboration that nurtures and develops the body and mind of each individual in ways that are consistent with the good of the whole – unless it can do that, it becomes the instrument of the dominant class and the agent of its own oppression.

Gary Cooper's performance as Will Kane suggests the following: if a man is going to change, to transcend his social identity as a member of a class, a race, or a gender, he will need to risk himself to the extent of falling apart, coming to the verge of the abyss in which you are lost to one community without having found your place in another. This point is driven home repeatedly by the great Westerns of the fifties. In *Shane*, the hero must die so that the empowered community can be born. In *High Noon*, the community must die – at least symbolically through the exposure of its corruption and implicit identification with Frank Miller – so that a new community can be born from the union of Will and Amy. The dialogical interactions that have led to Will's discovery of the limits of his courage and manhood and to Amy's discovery of the necessity of compromise between ideals and social commitment have made this new community possible. Will gets his posse through an alliance that crosses gender boundaries. However, the exit of Helen Ramirez reminds us that this alliance is only a beginning and has not sufficiently challenged the class and racial divisions that corrupted the community in the first place. By the same token, Shane's departure reminds us that as long as the nomad has no place in the community, as long as the community must exclude singularity as the condition of its social formation, it will not have achieved true empowerment.

The Men Who Save John Wayne

The other classic Westerns of the fifties that anticipate or respond to *High Noon* and *Shane* culminate in *The Man Who Shot Liberty Valance* (1962). In the best of these gunfighter Westerns, the masculine hero is always on the verge of a breakdown, either dramatized as a crisis internal to the subject or as a crisis externalized through a couple or group of male characters who embody different aspects of masculine subjectivity. Most of these films avoid the representation of class struggle either in the direct way of *Shane* or in the implicit way of *High Noon*. Still, there is usually a link between masculinity and the desire for money and power, with the implication that such a masculine desire ultimately destroys one's humanity, if not one's life. For example, in a series of Westerns with James Stewart, director Anthony Mann explores the destructive effect of masculine obsession, whether it takes the form of vengeance or the desire for wealth. Douglas Pye notes that "Mann's protagonists are prisoners of a masculinity coded in hopelessly contradictory ways" (1995a: 173). As in *Shane* and *High Noon*, a woman usually appears who challenges the masculine hero's values and mode of self-identification in such a way as to force him to a crisis where for a moment he loses all sense of self as the condition of his transformation.

After Delmer Daves's *3:10 to Yuma* (1957) and *The Hanging Tree* (1959), William Wyler's pacifist Western *The Big Country* (1958), and John Sturges's *Last Train from Gun Hill* (1959), the most interesting critical response to both *High Noon* and *Shane*, though it was particularly aimed at *High Noon*, is Howard Hawks's *Rio Bravo* (1959). Contradicting more recent feminist views, Hawks "didn't think a good sheriff was going to go running around town like a chicken with his head off asking for help, and finally his Quaker wife had to save him" (1982: 130). Hawks decided to make a Western that would do "just the opposite, and take a real professional viewpoint" (McCarthy 1997: 549). Despite this attitude Hawks respected and maintained a friendly relationship with Carl Foreman

(540), but John Wayne may have understood *High Noon* better when he inaccurately remembered the final scene as one in which Gary Cooper not only threw down his badge but "ground the star into the dirt with his heel." According to Wayne, this was "a sign of disrespect for the law itself" (Wills 1998: 273). As Drummond notes, Wayne disliked both the film and Foreman to such an extent that in the seventies the actor bragged about his role in expelling Foreman from the United States, even on the latter's new turf in the UK (1997: 38). Ironically, whatever Hawks's or Wayne's intention, in some ways their film only serves to validate the anti-Wisterian impulse behind *High Noon*.

The conflict in *Rio Bravo* that pits John Wayne and his two deputies against Nathan Burdette (John Russell) and his gang of gunslingers is a class struggle that echoes the allusions to the Johnson County War in *Shane*. As Wayne's John T. Chance says to Burdette, "You're a rich man, big ranch, pay a lot of people to do what you want them to do." Furthermore, when Chance's limping deputy Stumpy (Walter Brennan) explains his grudge against Burdette, he informs us that Burdette somehow robbed him of his 460-acre ranch through some twisted use of the law. The words of Stumpy and Chance imply class hatred and class warfare. Chance's voice is not the voice of the Virginian, especially when he tells Burdette that he and his two deputies are going to sit in the jail with Burdette's brother, the accused murderer, until the US Marshal comes. By contrast, the Virginian doesn't trust institutional law, hangs his best friend without a trial, and confronts the villain *mano a mano*. Chance has no intention of fighting alone and ultimately expects to be backed up by the US government. He no more identifies with wealth and power than does Cooper's Will Kane. Furthermore, though Chance does not go to the community looking for help, the community invariably comes to him – what little community there is.

Unlike Hadleyville in *High Noon*, there is no sense of a normal community in the town of Rio Bravo; and this fact enables Hawks to create an ideal community in the characters of Chance, his two deputies, who are respectively a drunk and a cripple, a teenage gunslinger Colorado (Ricky Nelson), the overtly sexual and independent woman Feathers (Angie Dickinson), and the Mexican American hotel keeper (Pedro González-González) and his wife (Estelita Rodriguez). Eventually, each one of these characters makes

ILLUSTRATIONS 17–18 Superego and alter ego. *Rio Bravo* (1959). Warner Bros. *Producer and director:* Howard Hawks *(shot/reverse shot sequence)*

some effort to help Chance, despite his protest, in his struggle against Burdette. Though Chance is a man who seems incapable of falling apart, the men around him manifest all of the qualities of self-doubt and anxiety that are excluded from the classic hero's identity (Ills. 17–18). Stumpy is an aging, somewhat broken man, while Dude (Dean Martin) is an alcoholic whose life has been shattered by his unrequited love of a woman. Finally, they are joined by Colorado, who is quick-witted and fast with a gun, but whose youth doesn't always allow the best judgment, as when he removes his pay from the dead body of his boss Pat Wheeler (Ward Bond), without thinking of the other hired hands. Throughout the film, Dude, the deputy closest to Chance, is on the verge of a nervous breakdown as he tries to recover from his alcoholism. Since Feather's courtship of Chance – and it is more her courtship of him than his of her – reveals his basic fear of women, it makes sense to see Dude as, in some ways, the embodiment of Chance's own fear of social commitment to the other, which ultimately would include the community itself.

As Robin Wood noted, though Chance is the strong pillar on which all of these characters depend, he rarely saves any of them, while they are saving him throughout the movie (1981: 46). Ultimately, Chance is able to embody the subjectivity of the multitude, not by acting alone and then absenting himself from the community as a critique of its corruption, as Will and Amy Kane do at the end of *High Noon*, but by ignoring the community at large and substituting for it an ideal version of itself, a small community of men who finally form a singing "posse" in the jail in one of the most peculiar scenes in the history of the Western. While Dean Martin and Ricky Nelson exercise their vocal cords, John Wayne and Walter Brennan stand around with big smiles on their faces as if to express the sheer joy of an "empowered" community when it works. In my view, this movie is so entertaining, such a pure aesthetic pleasure, because it creates this utopian sense of social bonding between men and at least two women, though at the price of eliminating the contradictions of the multitude itself and reducing gender, race, and class hierarchies to natural social divisions rather than forms of social corruption. Feathers, tough as she is, longs to be dominated by Chance; the Mexican Americans love to be patronized by the great white father of whom they are comic reflections; and the ruling class finally surrenders to the greater power of the masculine "posse." *Rio Bravo* exhibits a utopian representation of friendship and social bonding that works because it leaves out a community to which anyone is accountable.

In Hawks's film, the ideal masculine subject doesn't have to fall apart because his contradictions have been compartmentalized in the form of other characters who are managed by his superior moral force. Though the relationship that Chance, Dude, and the other members of the ideal community work toward is one "based on a balance of equality between free men," as Wood insists (1981: 50), such a relationship can only be achieved by eliminating the real contradictions of the community in capitalist culture. There is only the agent of raw power, which would be Nathan Burdette, who tells Dude that every man should get a little taste of power before he dies, and the subject that asserts its autonomy against power in the name of a law that transcends the community. *Rio Bravo* makes no reference to the ways in which power corrupts the law and the community. Still, as Chance's name suggests, in the end a true community is almost a matter of chance, a configuration of individualities that no one could have predicted. As Wood stresses, Dude's redemption comes only when he is beyond redemption, beyond the influence of Chance's example (51). Just as he lifts a glass of whiskey, he hears Burdett's Alamo music, which expresses the threat of "No quarter," and remembers why he stood with Chance in the first place. Beneath its surface, *Rio Bravo* is just as pessimistic as *High Noon* is about the possibility of a truly empowered multitude, a community of singularities. The two movies are mirror images of each other, one a utopia, the other a dystopia. Yet the object that each movie postulates as the goal of its representations is the same.

The Man Who Shot John Wayne

The Man Who Shot Liberty Valance brings to closure the classic Western itself. Furthermore, this movie ambivalently resolves the two traditions that emerged from the exemplary 1939 Westerns, *Stagecoach* and *Destry Rides Again*. Just as Destry comes to Bottleneck in a stagecoach, so lawyer Ranse Stoddard (James Stewart) is on the way to Shinbone in a stagecoach at the beginning of the long flashback that makes up most of the movie. After he is severely beaten by Liberty Valance (Lee Marvin) for trying to defend a woman on the stagecoach during a robbery, he is discovered and brought to town by Tom Doniphon (John Wayne), who keeps warning the lawyer that if he wants to bring justice to this territory he had better learn how to use a gun. In this respect, Tom ironically plays the same role for Ranse that the town-drunk-turned-marshal Washington Dimsdale (Charles Winninger) played for Tom Destry. Dimsdale's character is also echoed in the alcoholic Dutton Peabody (Edmond O'Brien), who edits *The Shinbone Star*. The critical scene before Ranse goes out to face Liberty Valance in a gunfight, the one in which he looks over the body of the beaten and nearly dead newspaper editor, echoes the scene in *Destry* when Tom holds the dying Dimsdale in his arms. Both Destry and Ranse are represented as feminized men; and, as I noted earlier, in *Destry* the women save the day, while in *Liberty Valance* Ranse goes to the showdown wearing an apron. Yet in the latter case, as we eventually learn, the feminized Ranse Stoddard's shooting of Liberty Valance is an illusion. When Tom tells Ranse the truth about who killed Valance, he has already fallen to the level of alcoholics like Dimsdale and Peabody. His clothes and unkempt appearance recall the clothes and appearance of Dean Martin's Dude at the beginning of *Rio Bravo*. The symbolic death of Tom Doniphon is the condition for Ranse Stoddard's political career in which he will employ his feminine attributes to transform the West. As Joseph McBride perspicuously notes, all the critical decisions of Ranse's career and the critical decisions that change Tom's life are actually made by Hallie (Vera Miles), the woman Ranse unintentionally steals from Tom (2001: 628).

At the end of *Stagecoach*, Ringo leaves the town of Lordsburg in a buckboard headed for the border, while in *Liberty Valance* John Wayne first appears on a horse accompanying a buckboard bearing the beaten body of Ranse Stoddard to town. Tom's shirt resembles the shirt John Wayne wore as Ringo. Tom is what Ringo would have become if he had not left civilization behind, and it's significant that when Tom shoots Liberty from the shadows of an alley he uses a rifle just as Ringo did when he killed the Plummers by unexpectedly falling to the ground. From this perspective, Ford's casting of John Wayne and James Stewart in roles that refer directly to their 1939 Westerns is more than simple iconography but a direct attempt to bring together and resolve the tensions between the two traditions that came out of the Depression era. McBride notes that Ford abused Wayne throughout the filming of *Liberty Valance*, while he treated Stewart rather gingerly (2001: 630–1). Yet in the film itself, Ranse Stoddard's character is the object of sadistic cruelty from Liberty Valance, who beats him up, trips him, and tries to kill him; from Tom Doniphon, who verbally humiliates him and tricks him when he tries to teach him how to shoot so that Ranse gets paint all over his dude's suit; and by Hallie, who makes fun of his dishwashing, points to the worthlessness of his education, and finally runs his life. Even in the final scenes, Ranse is virtually castrated by the recognition that his wife loved another man and that his whole life has been based on a fiction.

Though the film also refers to the entire scope of Ford's career (McBride and Wilmington 1975: 178–82), the two most critical references after *Destry* and *Stagecoach* are to *High Noon* and *Shane*, with a rarely observed debt to *Rio Bravo*. In fact, *Liberty Valance* makes explicit what is only implicit in the earlier movies. Valance and his henchmen recall the Frank Miller gang, only this time there is no ambiguity about who these men are, since they overtly attempt to enforce the political interests of the cattle barons who oppose statehood. Lee Van Cleef's presence in both gangs foregrounds the parallel. Ford said to Bernard Tavernier that *Liberty Valance* "was based on historical fact," which in my view could only be the

Johnson County War or a similar event (Ford 2001: 108). Though I can find no evidence that the cattle barons who participated in the 1892 invasion of Johnson County fought against Wyoming statehood, which was achieved in 1890, they surely were not pleased when the first state legislature "reversed all previous policy [concerning mavericks and the control of the open range] *in toto*, erasing the word *maverick* from the books, leaving a void." As it turned out, the repeal of the law did not benefit the small ranchers, since the Johnson County chapter of the WSGA decided that, "in the absence of a maverick law, the mavericks were to be divided up daily by the roundup foreman in the ratio of the number of calves branded by each outfit. This arrangement excluded the small owners, many of whom were barred from the roundups anyway" (Smith 1966: 88). In effect, the statehood that seemed to limit the power of the corporate cattlemen became the incentive for the consolidation and assertion of their power and ultimately precipitated the Johnson County War as an overt class struggle. As Slotkin stresses, when the WSGA used the territorial legislature to develop "a policy of deliberate discriminations against the interests of small ranchers as a class," the latter entered "the electoral lists as Grangers and Populists, taking control of individual towns and counties and eventually united within the Democratic Party to contest control of the legislature with the WSGA-oriented Republicans. Johnson County was dominated by these small ranchers and provided a political base for the Democratic opposition" (1992: 172–3).

Liberty Valance symbolizes the use of raw physical force to justify a socioeconomic structure that privileges wealth at the expense of the common man. As in *High Noon*, a single man is required to face Liberty Valance, only this time the woman he presumably loves encourages rather than discourages his action, while at the same time she seeks help from an outside force. Tom Doniphon is the Shane figure in *Liberty Valance*, and this time the woman he loves does not discourage his taking action. In the end, Tom doesn't get the glory of the gunfight and formal self-sacrifice that Shane gets at the end of Stevens's movie. He shoots Valance surreptitiously and then, instead of immediately dying or riding away into symbolic death, he enters into a gradual decline that culminates in the man who hadn't worn a gun in years and is about to be buried without his boots on. Finally, *Liberty Valance* pays tribute to *Rio Bravo* through its confinement of the action to the claustrophobic space of the town, though there are a few glimpses of a very un-Fordian countryside in the scenes at Doniphon's ranch.

Ultimately, Ranse and Tom represent the two sides of a social identity that, within the frame of the film, can never be unified. Ranse imagines a legal system that would articulate the subjectivity of the multitude through its dis-identification with the agents of social violence. For this reason, he falls outside of the "norm" of the dominant masculine subject: he is always nearly hysterical and on the verge of breakdown, even as he struggles to assert himself against Valance in the name of a community that doesn't really exist within the frame of the movie. Tom, by contrast, almost completely identifies with the use of force that Ranse opposes; and though he uses his guns outside the rule of capital, he doesn't necessarily oppose capital. As he says to Ranse at the very outset, "Liberty Valance is the toughest man south of the Picket Wire – next to me." If anyone challenges the force that justifies the right to wealth, they must somehow do it without the use of force or end up validating the very principle that justified social inequality in the first place. Yet it seems impossible to challenge force without force. Thus, when Tom shoots Liberty Valance, which is a crime he can live with, he effectively undermines his own social identity. He has virtually shot himself, which puts an end to the kind of world in which an identity like his can have a place. At the same time, Tom subverts Ranse because he forces the latter to become the agent of a lie. Ultimately, neither Tom nor Ranse is the man who shot Liberty Valance, because to the public this heroic figure is a David going up against and defeating a Goliath, when the truth is that Ranse didn't kill Liberty Valance and Tom wasn't that heroic. In *Liberty Valance*, the culminating showdown is a phony, whether it's from Tom's or Ranse's perspective.

According to Peter Bogdanovich, despite the newspaperman's phrase, "when legend becomes fact, print the legend," Ford himself "prints the fact" (1978: 34). Furthermore, as Pye stresses, "the 'fact' (*Tom* killed Liberty) *explains* the death of the old West, the otherwise unaccountable (impossible) triumph of an inferior civilisation" (1995c: 122; original emphasis). Though Ford may have felt that the past was superior to the present, he suggests through his presentation of the facts that neither the present nor the past is all that heroic. Assuming that Tom could easily take Liberty in a gunfight, why didn't he before the showdown with Ranse? Tom is willing to gun Liberty down over a steak that falls to the floor but seems largely indifferent to the fact that Liberty has robbed stagecoaches, beaten up his friends, and murdered "a couple of sodbusters" south of the Picket Wire who don't support the political interests of the cattle barons. Tom knows that Valance has been recruiting hired guns and insists, against Ranse's arguments, that votes won't stand up against guns. Though Tom claims he killed one of Liberty's men when they tried to bushwhack him, he shows almost no inclination to confront Liberty himself. When Liberty fails to disrupt the voting process in Shinbone and challenges Ranse to a gunfight, he shows no concern for Doniphon's position or presence, even though he clearly fears Doniphon. The simple truth is that Doniphon identifies with Liberty more than he identifies with Ranse. For most of the film, he doesn't use his skill with a gun to confront Liberty and put an end to his reign of terror because he doesn't want to. When he finally kills Liberty for Hallie, he acts more or less against his own desire. Once he realizes that he has miscalculated and lost Hallie, he virtually falls apart and burns down his own house, just as he has destroyed his identity in killing Liberty. Tom may not be a gunman for the cattle barons, but he nonetheless identifies with the principle that guns determine the right to wealth; and though he sympathizes with the sodbusters who may become Valance's victims, he doesn't act on their behalf until he is prodded to do so by Hallie. Tom is another antithesis of the Virginian only in the sense that he doesn't need to confront his enemy out in the open in order to kill him. He can live with his crime because he believes in the force that entitles him to commit it.

The Man Who Shot Liberty Valance is probably the most pessimistic Western ever made, one that borders on nihilism. If *High Noon* and *Shane* try to articulate forms of social identity that can represent the multitude in opposition to the domination of capital, Ford's meta-Western suggests that no true opposition is possible, that the past and the present are mirrors of one another. To me, this is the real significance of a fact often noted by critics: Ford's actors are too old for the parts they're playing. As Lee Clark Mitchell stresses, the film explores "age's reconstruction of its own youth" and the attempt to subordinate the past to present needs. We are made "to see distinctly older figures imagining themselves *as* young, trying dimly to put a past to rest that has not yet been resolved" (1996: 178). Events like the Johnson County War teach us that the Old West never was a haven for individuality and personal autonomy beyond the class conflicts and direct exploitation of eastern capital. In this film, the images projected onto the past disavow the present but nonetheless harbor its truth. For example, in the past Pompey (Woody Strode) was Tom Doniphon's servant, and in the present Ranse Stoddard treats him as a subordinate when he gives the black man "pork-chop money." Ranse's present-day pomposity and paternalism represent a new social authority and a new class structure that is probably no better than the system he supposedly challenged and for which Tom Doniphon destroyed himself.

Yet *Liberty Valance* offers one hope, one possibility beyond the disunified masculine subject that can never resolve the contradiction between the singularities of the multitude and the power it must deploy in order to assert itself as a historical force. According to McBride, Hallie's "choice of Ranse over Tom . . . was a tragic mistake" (2001: 628). He assumes that when she puts the cactus rose on Tom's coffin, she expresses her regret for having chosen the lesser man. But the truth may be more complicated than that. If Hallie makes all the critical decisions in the film, as McBride argues, one could say that her desire has driven the plot and the history it registers. Perhaps the truth is that Hallie loves both men but that her desire exceeds what either man has to offer her. In the past, Hallie rejected Tom for Ranse, and in the present she seems to reject Ranse for Tom; but the truth is that Hallie harbors a desire that can't be reduced to the love of a man, a desire that inhabits her feelings for Tom and for Ranse but ultimately exceeds both of them. The cactus rose symbolizes this desire; and when she puts it on Tom's coffin, she is not rejecting Ranse, but recognizing that her love for Tom like her love for Ranse were the supports of her desire – a desire that is not yet dead. Both McBride and Andrew Sarris have pointed to the great shot, just before the last scene on the train, when Ranse realizes that Hallie still loves Tom (Ill. 19). As McBride notes, Ranse "moves forward in the middle frame to shut the door of the coffin room when he sees the rose [in the foreground], with the door half-closed and Hallie's solitary figure visible in profile in the far background" (2001: 633–4). As Sarris

ILLUSTRATION 19 Cactus rose as symbol of impossible desire. *The Man Who Shot Liberty Valance* (1962). Paramount Pictures. *Producer:* Willis Goldbeck. *Director:* John Ford

put it, "everything that Ford has ever thought or felt is compressed into one shot . . . photographed . . . from the only possible angle" (1975: 182). Though one might think that the angle represents the viewpoint of the dead Tom Doniphon, it would be more correct to say that it is the perspective of Hallie's desire as something distinct from Hallie's social position as the wife of Ranse Stoddard. In the next scene, Hallie asks Ranse if he isn't proud of the garden he has made out of the desert, but the garden is not the end of history but the force that drives it in the present and the past. In the past, Ranse won Hallie with the dream of a real rose, but now her actions stress that her desire is a cactus rose, a kind of beauty that comes out of nothing and that nothing can stop. *Liberty Valance* explodes masculine identity as a possible ground for the subjectivity of the multitude. Yet in that act of destruction lies the possible ground of a new political subject, one that responds to a desire that must be coded feminine in a social system that has always coded the dominant viewpoint of power and capital as masculine.

In foregrounding the impossibility of a revolutionary subject that has not transcended traditional masculinity, *Liberty Valance* necessarily posits the dead end of the Western itself. The class struggle that the Western encodes and attempts to transcend through the postulation of revolutionary masculinity cannot be transcended within the boundaries of the masculine itself. Either the masculine hero becomes an authoritarian figure whose ability to liberate anyone is cancelled by his failure to envision and represent the singularities of the multitude as anything more than mirror images of himself; or the masculine hero falls apart, falls into revolutionary hysteria that promises social transformation but fails to achieve it because it cannot hold itself together or find its way back to the community in whose interests it has tried to act. In the end, the same social hierarchies keep replicating themselves. The only hope lies in the rare representations of a feminine desire that breaks through the masculine to the expression of a subject-position that cannot be coded fully by gender, race, or class. That position is hinted at in the feminocentric Westerns like *Duel in the Sun* and *Johnny Guitar* and their occasional avatars; but even in these Westerns, such a feminine desire is usually contained by some kind of return to the masculine or by death. For the paradigmatic Western heroes, like Shane and Will Kane, the feminine intrudes upon the domain of the masculine with the force of a desire that breaks down traditional identities. These men must go away or die because they cannot live in a society that still protects the class system through the naturalization of gender and racial hierarchy. With *Liberty Valance*, there is no masculine force that can succeed against the hegemony, and there is no feminine counterforce that can take its place. There is only feminine desire, a desire that transcends the dominant subject-positions without postulating a new one. From this point forward, the greatest Westerns can only imagine the transformation of the social system and the destruction of class as the destruction of man. The only *masculine* heroes are the ones who destroy themselves in an act of revolutionary suicide or some simulation thereof. To go on living, as Tom does after killing Liberty Valance, or as Ranse does after learning the truth about who killed Liberty Valance, is to become a hollow man.

CHAPTER 7

MAGNIFICENT CORPSES

Redemption through Destruction

In 1969, both Sergio Leone's *Once Upon a Time in the West* and Sam Peckinpah's *The Wild Bunch* were released in the United States within a month of each other. By the fall, *Butch Cassidy and the Sundance Kid* was playing on American screens. These movies were the culmination of a decade in which the Hollywood Western had been turned inside out – the decade of the Kennedy assassination, the Vietnam War, the emergence of postcolonial nation-states across the globe, the international youth movement, and, generally speaking, the American loss of innocence. If the classical Western both articulated and disavowed the class contradictions of American society, usually through a false resolution that hinged on the action of an individual, it nonetheless postulated a kind of hope for a world beyond class, and, consequently, beyond the distributions of wealth that have resulted from exploitation based on race or gender. The very ambiguity of the last image in *Shane* that has spawned debate and numerous cinematic responses – the ambiguity as to whether Shane is dead or alive – ironically points to a kind of hope that the community he leaves behind will have justified his life, given it a meaning and a purpose. His death is not the end of things but the beginning – a new kind of life. The sixties were not devoid of such hope, but they inflected that hope differently. In the Westerns of that decade, the power of the dominant class – whether it materializes itself in the image of the railroad magnate, the big rancher, the Mexican counterrevolutionaries, the bandits who prey on the poor, or any lawman or gunfighter who defends the dominant property relations against the interests or desire of marginalized individuals or groups – cannot be defeated. The commitment of the apocalyptic hero is not to victory but to a kind of permanent struggle – perhaps even a permanent revolution.

The shift toward an apocalyptic tone in the Western does not emerge out of the void; and the elements were always there in the classic Western. When Shane tells Joey that there's no going back on a killing, he expresses the view that, while there is hope for the community, there is none for himself – at least not for his current social identity. Shane must die in order to be reborn as a new political being who can survive in such a community. In the apocalyptic Western that comes after *Shane*, there is little faith in the community as it currently exists, even though the hero may risk or even sacrifice himself for it. In some ways, Tom Doniphon anticipates the future of the Western when he sacrifices his identity for the woman he loves. Though he expresses affection for the individual citizens of Shinbone, he exhibits no faith in their ability to create a future that he would choose to live in. His killing of Liberty Valance is apocalyptic, not because good destroys evil in the manner of the Christian apocalyptic vision, but because in a moment of temporal crisis Tom brings about the end of the world as he knows it, but not the prospect of a new paradise that he can enter. The garden Hallie refers to at the end of the film is not for Tom. One can only imagine Tom's slow withering away and wonder if he continued to think that his sacrifice was worth the new community that would rather print a lie that justifies the present than the truth that founded it.

In an essay on apocalyptic themes in films of the last quarter of the twentieth century, Conrad E. Oswalt notes that such films articulate a modern apocalypse that "transfers the messianic kingdom from a new-age heaven to a second-chance earth." The result is to place the ordering of time "completely in the control of humankind," granting them "the ability to control the end." Thus, "Hollywood has captured and fostered the secularization of the apocalyptic tradition" (1995: 62–3). In the apocalyptic Western, good does not destroy evil even when that appears to be the case. On the contrary, evil destroys itself. The secularization of the apocalyptic tradition means that humanity has the power to bring about its own redemption through its own destruction.

The Winners Are the Losers

The hope in these Westerns might be described by the word "magnificence." In one of the first Westerns to foreground the apocalyptic sense of an ending, John Sturges's *The Magnificent Seven* (1960), the Seven constitute a small army of Shanes; yet the difference between these men and the classic gunfighter lies precisely in their relation to the community they defend. Though *Shane* exhibits the weaknesses of the homesteading community and the difficulty of empowering it, the movie never mocks the community per se or suggests that it can be anything but the bedrock of any possible future. By contrast, the Seven never seriously attempt to become members of the Mexican farming community they come to defend; and only at the end does one of them, the one who comes from a similar Mexican village, decide to stay with the young woman with whom he has fallen in love. Though he is fast enough with a gun and courageous enough to be one of the magnificent, he is nonetheless not a true gunfighter but one of the people. His last act in the film is to return to the village and take off his gun, an act which signifies his surrender of the gunfighter's identity. The leader of the Seven, Chris (Yul Brynner), is impressed when the villagers offer him everything of value they have so that he will come and defend them against the bandits; but though he is willing to fight for them, he would never be willing to work with or for them in the fields in the way that Shane works for Joe Starrett.

Unlike Akira Kurosawa's *Seven Samurai* (1954), which explores the class tensions between the samurai warriors and the peasants, *The Magnificent Seven* largely obscures these class divisions through what Slotkin describes as "the translation of class difference into racial difference, and the projection of an internal social conflict into a war beyond the borders" (1992: 475). In *Shane*, the hero sacrifices himself for a community in which he believes more than he believes in himself or in the social viability of his skill with a gun. In *High Noon*, the hero turns away from a community that has betrayed itself and presumably seeks to create a better community that does not accept or identify with the viewpoint of capital. Aside from the young Chico (Horst Buchholz), who initially must struggle to prove himself one of the Seven, none of them seriously contemplates integration with the Mexican community. Even Bernardo O'Reilly (Charles Bronson), who presumably is part Mexican and shows the greatest affection for the people, or at least for their children, can never imagine himself as one of them (Buscombe 1993: 20). Though he would never put it this way, his actions suggest that he would rather be dead; and eventually, he is.

When the Seven come to the community, they are warned immediately by the Old Man that these farmers are "afraid of everyone and everything." When Chico rings the church bell to summon the farmers from hiding, he calls them "chickens." Later the Mexican bandit leader, Calvera (Eli Wallach), says of the villagers, "If God didn't want them sheared, he would not have made them sheep." Though the Seven befriend the Mexicans in "liberal" fashion, they frequently grow frustrated with them. The Mexicans are usually presented in a comic light, and even Chico engages in a form of hero worship of the American gunfighters that marks him as strictly subordinate. Only the wise Old Man, the brave peasant leader Hilario, and the tavern- keeper Sotero (who is shrewd enough to betray the Seven when he feels it is necessary) show any independence of mind. When Chico discovers the women whom the peasants have been hiding for fear they might be raped by the gunfighters, Chris says that the Seven might have done such a thing, though in his opinion they should have been given the benefit of the doubt. His view of these people is fairly condescending and paternalistic. Though Vin (Steve McQueen) frequently expresses interest in the village girls, he never acts on it, while the others, except for Chico, show no interest at all. When the Seven realize that the peasants are going hungry so that the gunfighters can eat well, they start redistributing the food; but this gesture only signifies more dramatically the distance between the gunfighters and the people. The truth is that Calvera hits the nail on the head when he says to Chris and Vin, "We're in the same business." Vin quickly responds, "Only as competitors," but this doesn't draw a very sharp distinction between the bandits and the gunfighters. Early in the film, Vin and Chris have expressed some degree of regret over not being able to find any action in the West since everyone has apparently settled down. Though this phrase may imply that these gunfighters have defended poor settlers against more rapacious forces, historically gunmen work for those who can pay; and these men are used to making a lot of money. Chris can hire gunmen so cheaply only because they are currently unemployed.

The ambivalence of the gunfighters' relation to the Mexican community comes to a head when the tavern-keeper Sotero argues for surrender and Chris, after winning what Slotkin calls a "pseudo-plebiscite," responds that he will kill the first man who says anything about giving up. As Slotkin stresses, Chris treats Sotero and the Mexican fathers in the same way O'Reilly treats the children: "he 'spanks' or disciplines them coercively, replacing their authority with his own in everything but name. Yet he asserts that this paternalistic coercion will make them free and independent adult men" (1992: 480). A few scenes later, Vin accuses Chris of starting to care about these people and then admits that he himself has been thinking about getting some land and settling down. But the unreality of these emotions is driven home when Chris confronts Chico with the fact that he comes from a peasant background himself and a village like the one they're defending. In a scene that is close to one in *Seven Samurai*, Chico responds by expressing his hatred of the peasants' cowardice and then turns it against the gunfighters when he says, "Who made us the way we are? Men like Calvera and men like you." In the end, all talk of settling down is ridiculous because six of the Seven are men like Calvera, men who have historically identified with those for whom the right to wealth is determined by force.

Slotkin reads *The Magnificent Seven* as one of several Mexico Westerns that anticipate "the American approach to the Vietnam war" (481). Most critically, he notes that when the Seven go back to the village, after they have been betrayed by Sotero and some of the other peasants, they go "in the teeth of evidence that the village polity does not fully sustain them and that its culture is alien to them" (482). In fact, their "commando-style attack" looks as much like "an attack on the village that has betrayed Americans" as a final attempt to drive away the bandits. Ideologically, it visualizes the "mythical 'surgical strike,' so central to the fantasies of military scenario-makers, and the counterinsurgency fantasy of blasting the guerrillas with bomb and shell without harming the peasants" (483–4). The only problem with this reading is that Calvera and his men are not guerrilla revolutionaries or insurgents of any sort. Though they may technically operate outside the law, they represent the historical reality of the domination of peasants by rapacious social groups that expropriate the products of a laboring class simply because they have the power to do so. Such forces frequently use the law to achieve their goals. Ultimately, it is the peasants who are the insurgents in this case, refusing to accept a situation that might be considered a fact of life in the world in which they live (see Carroll 1998).

In the same way, the small farmers and cattlemen of Johnson County became insurgents when they opposed the monopolistic practices of the WSGA and challenged the legal system that protected the corporate cattlemen. They challenged the legal system by refusing to convict the men who were accused of cattle-stealing, though the number of such cases was exaggerated by the WSGA (Smith 1966: 115–16). In other words, they tried to use the law to fight an abuse of law. In *The Magnificent Seven*, the peasants do not seek help by going to the proper legal authorities and demanding protection against the bandits, a fact that implies that the bandits probably have more access to legal authority than do the impoverished peasants, or rather that the right to legal protection is determined by wealth. The American gunfighters understand this fact because they have made a career out of selling their skill with guns to those who can pay. In the end, the gunfighters go back to the village not only out of pride and honor, as Slotkin notes (1992: 482), but because in a sense this is the end they have been looking for all along. The racial and cultural difference between the Americans and the peasants or between the Americans and Calvera becomes the means to their final act of self-destruction.

In their own eyes, the Seven realize the utopian dream of a posse, as Hardt and Negri use the term – an empowered community in which each member contributes his particular skill to form a group identity that protects the singularity of each and can oppose the force of the dominant class. The incorporation of Chico into the group at least implies the elimination of racial divisions in the empowered community, though in the end the Seven cannot live up to that promise. The condition that makes the Seven possible is that they do not live in real time. The peasants live in the real time of seasonal change that can support their labor or destroy it, though the hope is always for consistency and survival. Because they live in real time, they are afraid of everything, because for them the end of time is a hypothetical goal that has no bearing on the day-to-day struggle for life. Even the periodic incursions of the bandits represents the fluctuation of real time in the life of the peasants. The bandits themselves seem to live in real time, since, though they want wealth without labor, they too experience periods of plenty and periods of scarcity; and their conflict with the peasants is really over the distribution of resources that enables both groups to survive. Unlike the gunfighters, neither the peasants nor the bandits see themselves or their way of life as an anachronism. For them, the future lasts forever and takes the shape of cyclical patterns. The American gunfighters, by contrast, are obsessed with the sense that their world is ending, though they have no expectation that some transforming apocalyptic event is about to take place.

Their relation to time recalls an important element within the apocalyptic tradition that Frank Kermode points out: "Before the End there is a period which does not properly belong either to the End or to the *saeculum* [or time period] preceding it. It has its own characteristics" (2000: 12). This myth of transition, as Kermode calls it, registers "the conviction that the end is immanent rather than imminent; it reflects our lack of confidence in ends, our mistrust of the apportioning of history to epochs of this and that. Our own epoch is the epoch of nothing positive, only of transition" (101–2). Chris beautifully sums up his relation to time in spatial terms when the traveling salesman in the border town asks him where he comes from. Chris just points vaguely back over his shoulder with his thumb. When the man asks where he's going, he wordlessly points in the opposite direction with his index finger. In other words, he comes from nowhere in particular and is going nowhere in particular. One can assume that his relation to time is more or less the same. As Kermode defines the modern version of apocalyptic time, "we may suppose that we exist in no intelligible relation to the past, and no predictable relation to the future. Already those who speak of a clean break with the past, and a new start for the future, seem a little old-fashioned" (102). The peasants want such a break from their history of exploitation by the bandits, a break that will give them a new start. The bandits think in similar terms when they release the Seven and even give their guns back to them. For them, history moves through breaks and starts in a cyclical pattern. For at least six of the Seven, history is meaningless except as a form of permanent struggle until death.

This struggle until the end of time is a class struggle only in the sense that it is a fight for a form of group or collaborative identity that transcends the class system and the contradictions that derive from it. As Chris tries to explain to Chico, who is enamored of the power that derives from knowing how to use a gun, the relation of these gunfighters to their weapons and their way of life is ambivalent at best. To identify with the gun is to identify with the position of social dominance, and everything suggests that in their lives these gunfighters have rarely been on the side of the poor and the dispossessed. With the power of the gun comes the inability to lead a normal life made up of breaks and starts. As Vin and Chris point out, the life of a gunfighter is a life without family or community, without social ties. Only Lee (Robert Vaughn) suggests a positive side to the gunfighter's profession when he says you don't accept insults or have any enemies who are alive. Yet later he is the one who reveals the underlying truth about these men – that they are the ones on the verge of a nervous breakdown, because they live in constant fear, not of the weather or of bandits, but of the truth behind the lies they tell about themselves. To the peasants who try to comfort him when he wakes up from a nightmare, Lee admits that he has stopped counting his enemies; and though the peasants say he is among friends, Lee sees his participation in this struggle as the "final supreme idiocy."

Lee calls himself a "deserter hiding out in the middle of a battlefield," which implies that what the Seven fear is the social tie itself, a commitment to community. When a peasant sympathizes with Lee's fear and says, "Only the dead are without fear," the look on Lee's face suggests that death may be the only answer to his dilemma (Ill. 20). Ultimately, four of the Seven die in the final raid on the village, though in reality one could just as easily say that they all die, except for Chico. In the film's last shot Chris and Vin ride off like Shane,

ILLUSTRATION 20 "Out, out, brief candle!" Death as the absence of fear. *The Magnificent Seven* (1960). The Mirisch Company. *Producer and director:* John Sturges

but their fates are still sealed. They are riding off into apocalyptic time that has no before or after, but only the present of transition that finds its only closure in death. They will not wither away like Tom Doniphon but find some other bloody mode of self-transformation. Despite the line that echoes the ending of Kurosawa's film, "Only the farmers have won," the truth is that the winners are the dead, and those who will soon be like them. The farmers may last forever, as the Old Man says, but no one should have the illusion that the bandits will not come back sooner or later; or if it is not the bandits, it will be the bankers. The Seven have realized the dream of an empowered communal subject only in the act of dying. It is an illusion because it excludes almost all of the community that exists in real space and real time. Chris says to Vin, "We lost. We'll always lose." Then the camera cuts to the village boys tending the grave of O'Reilly and the other dead gunfighters. They lost because in defeating the bandits they were defeating themselves. In a world where men have lost faith in the community, the only hope lies in revolutionary suicide that produces magnificent corpses. The bad men must finally kill themselves if the good men are ever to inherit the earth.

Only Death Will Do

Though it was not the first "professionals" Western, *The Magnificent Seven* started a trend that would eventually culminate in *The Wild Bunch*, however different those two movies may be. Marlon Brando's

One-Eyed Jacks (1961) also anticipated the later movie as well as Peckinpah's *Pat Garrett & Billy the Kid*, though critics of the Western have generally dismissed it with the notable exception of Philip French, who thought that "Brando has less reason to be ashamed of it than he has for many of his pictures since *On the Waterfront*" (1977: 16). Peckinpah worked on the original version of the screenplay (Weddle 1994: 143–6), and the movie bears his signature in its unapologetic representation of bad men. Furthermore, its relatively progressive view of racial difference probably owes a lot to Brando's own eccentric sense of social justice (Manso 1994), but there may have been an element of Peckinpah in it. One imagines that the Peckinpah version would have made more sense, since Brando's Rio Kid would have died (Weddle 1994: 144) and thus have become a figure of transformed masculinity, according to the logic of the sixties Western that the only good "macho man" is a dead one or one committed to death. *The Professionals* (1966) also anticipated *The Wild Bunch* with its Mexican fantasy of a revolution that is legitimate as long as it is outside of the United States. In the group Western, the revolution is always somewhere else.

The Wild Bunch is the culmination of the group Western and makes explicit a tendency often implicit in the classical Western. Long ago Jim Kitses referred to this tendency as "a deep stream of anarchy, a subversive current that insists that society is too oppressive, love is not possible, living with other people is not possible, community is not possible" (1970: 154). In many ways, *The Wild Bunch* epitomizes what the theorist Adorno meant by determinate negation when he referred to the way artworks "must assimilate themselves to the comportment of domination in order to produce something qualitatively distinct from the world of domination" (1997: 289). The movie negates the social categories that determine its content and form through the way in which it makes visible its own contradictions. As in other Westerns that came after *High Noon* and *Shane*, *The Wild Bunch* articulates a conflict of identifications that challenges any simple alignment with the status quo – "the law" that the railroad executive Harrigan (Albert Dekker) represents – or any simple opposition to law, such as the Bunch themselves. As Michael Bliss points out concerning the latter position, "The Bunch's robberies serve to strengthen the ruling classes by giving them a very visible, apolitical antagonist that they may oppose for the supposed benefit of 'the people'" (1993: 103). In contrast to most Westerns, *The Wild Bunch* has accumulated a significant body of criticism; yet one of the hallmarks of this criticism is ambivalence about the Bunch themselves and about the film's use and representation of violence, particularly in the final battle of Aqua Verde, which is almost unanimously described as "apocalyptic" (Bliss 1993, 1999, Dixon 1999, Graham 1983, Doug McKinney 1979, Devin McKinney 1999, Prince 1998, Schrader 1994, Seydor 1999, Sharrett 1999, Simons 1994, Torry 1993, Weddle 1994).

Slotkin discusses *The Wild Bunch* in the context of the My Lai massacre in Vietnam, a perspective that rejects the idea that the final battle could be "a complex attempt at redemption" (1992: 607). Though I would hesitate to explain the film's ambivalence or any specific reference to Vietnam as Peckinpah's strict intention, especially since news of the My Lai massacre did not reach the American public until after the release of *The Wild Bunch* (598) – still, I do think that these elements help to explain its controversial impact at the time of its release and its historical significance since that time (see Prince 1998: 35). As Marshall Fine notes, by comparison with the more financially successful Westerns of 1969, Henry Hathaway's *True Grit* and George Roy Hill's *Butch Cassidy and the Sundance Kid*, "Only *The Wild Bunch* stands the test of time." The reason for this critical success, however, is not simply that the film is "about loyalty and changing times," as Fine argues (1991: 155), which would describe Hill's film just as well. Rather, it has to do with the film's dramatization of the contradictions in the relationship between subjectivity and power in the postmodern world. *The Wild Bunch* could be considered a test case for the possibility of agency that emerges from complicity and ambivalence. The numerous films that have imitated Peckinpah's method of representing graphic violence have, for the most part, eliminated such ambivalence and neutralized the contradictions that Peckinpah's characters epitomize (see Prince 1998: 229–53). In this way, they have disengaged the audience from the recognition of their own implication in the social violence that produces stable social structures. Spectators do not see or recognize the violence that supports their mode of living, their free time, and their right to wealth.

Several critics have noted that, in the opening sequence, Pike Bishop (William Holden), the leader of the Bunch, makes the conscious decision to use the parade of the Temperance Union as a cover for the gang's escape from the railroad office. When Bishop says, "We'll join them," his apparent second-in-command, Dutch Engstrom (Ernest Borgnine), giggles, suggesting the inhumanity of these men in their lack of concern for the lives of innocent people. However, this decision is made before the Bunch learn of the ambush that has been laid for them by the railroad posse. When Angel (Jaime Sánchez) spots the rifles on the roof across the street, Bishop makes a series of quick decisions that are given almost no verbal expression. He quickly grabs the railroad office manager – the one whom, as the Bunch entered the office, is overheard saying to an employee, "I don't care what you meant to do, it's what you did that I don't like" – and sends him out the door to see what the men on the roof will do. Despite the obvious callousness of these decisions, even Slotkin recognizes that at this point in the movie "It is still possible to imagine that the escape will pass off bloodlessly, that the posse will refrain from shooting at the Bunch while there are civilians in the way, and that the Bunch will simply back out of town behind that cover" (1992: 596).

Bishop assumes that the forces of "the law" will not risk taking the lives of innocent civilians in the war they are waging against the Bunch. Ironically, this assumption is almost certainly shared by the citizens of Starbuck, including those who march for the Temperance Union. Bishop identifies with the "normal" subject of the dominant culture to the extent of believing that "the law" will put the interests of the community above the interests of corporate capital. Dutch presumably shares this view, since everything we learn about him in the rest of the film suggests that he would not giggle at the pointless murder or exploitation of innocent people. However, when the office manager is brutally gunned down by the railroad posse, both Bishop and Dutch must realize that, in this case, the law may be willing to sacrifice the innocent to get at the guilty or, more to the point, that it may regard its war against the Bunch as a class war in which the distinction between criminals and citizens gets blurred – so that the deaths of the latter can be considered "collateral damage." This knowledge doesn't prevent the Bunch from making their escape anyway, during which Bishop unintentionally tramples a woman to death. Furthermore, Bishop has instructed Crazy Lee (Bo Hopkins) to keep the civilian hostages under guard until the shooting starts. However, when the not overly intelligent Lee says he'll keep them until Hell freezes over or Bishop says different, Bishop makes the implicit decision to leave the man behind since he represents a liability in the gang's attempt to escape. He may not know for sure that Lee will execute the hostages, but he's clearly willing to take that risk in order to escape apprehension by the law. In effect, though Bishop does not explicitly wish for the murder of the innocent that is unleashed on the streets of Starbuck, he nonetheless acts without full regard for the human consequences of his actions. One could say the same thing of the posse, though there is a significant difference between their position and that of the Bunch: technically, the members of the posse, with the exception of Deke Thornton (Robert Ryan), don't have to choose between their own freedom (including the freedom to live) and the freedom of others. The corporate representative, Harrigan, makes the unambivalent decision to sacrifice innocent civilian lives in his pursuit of the Bunch in order to protect the railroad's capital.

This distinction between the agents of "the law" and the outlaws may seem arbitrary, but it is important to understanding the cultural significance of the film. The outlaws are not presented as ideal figures, Robin Hoods out to defend the poor; and, and with the possible exception of Angel, they don't fit neatly into the category of social banditry, as Eric Hobsbawm uses that term to describe "peasant outlaws whom the lord and state regard as criminals, but who remain within peasant society, and are considered by their people as heroes, as champions, avengers, fighters for justice, perhaps even leaders of liberation, and in any case as men to be admired, helped and supported" (2000: 20). Though the Bunch are well received by Angel's village, they are never seen as liberators, even in the way that the Seven are. On the contrary, their primary motivation for robbing the railroad, which they do twice in this film, is greed and the desire to appropriate wealth without selling their labor at too low a price. After the massacre at Starbuck is over, the Bunch realize that their robbery has been in vain because all they got away with, after the slaughter of most of their men and numerous innocent bystanders by the railroad posse, are a few bags of washers. Yet their response to this situation is laughter – laughter at themselves for the futility of their actions. This may seem to be another sign of callousness, but it also exhibits a different relation to wealth than that of Harrigan, who only exhibits something resembling a sense of humor when he takes pleasure in shooting Crazy Lee and when he brags about how good its feels to be on the right side of the law to Deke Thornton. To Harrigan, wealth represents power and the ability to dominate and control other people, even to the point of taking their lives. As Stephen Prince comments, "Harrigan's boast emblematizes the looming historical forces – the concentration of ruthless political and economic power sustained by violence – that Peckinpah believed posed a significant antidemocratic threat in the twentieth century" (1999b: 22). Later at the Bunch's campsite, Pike and Dutch conclude that their attempt to hold up the railroad office in Starbuck was a mistake. By contrast, Harrigan believes himself incapable of error and boldly tells the angry citizens that he and his gunmen "represent the law." In effect, the film explores the relationship between law, violence, and the formation of the normal self. Three crucial positions are identified in the Starbuck sequence: the law as the expression of social dominance (the viewpoint of capital), the outlaw as the refusal of social dominance but without any effective concept of an alternative community, and the "normal" subject of the community that identifies with the law but without the conscious knowledge of the community's subjection to and implication in the violence of social domination.

Though the film should not be read as a simple commentary on the Vietnam War, it nonetheless reproduces in a microcosm the contradictions in American culture that became visible during that conflict and are still operative at the present time (see Prince 1998: 1–45). The outlaws are not the heroes of this scenario, but some of them do possess a social consciousness and sense of responsibility that the normal citizens lack. Historically, a significant number of US citizens, initially at least, supported their government's direct intervention in Vietnam and its indirect intervention in other countries before, during, and after that war, especially in the Philippines, Latin America, and the Middle East. They may not have specifically endorsed those ventures and alliances with dictatorial regimes, but most did not protest and continued to elect conservative politicians to office who explicitly endorsed such a foreign policy. Though US citizens eventually became aware of the brutality of the Vietnam War and had some knowledge of US involvement in regimes that used torture and murder as a means of social control, they continued to live as if there were no relation between such violence and their own social positions and personal wealth. In the case of Vietnam, despite a vociferous antiwar movement, the average American saw the Viet Cong (a phrase equivalent to "commie," and coined by Ngo Dinh Diem for the Viet Minh in the South who opposed his regime after he began returning the land of peasants to their former landlords and forcing them to relocate) as a disreputable band of outlaws and traitors to American democracy and goodwill. Only when significant numbers of Americans began to die, sometimes from friendly fire, did the people of the United States begin to turn against the war, just as the good citizens of Starbuck turn on Harrigan. However, after Vietnam, US interventions in Latin America (especially in El Salvador and Nicaragua), Africa, and the Middle East, culminating in two Gulf Wars, were largely supported by US citizens; and rarely did any mainstream politician or public figure point out any relation between US affluence and the use of violence against other nations and individuals.

Those members of the Bunch who survive the Starbuck massacre – Bishop, Dutch, Angel, and the Gorch brothers, Lyle and Tector (Warren Oates and Ben Johnson) – are not a homogeneous group. The brothers are the least disciplined and the ones most lacking in principles. Self-interest and personal pleasure seem to be the only motives that keep them in the group. As soon as they get to the rendezvous with Sykes (Edmond O'Brien) after the robbery, they begin to demand a larger cut for themselves and less for Angel, because he is Mexican, and for Sykes, because he is old and only looked after the horses. To some extent, one can measure the character of each member of the Bunch by the history of his relation to women, insofar as this is made apparent in the film. In each case, there is ambivalence in that history. For the Gorch brothers, women seem to be objects of pleasure that can be enjoyed, to use the phrase that confuses Lyle, "in tandem" like so many commodities. Yet, after they get drunk in Mapache's headquarters at Aqua Verde, their blatantly lascivious relation to the three prostitutes they share is ironically transformed into the most conventional and sentimental of desires when they show up in the hot bath to introduce the rest of the Bunch to Lyle's fiancée. Furthermore, their behavior with the young peasant girl in Angel's village has already underscored their childlike relation to women despite their apparent crudity. In both cases, their maudlin amorousness evokes laughter from the rest of the gang. Angel is the most socially proper since he loves a woman of his village, Teresa, whom he has never touched because he puts her on a pedestal. When he learns that she has run off to be the woman of Mapache by her own choice, he goes ballistic, literally, and upon encountering her in Aqua Verde, shoots her dead. Pike Bishop is a more seasoned romantic who, in a flashback, recalls the one woman he wanted to marry, a Mexican named Aurora. Though he didn't put her on a pedestal, he nonetheless indirectly brought about her death when her estranged husband broke into the room where they were about to make love and shot her dead. Dutch is the eternal bachelor whose closest bonds might seem to be exclusively with men. Christopher Sharrett comments on the fact that he "appears to be gay since he doesn't enter the brothel in the scene just before the Battle of Bloody Porch" (1999: 88–9). Yet he dances with one of the women in Angel's village; and in the march out of the town, a woman comes up to him and gives him a flower. In this critical scene, Dutch and Pike ponder the flower and give each other knowing looks. Then Dutch turns to look at the children and their mothers waving goodbye. The flower symbolizes the social ties they have left behind in order to pursue the lives they have chosen.

All these relations to women indicate the dysfunctional construction of the Bunch as social individuals. They are incapable of socially productive relationships, yet the unconscious objects of their desire could not be more conventional. Pike wants permanent romantic love with a sensual woman he respects and who will stand up to him, as Aurora did when he showed up late for their encounter; but he can never conform to the conventional rules of heterosexual union long enough to sustain a relationship. One gets the feeling that he chose a married woman to fall in love with precisely as a way of avoiding commitment. Tector and Lyle want, if you will, a kind of return to infantile narcissism, a nurturing sensuality without any responsibility to the other. Their inseparability and tendency to share women suggests their fixation at the earliest stages of development when the only compelling social ties are within the family, particularly to the shared mother. Angel wants ideal love that transcends sexuality and supports his own identification with patriarchal authority. When Teresa betrays his love, she forsakes that authority and the community it supports, which has already been subverted by Mapache's pillaging of the village and murder of Angel's father. Shooting her is his way of reasserting such authority. Dutch may be the classical image of the repressed homosexual who channels his desire into activities that imitate sexual contact between men, including acts of violence, as Sharrett implies. Yet the scene in which a woman gives him a flower points to the possibility that Dutch is more capable of real intimacy than anyone else in the group, including Pike. The difference is that Dutch, ever the realist, recognizes the futility of trying to substitute paid sex for real relationships. He seems to accept the loss of social ties more consciously than the other members of the group, though Pike also recognizes the significance of the flower. In the final battle, both men will unleash their misogyny when Dutch uses a woman as a shield and Pike screams "Bitch!" before shooting the woman who has shot him. In their desires, the Bunch are pathetically conventional. Yet they disclose the misogynist violence that underlies conventional relationships, which are not founded on social equality or the recognition of the singularity of desire and the demand for autonomy. They manifest all the dysfunctions common to the hegemonic patriarchal society against which they are supposed to be rebelling. Yet the very dysfunctionality of their relation to women and to society in general inadvertently drives them in a subversive direction, not so much as individuals but as a group.

As Tompkins notes, women in the Western embody society and civilization through their identification with the "genteel tradition." This is the tradition that the Virginian's Molly derives from in the East: "a matriarchal society that values social position, manners, education, good grammar, the correct accent, and the right clothes" (1992: 142). Tompkins asserts that the Western "owes its popularity and essential character to the dominance of a women's culture in the nineteenth century and to women's invasion of the public sphere between 1880 and 1920" (44). This culture, through the bestsellers of women like Harriet Beecher Stowe, Susan Warner, and Maria Cummins, "spoke to the deepest beliefs and highest ideals of middle-class America" (38). To support her view, Tompkins refers to the opening scenes of The Wild Bunch: "a temperance leader harangues his pious audience; in the next scene a violent bank robbery makes a shamble of their procession through town. The pattern of talk canceled by action always delivers the same message: language is false or at best ineffectual; only actions are real" (51). Though Tompkins's general observations are undeniably true, she tends to gloss over the specific details that add complexity to the problem she points out. In the first place, despite the insane explosions of violence with which *The Wild Bunch* begins and ends, it is an oversimplification to say that it treats language as false or ineffectual against the reality of violence. Ironically, the Wild Bunch as a group are among the talkiest Western figures ever put on film, with lines utterly uncommon in the Western such as Sykes remark to Pike, "That was a mighty fine talk you gave the boys back there about sticking together." Though Deke Thornton has no one in whom he can verbally confide among the even more lumpen characters he leads for the railroad, he still spends most of his screen time in the movie talking away about what imbeciles he leads and how much he would rather be with the men he's pursuing. The temperance leader at the beginning of the film is a man; and if the women's culture Tompkins mentions represents the beliefs and ideals – or the ideology – of middle-class America, then the contradictions in that ideology are made apparent when the forces of the law brutally slaughter the very citizens who support them. The critical point is that the authority of the temperance speaker and his mostly female followers is still identified with the law and the power of capital that uses it as an instrument. The most critical and subversive aspect of *The Wild Bunch* is the way the dominant masculine hero of the Western splits into two figures: a masculine figure bent on self-destruction, and another masculine figure who, after undergoing a sort of feminization, gropes toward some limited form of critical consciousness. This consciousness cannot be correlated with "social position, manners, education, good grammar, the correct accent, and the right clothes," but it does suggest a radical critique beyond the death wish of the outlaw subject.

Tompkins emphasizes Deke Thornton's desire to be with the Bunch, whom he regards as real *men* by contrast with the "gutter trash" he travels with (18). Yet she ignores the critical remark that Thornton makes to Harrigan: "What I like and what I need are two different things." He says this when Harrigan hesitates to let him ride with the bounty hunters in pursuit of the Bunch. Harrigan worries that Thornton may join up with the Bunch; and though no critic so far as I know has ever commented on the fact, nothing could prevent Deke from doing just that, certainly not the men he travels with. If he wants so badly to join *the men*, as Tompkins suggests, why doesn't he do it? After all, at the end of the film he has no intention of going back to the United States and submitting to the law represented by Harrigan. The answer to the question lies in the conflict between Thornton's critical consciousness, which is suggested throughout the film, and Pike Bishop's ideological leadership of the Bunch. From the beginning, Thornton is presented as a feminized counterpart to Bishop's apparent hypermasculinity. Shortly after the Starbuck massacre, in his exchange with Thornton, Harrigan insists that the latter will either lead the posse of bounty hunters after the Bunch or go back to prison. In a critical flashback, Thornton is stripped to the waist and being whipped by a prison guard, who has obvious pleasure on his face, reminiscent of the pleasure on Harrigan's face when he tells Thornton how good it feels to be right, which means to do your killing or hire others to do it through the agency of the law. This image superimposed over Thornton's face as he stands before Harrigan suggests his emasculation by the law, which has brought about the change in his critical consciousness (Ill. 21). As there is no explanation as to why Deke doesn't join the Bunch, one is forced to conclude that, despite all of his protests to the contrary, he simply doesn't want to because he no longer sees the identity of his friend Bishop as viable.

Pike Bishop is the political center of the Bunch, the spokesman of the ideology that holds them together and distinguishes them from the railroad posse, who, with the exception of Thornton, are

ILLUSTRATION 21 The subject of discipline and punishment. *The Wild Bunch* (1969). Warner Bros. *Producer:* Phil Feldman. *Director:* Sam Peckinpah

only interested in the bounties on the heads of the men they pursue. As Bishop sums it up when Tector Gorch tries to shoot Sykes, "When you side with a man, you stay with him. And if you can't do that, you're like some animal. You're finished. We're finished. All of us." The inadequacy of this ideology, however, is on display throughout the film. Though Pike's loyalty to the men who follow him is fairly consistent, his history and the events unfolding during the course of the film suggest that such loyalty must be compromised. In a flashback, we learn that Bishop was the reason Deke Thornton was captured and imprisoned. After a robbery, they went to a nearby bordello under Pike's optimistic assumption that a posse wouldn't look for them in its own backyard (a strategy that works in *Butch Cassidy*). When Deke warned him that they needed to move on, Pike resisted with the comment that he was sure they were safe and being sure was his business. Shortly thereafter, the police broke in and shot Deke while Pike made a quick escape. Though Deke doesn't seem to blame Pike for his capture, the latter obviously feels responsible. Later, he defends Deke's working for the railroad by insisting that Deke gave his word and has to stick by it; but Dutch calls that into question when he says, "That ain't what counts. It's who you give it to!" Yet Pike's sympathy with Deke may lie in the fact that he has made a similar compromise with power in giving his word to Mapache (Emilio Fernández), the fascist leader of the counterrevolutionary forces who are destroying the people of Angel's village and, by implication, the people of Mexico. Though he compromises his agreement with Mapache by giving Angel one case of guns for his people in return for his share of the payoff, Pike still allows Angel to ride into Aqua Verde, which leads to his capture by Mapache; and the only reason for this, apparently, is so that Mapache will not suspect the Bunch of giving Angel the guns. Furthermore, Pike decides to leave Sykes behind after the old man has been shot by one of the railroad posse.

Pike's inconsistencies derive from the ambivalence of his relation to power. This ambivalence is visually imagined through the opposition between Angel's village, an egalitarian utopia, and Mapache's headquarters at Aqua Verde, a fascist dystopia. After the Bunch ride out of the village to the singing and celebration of the community, the next shot is a close-up of a child nursing on a woman's breast with a gun belt draped across it. Mapache's fascistic vision of the world perverts the nurturing, maternal foundation of an imaginary Mexican culture, which has just been epitomized by Angel's village. After the Starbuck massacre, Pike says that the Bunch need to start thinking beyond their guns, but he never succeeds in doing that. On the contrary, the Bunch's next job is to steal guns for Mapache, which culminates in their gift to the fascist of the most symbolic weapon of all, the machine gun. If Pike is the ideological center of the Bunch, Dutch is its conscience, the voice that consistently points out Pike's contradictions and tries to keep him consistent with himself. Dutch's criticism usually pushes Pike toward an identification with the common people as opposed to fascists like Mapache or the corporate capitalist who appears to control Thornton. When Pike laughingly suggests the similarity between the Bunch and Mapache's men, since they're all thieves, Dutch takes offense and says, "We ain't nothin' like him. We don't hang nobody. I hope someday these people kick him and the rest of that scum like him into their graves." Later, when he insists that it matters who you give your word to, Pike Bishop is literally struck dumb. At that point, he makes the decision to go back to Aqua Verde, which leads inevitably to the apocalyptic destruction of the Bunch. Once again, while Bishop and the Gorch brothers spend time in the bordello, Dutch waits outside, as if to signify Bishop's conscience waiting for him to rethink his obligations – not only to Angel but to the part of himself that sides with the angels.

Of course, Angel is no angel, as his brutal murder of Teresa makes clear. Though Bishop does not idealize women to the same extent as Angel, he moves through a world that he understands largely in terms of polar oppositions. His masculinist ethos blocks him from the belief that the angels (who as victims have been feminized like Deke Thornton) could ever triumph over the fascists or the capitalists. He sees no middle ground between identification and collaboration with Mapache, on the one hand, and an apocalyptic war to the death, on the other. As Sharrett argues, in this film, as in most of the Mexico Westerns after John Huston's *The Treasure of the Sierra Madre* (1948), "The Mexican, like the Indian, is alternately demonized and romanticized, with death being 'the right place to go'" (1999: 84). For the Bunch, only death will do. In imaginary Mexico, one sees the basic social contradiction between power and subjection, wealth and poverty, and good and evil, in stark, elementary terms. Revolution is still possible in such an environment, whereas in the United States it is no longer possible to fight against men like Harrigan and everything they stand for, because the hegemony has been so effective that it has incorporated the subjected into the structure of power itself, as *High Noon* demonstrated. Though the people of Starbuck are furious that representatives of the railroad turned their town into a battlefield and made no distinction between the innocent and the guilty, there can be no doubt that they will go on identifying with the same power that has murdered them.

Angel's contradiction, as Sharrett notes, lies in his identification with and admiration for Bishop, which effectively cancels "his stated beliefs in democracy and community" (86). Yet we may still wonder why Angel is sacrificed. In the scene before the sequence that concludes with Angel's capture by Mapache, Pike returns to the Bunch's hideout in the mountains with several bags of gold. He tosses one bag to Dutch who then tosses it to Angel. The camera cuts in close to accentuate Angel's reaction to the sight of wealth. Though Angel has already sacrificed his share to give guns to his people, he is clearly seduced by this sight, which reinforces his commitment to the Bunch. Ironically, at this moment, he has succumbed to exactly the same temptation to which his woman Teresa succumbed when she decided to leave behind the poverty of the village and join Mapache. Angel has unconsciously identified with Mapache himself through the mediation of Pike and the Bunch. Angel could easily leave the gang and join his people to fight with the guns he has stolen, but the sight of the gold precludes such an action. Angel has signed his death warrant at that moment.

Yet, if Angel admires Pike and his masculinist ideology, Pike in return identifies with Angel and his contradictions. Though Pike tries to prevent Angel from reacting violently to Teresa's betrayal, he nonetheless sympathizes with Angel's claim that she was "his woman" with the words, "I know, I know." As Sharrett stresses, "Pike's consolation refers us to his own culpability in the murder of Aurora and the misogyny at the base of romantic love" (103). It isn't that Pike wanted Aurora dead, but his romantic attachment to her lacked any realistic understanding of what it takes for a relationship to work. By avoiding the responsibility and commitment that would have required him to get her as far away from her husband as possible and to lead a different kind of life, he created a situation that resulted in her death. Pike sees in Angel and, by implication, in Mexico itself, the contradictions that have consumed his life and destroyed any possibility of real social relationships. In witnessing Angel's torture by Mapache, he witnesses the destruction of Angel's masculinity and his patriarchal identity. Angel is being feminized just as Deke Thornton was feminized in prison. Pike knows that sooner or later the same will happen to him, if not by Mapache then by old age; and since he can't imagine that effective action could emanate from such a feminized masculinity, he concludes that the only alternative is to choose death and go out in a blaze of masculine violence.

His last act is to surrender all hope for love or any kind of permanent social tie. In the bordello at Aqua Verde, when Pike looks at the young prostitute and her child, he realizes his own complicity with the world that has left this woman destitute and forced her to sell her affection for money. Immediately, he hears the Gorch brothers in the next room bickering with another prostitute over the price. At this moment, Pike realizes that he is fundamentally not different from these men – that however much he may identify with Angel's romanticism, in the end everything comes down to the price of gold, even for Angel. The life Pike has chosen to lead has made him no different from Mapache. The only love he has is the love he can buy, and he knows that this woman is forced to sell herself because of men like him. In fury, he throws his empty whiskey bottle to the ground, picks up his gun, and walks into the other room. He stands in the door in the image of the crucified, which clues the spectator that he has decided on death as the only viable form of self-transformation in the world as he imagines it. In a last ironic gesture, he gives what appears to be a substantial payment of gold to the prostitute. Some critics have read the expression on her face as insulted and disappointed; but to me it seems clear that, though she maintains her dignity, she is surprised at how much he has given her. Yet Pike looks back at her one last time in a way that expresses his recognition of the futility and self-serving nature of this gift (Ill. 22). His face at that moment is half-shrouded in darkness as if to suggest that he is already dead, already too much committed to the negation of human life. He cannot possibly give this woman what she deserves or make up for

ILLUSTRATION 22 Self-recognition as death wish. *The Wild Bunch* (1969). Warner Bros. *Producer:* Phil Feldman. *Director:* Sam Peckinpah

what he has lost, and in his own view he can't change the world that has put them both in this situation. What he can do is take himself and Mapache out of the equation. Yet the final irony is that in a few minutes Pike will be screaming "Bitch!" while he shoots the woman, similar in appearance to the young prostitute, who has just shot him in the back. With one hand he proffers payment in the attempt to erase his exploitation of women and everyone else in a subordinate relation to power, and with the other hand he strikes back brutally against all women for having betrayed his romantic fantasies by aligning themselves with power in exactly the way Pike has done himself. Dutch, whose approach to women is usually "genteel" by comparison with the rest of the Bunch, uses another woman as a shield in the final battle. Since these women have sided with Mapache, they are fair game; but this political judgment is contradictory and hypocritical because the Bunch have themselves sided with Mapache – even to the extent of giving him the machine gun that, for a while, symbolizes his power – and have never clearly stood with the peasant opposition, not even in their act of revolutionary suicide.

From a distance, Deke Thornton witnesses the final battle in a way that recalls the moment when Pike and Dutch looked over at the children torturing scorpions on an anthill at the beginning of the film. Like the scorpions, the Bunch are trapped in an enclosed place that ultimately signifies the enclosure of their minds, the limits of their social vision (Bliss 1999: 107–8). When they looked at the children torturing scorpions, their faces expressed confusion, suggesting that they recognized themselves in the image but couldn't come to terms with it. Deke's experience in prison has made it necessary that he come to terms with what the death of the Bunch and of the scorpions signifies: according to David Weddle, "the cruel self-devouring world that the Bunch were born into, a world devoid of grace" (1994: 331). Later, walking through the aftermath of the battle, while his men glory in the final capture of their prey, Deke comes upon Pike and takes his gun. By doing this, Deke makes it clear that he has not fully escaped the rule of Pike's masculinist ideology; but he has accepted a more passive and feminized relation to history than Pike and the Bunch did. Ironically, of the two Americans who survive at the end of the film, one has been broken by the brutality of prison and the other has been diminished by old age. Yet precisely because they have surrendered some of their masculine purity, old Sykes and Deke are finally able to choose sides in a way that the Bunch never could. In a sense, these two men achieve what the Bunch promised but never delivered, what Sharrett calls a "gay utopia," though not one in which, as he argues, "the male libido is unfettered, and takes a direction both destructive and liberatory" (1999: 90). Precisely because Deke and Sykes have had to accept the loss of libido both to time and to power, they have come to realize that force and sexuality do not make the man, and that it is possible for men to love one another without killing themselves or having to prove their sexual prowess. This enables them to join forces with the people who struggle for liberation through cooperation and a surrender of masculinist purity. In effect, they go back to the green world of the village, and the last image in the film is a flashback to the Bunch leaving the village behind and with it all the possibilities for social transformation that an identification with the village would make possible. Yet the path to the green world is through the desolation of a desert landscape.

At a critical point, while Deke sits outside Aqua Verde against the wall, he hears the gunfire that represents the final end of the posse of bounty hunters, and his only reaction is an ironic smile. There can be no escaping the consequences of an identification with power; and sooner or later it destroys the being who aligns with it, either directly or indirectly. Bliss argues that the recollected images of the Bunch seized by laughter, superimposed over the image of Deke and Sykes riding off with the peasant revolutionaries, tell us "more successfully than words that because fidelity is now linked to political purpose, it's not only like it used to be, it's better" (1993: 126). This is a rather romantic way to put it, but it is still true that the laughter signifies what was best in the Bunch, the possibility of their humanization and transformation. Still, Prince argues that by keeping this ending, which Peckinpah had tried to remove, he undid the moral vision that he had produced at the end of the Aqua Verde slaughter. If the film had ended with Deke Thornton seated against the wall, "a mute witness to the carnage," Peckinpah "might have had an aesthetic and narrative structure that could control the extended, climactic, violent spectacle," instead of "a sentimental conclusion" (1998: 124). Aesthetically speaking, I would have to agree with Prince and Peckinpah that the other ending would have been preferable, though Prince's certainty about the damaging effects of screen violence on spectators, based on inconclusive empirical evidence (Felson 2000: 258), leaves out a much larger context of socially-sanctioned state violence that has to be taken into account.

There is no innocent, intrinsically nonviolent location from which we can sit and pass judgment on the Bunch. But it is possible to see where they went wrong in sacrificing the possibility of utopia, gay or otherwise, for an act of self-destruction that finally only serves the purpose of transforming them into monuments to a form of masculinity that must be left behind. The ending of *The Wild Bunch* may seem sentimental or naïve, but these final images of laughter do not mourn loss in the way that the freeze-frame shot at the end *Butch Cassidy and the Sundance Kid* mourns the loss of such colorful characters. The Bunch wasted their lives, but their legacy is the laughter that points toward what they could have been if they had transcended the contradictions of their own social identities.

CHAPTER 8

DEATH'S LANDSCAPE

The Uses of the Dead

Sergio Leone may seem out of place in a book on the Hollywood Western. Yet his movies are largely responses to and revisions of that tradition and, after the success of his first two Westerns, were largely made with Hollywood money (Frayling 2000). Furthermore, the concept of "Hollywood" shares in the Americanism that Marcia Landy, in her discussion of Leone, has described as "a phenomenon that is larger than the geographical and cultural boundaries of the United States and its cold war domination, coming to represent worldwide transformations and conflicts" (1996: 46). Though Leone's most important Westerns were made before the release of *The Wild Bunch*, the world they imagine is on the other side of the apocalypse that ends Peckinpah's masterpiece. It is a world in which the unveiling of the end of things is an everyday event, having, to repeat a line from *Once Upon a Time in the West*, "something to do with death." Leone said of the director of Westerns he cites more than any other in *Once Upon a Time*: "Ford was full of optimism, whereas I on the contrary am full of pessimism" (quoted in Frayling 2000: 258). Yet, as Antonio Gramsci has taught us, pessimism of the intellect can be revolutionary when it is allied with optimism of the will. Even more than Peckinpah's, Leone's vision is of a time when, to echo Kermode, there is nothing positive, only transition. In such a world, the will may be the only remaining force of change, or at least that is how it appears; but the intellect that lies behind this will cannot afford any illusions about the acts that result from it. There are no true heroes in Leone's world, only men who have lost all hope and yet discipline themselves to perform acts of the will driven by vengeance, greed, or simply the inexplicable desire to prevent a strong person from exploiting a weaker one. Their motives are usually mixed, and Leone seems to imply that anything good can only come from a willingness to risk the possibility of doing something evil. His films strangely illustrate the ethical proposition of French philosopher Alain Badiou: "If Evil exists, we must conceive it from the starting point of the Good" (2001: 60).

The world of the Man with No Name is a world that comes to pass after an apocalyptic event. Such an event is one that calls into question all the assumptions that have underlain the situation of the world as it has existed up to the moment of the event, including assumptions about the nature of the good. Most particularly, such an event calls into question the assumption that evil or good can be identified *a priori*. Apocalyptic events unveil the truth about a situation that was always present as a possibility but not previously grasped from within that situation. Events of this sort, as Badiou comments, "are irreducible singularities, the 'beyond the law' of situations" (44). When Clint Eastwood's Man with No Name rides toward the town of San Miguel in Leone's first Western, he emerges out of the desert landscape that in some way has been created by the apocalyptic event. Ultimately, the symbol of this event is the railroad, which in the imagery of these films, as in *The Wild Bunch*, is linked to the desert landscape as the landscape of death that it has symbolically created. Yet this death is the condition of life, the radical possibility of social transformation.

The Man with No Name is already symbolically dead, and that's why he has no name, though he is called by various names in Leone's Westerns: Joe in *A Fistful of Dollars* (1964; US release 1967), Monco in *For a Few Dollars More* (1965; US release 1967), Blondie in *The Good, the Bad and the Ugly* (1966; US release 1968), and Harmonica in *Once Upon a Time in the West* (1968; US release 1969). In *Duck, You Sucker*, which was retitled *A Fistful of Dynamite* for US distribution (1971; US release 1972), Sean Mallory is the character closest to the Man with No Name, though this film functions in many ways as an epilogue to the first four and a response to Peckinpah and other Italian "revolutionary" Westerns. In the trilogy and *Once Upon a Time*, the Man with No Name derives whatever name he has from others and never names himself. In *Fistful of Dynamite*, by contrast, Sean Mallory calls himself John and avoids revealing his true name, since it signifies the being he no longer is, a loss as permanent for him as death itself. The whole of Leone's Western *oeuvre*, and the Eastwood *oeuvre* that derives from it, could be summed up by the comment of the Man to the barkeeper Silvanito in *Fistful of Dollars*: "The dead can be very useful sometimes." In that movie, The Man makes use of dead bodies, which are not so magnificent, to create the illusion of life in order to "sucker" two warring families into continuing the process of killing each other off. Critics have sometimes commented that Leone's use of close-ups of the human face and the choice of actors for these shots transforms the face itself into a landscape. As Mitchell remarks, "the camera follows faces not to probe psychology but simply to register the impossibility of any greater knowledge of character than one has at first glance" (1996: 230). The face itself becomes a desert, empty of any social significance that can point toward a meaningful past or a future that can be the object of hope. The Western as a genre is declared dead by these movies, which means that its signifiers have lost all referential value, all historical meaning, except to the extent that they congeal in themselves the absence of any meaning or hope in the contemporary world. Paradoxically, through this apparent negation of hope, these faces and landscapes nonetheless convey an emotion, a significance, and even an odd form of hope.

Two Kinds of Men

A Fistful of Dollars, although it is a remake of Kurosawa's *Yojimbo*, is also structured through an explicit reference to *Shane*. In the first scene, the Man with No Name stops at a well set off to the side between two adobe buildings, seemingly in the middle of nowhere. He watches a small boy harassed by a gang of hooligans for trying to see his mother who is being held against her will. At one point, the mother Marisol (Marianne Koch) appears in the window and stares out at the stranger through the bars that hold her in, recalling Marian's first look at Shane through the kitchen window. The comparison suggests that by the sixties, just before the second wave of feminism burst on the scene, the family had been recognized as a prisonhouse for the woman. Eastwood's face is difficult to read, as he shows almost no emotion at the sight of the boy's being abused, though he smiles slightly at the sight of the woman. There seems to be some kind of attraction between them, though it will never be consummated. Yet this scene clearly motivates the events that follow. Like Shane, the Man comes upon a family in distress and, in his own way, sets out to reverse the situation and set them free. Unlike Shane, however, the Man never develops any kind of relationship with the family or overtly expresses affection toward any of its members, including the little boy. Aside from smiling at the woman, his only real contact with her comes when he knocks her out by accident. After he kills the Rojo gunmen who hold her prisoner, he hands her over to her husband and child and then gives them the money he has received from the two warring families he has been playing off against one another. When the woman asks him why he does this, his answer is enigmatic: "I knew someone like you once, and there was no one there to help." Though the family walks off into the night with enough money to last them for a while, there is nothing to suggest that the new life they will find will be substantially better than the one they have left behind. Like the flight of the holy family (whose names are echoed by the names Marisol, Julio, and Jesús), they will escape an immediate threat but not the ultimate crucifixion. One imagines that everywhere they go in this world, they will find another set of Rojos and Baxters.

As Robert C. Cumbow stresses, the Man "does not 'clean up' San Miguel out of any high-minded notions of right and wrong, or because he honors the law or any other absolute authority" (1987: 8). On the contrary, the only representative of the law in the town of San Miguel is Sheriff John Baxter, who is described by Silvanito as a bandit and a gun merchant who buys cheap in Mexico and then sells at a high price to the Indians in Texas. The Rojos apparently do the same thing with liquor. In this world there is no longer any clear distinction between capitalism and gangsterism, or between the law and the outlaw. Authority, to echo Chairman Mao, is the power that comes out of the barrel of a gun. The only motivation that we can ascribe to the Man is annoyance at "the victimization of the innocent" (8), although even this is questionable. In *Fistful of Dollars* and the other Westerns in Leone's trilogy, class struggle is never a conflict between two autonomous parties that are strictly external to one another and whose antagonism points to a dialectical shift toward a different social organization that would destroy the class system. On the contrary, it is a conflict internal to the class system, one that motivates the system itself to readjust and contain the contradictions that it generates, and internal to a class, with the exception of a subject that has no visible historical identification with any class. Nonetheless, there can be redistributions of wealth; and the Man himself brings this about by playing the different wings of the ruling class against each other in order to subvert their domination. But the agency of the exploited remains almost unimaginable within this framework. The family is virtually all that we see of the community, with the exceptions of the barkeeper, the bellringer, and the coffinmaker. None of these representatives of a diminished community can articulate the possibility of a radical social identity that can become the agency for the overthrow of capitalist power. The Man himself functions as a place holder. He does not manifest revolutionary consciousness but rather a viewpoint from within the system that can recognize the blindness of the different ruling parties, the different modes of social domination, and the relative innocence – but also ineffectuality – of the dominated.

To apply a rather crude allegorical interpretation, the Baxters represent the capitalist establishment of the United States that tries to operate as the international policeman, in the tradition of Ford's Wyatt Earp, though here there is no illusion of integrity. The Rojos are the Reds – based on the Spanish meaning of the surname – not as social revolutionaries but as Stalinist gangsters, who have expropriated the wealth of the masses largely through their extermination. Ramón Rojo (Gian Maria Volonté) is the psychopathic Stalin figure, whose passion for the peasant woman, Marisol, correlates with the Stalinist claim to love and represent the interests of the people. The Man is able to play these two families against each other because he sees through the fantasy with which each group operates. He recognizes that the real power of the Baxters resides in the mother, whose fundamental illusion is that her family legitimately possesses power and social authority, despite her Machiavellian willingness to use violence and any other means necessary to protect their interests. An implicit racism lies behind her war against the Rojos, even though she herself appears to be Mexican. Ironically, the matriarchal structure of the Baxter family aligns it with conventional morality by contrast with the Rojos, a family in which there is no woman, no mother or father, but only brothers, who have no compunction about destroying the traditional family and can be assumed to have devoured their own mother and father at some previous point in the film's imaginary history. Their family illusion reveals itself in Ramón's passion for Marisol and in his belief that he can force her to love him. Ultimately, this illusion derives from the larger belief that power is unidirectional and without dependence on the others who are its objects. The Man exploits Ramón's conviction that a man with a rifle will always defeat a man with a forty-five as long as he shoots at the heart. Though Ramón worries about the Man because he is too smart, he fails to recognize his own blindness and succumbs to the Man's craft in constructing a bulletproof iron vest to wear over his heart. The Man realizes that Ramón's weakness, his blind spot, lies precisely in the illusion that power really does come out of the barrel of a gun.

Though the Man with No Name is not identical with himself in the three Eastwood films, one can read these stories as a reverse evolution, leading backwards in time to the moment in *The Good, the Bad and the Ugly* when the Man first dons his signature green poncho. From this perspective, the hero of *Fistful of Dollars* is the more mature figure and the more ironic one, who almost always says the opposite of what he means. When he tells Silvanito that there's money to be made in a town where there are two bosses, he creates the impression, which most critics have accepted, that greed is the only motive driving him, which is more true of Monco in the second film and of Blondie in the third. Yet the Man is different from someone like Shane. He cannot afford the illusion of his own objective goodness or assume any moral superiority in relation to the men he finally faces in the showdown, the Rojos. Shane is still in the tradition of Henry Fonda's Wyatt Earp. Even though he implicitly questions his own reliance on the gun and on violence as a solution to social conflicts, there is never any question but that he has sided with those who are in the right and is himself morally superior to the men he kills at the end of the film. The Man, by contrast, can make no such claim. His decision to play the opposing powers against each other and to transfer wealth and the possibility of autonomy to Marisol and the holy family does not derive from any apparent sense of moral or legal right but from the personal decision of the Man himself (Smith 2000: 85). He is noble in the Nietzschean sense that he legislates his own values.

The other two parts of the trilogy explore the symbolic genealogy of the Man's eccentric relation to society. In *For a Few Dollars More*, though the title suggests a continuation of the greed theme from the first film, the movie actually shows the obsession with money in the Man for the first time, an obsession that can be juxtaposed ironically against the Man's actions in the first film. During the course of the film, the relation between Mortimer (Lee Van Cleef) and Eastwood's Monco gradually evolves into something resembling a father-and-son relationship, so that by the end of the film, when Mortimer finally faces Indio (played by Volonté), Monco intervenes on the Colonel's behalf when Indio gets the drop on him. He sees to it that they have a fair fight, which Mortimer wins. At this point, though Monco realizes that Mortimer is less interested in the bounty than in avenging his sister, who killed herself while being raped by Indio, he has no reason to believe that Mortimer doesn't want his share of the bounty. Though he could easily allow Indio to kill the older man and then kill Indio himself in order to keep all the reward money, Monco has bonded with Mortimer; and, despite the typically ironic mode of the Man's speech, he looks up to the older man.

The last shot of Mortimer riding into a sunset (Ill. 23) aligns him with Shane and all the other Western heroes who ride off alone in the end. One could argue that Mortimer's decision to choose vengeance over money in response to his sister's violation later determines the Man's decision to save the holy family, or at least to redistribute the wealth in order to give them the means to start a new life, however problematic that may turn out to be. Furthermore, by entering into an alliance with Mortimer, though that alliance remains uneasy until the final scenes of the film, Monco implicitly

ILLUSTRATION 23 Riding off into the "unreal" sunset. *For a Few Dollars More* (1965). United Artists. *Producer:* Alberto Grimaldi. *Director:* Sergio Leone

develops a more critical understanding of his own socioeconomic situation. When he learns the identity of Colonel Mortimer from the Old Man who lives in the rickety house next to the train tracks, a house that shakes violently every time the train passes, he is told that Mortimer has been reduced to being a bounty hunter "same as you . . . because of trains." Trains will continue to function as a synecdoche for modern industrial capitalism in every Leone Western after *Few Dollars More*.

In *The Good, the Bad and the Ugly*, the Man with No Name is strictly displaced from the center of the action by the predominance of the character Tuco, played brilliantly by Eli Wallach. This film takes place during the Civil War, or the period immediately preceding the time frame of the classical Western that the earlier movies presumably referenced, though the war has been displaced to Texas, where there was at least one battle for which Leone found documentation in the Library of Congress. It was over the ownership of gold mines, which fits perfectly into the thematic concerns of the film (Frayling 2000: 206). Displaced history and derealized characterization suggest that Leone is using the Western not so much as an object of parody or of critique, but as a medium through which he can articulate the contradictory social drives and desires that modern capitalism produces as its by-product. In the opening sequences of the film, each character is labeled by a moral or aesthetic term that appears on the screen over a freeze-frame of his image. The last to be identified is the Good, Eastwood's character; and it can be inferred from his role in the film that the word "good" applied to him can be read as both an aesthetic and a moral category and probably is meant to represent the confusion of the two in the modern Nietzschean world.

Morally, the Good is only good by comparison with the Bad, who goes by the name Sentenza in the Italian version and Angel Eyes in the English. The name "Sentenza" means sentence or judgment; and at the beginning of the film the character pretends to carry out the judgments of his social superiors, men of wealth or power who hire him to do their dirty work (a situation that recalls the gunfighters who sold their services to the WSGA in the Johnson County War). Later he poses as a legitimate member of the Union army holding guard over prisoners of war, though his social legitimacy is only the means to an end that has no social justification. The spectator learns nothing about Angel Eyes's history or origin, anymore than he or she learns anything about the Man; but the ease with which the Bad is able to pose as a respectable member of society, a conventional form of the good, suggests that he has always identified with the dominant social powers when he could use them. It is no accident that Leone cast Lee Van Cleef in this role, which reverses his role in *Few Dollars More* just as the first shot in which he appears reverses his last appearance in the earlier film. The composition of the shot suggests that Angel Eyes is a Shane figure, a view that is initially reinforced by the fact that the first person to see him in the film is a boy. Yet this boy is a dark-headed Mexican, not a blond-headed American; and he is not playing but working, as he rides a donkey in circles to pump water out of a well. Before the end of the scene, the boy's father and brother will be gunned down by Angel Eyes with little or no apparent justification. Unlike Wilson in *Shane*, however, Angel Eyes then kills the rich man who hired him because he doesn't want to share the gold he is after with anyone.

In contrast to the relation between the Man and Angel Eyes, the category of the Good takes on an aesthetic significance in the relation between the Man and Tuco: if the latter is ugly, then the former is "good" in the sense of good-looking. Yet the aesthetic difference between them also reflects a social difference. Tuco is Mexican and lower class; he has a history and a family, both of which we learn something about when he meets with his brother, who is a monk. His family was so poor that the two brothers had only two possibilities of escape from their class, the priesthood or banditry. According to Tuco, he chose the harder path by becoming a bandit. In several ways, Leone drives home the fact that Tuco's "ugliness" is relative to an idealized norm that derives from the class system and the racial divisions it fosters. Throughout the film, everyone refers to Eastwood's character as "Blondie," though his hair is obviously not blond. Yet this signifier pinpoints his archetypal status as the "white" American, Tuco's racial and ethical superior. While Tuco is loudmouthed and quick to emotional outbursts, Blondie is soft-spoken and says very little. While Tuco can be forced to talk and reveal the location of the gold under torture, Blondie claims that he would probably not talk and Angel Eyes agrees with him. Blondie's name aligns him with the pale-skinned, blue-eyed, blond hero of *Shane*.

Since the difference between Tuco and Blondie is an aesthetic one, it tends to subvert itself, if only because Tuco is the real human being while Blondie is a fantasy. Tuco's ugliness cannot be separated from a gaze determined by class, race, and national identity, a gaze that constructs the blond, blue-eyed, soft-spoken man as the idealization of itself. In other words, the differences between them are largely matters of surface. If Tuco forces Blondie to march through the desert without any water, he is only doing unto his brother as his brother has done unto him, when Blondie left Tuco in the desert earlier in the film. One could argue that Blondie's treatment of Tuco is necessary because he recognizes the threat and potential violence of a person who has been dehumanized by the sustained brutality of the class system. Yet throughout the film, as the relationship between Tuco and Blondie develops, it becomes increasingly obvious that Blondie feels empathy for Tuco, starting from the moment he overhears the latter's conversation with his brother the monk, who faults Tuco for deserting his mother and father. When they ride off in a coach, Blondie offers Tuco a smoke after listening to his lies about the warm relations he has with his brother. This act signals a compassion in their relationship that wasn't there before, and when Tuco later takes on Angel Eyes's gang by himself, Blondie joins him to seal their partnership. Nonetheless, the closer they get to the treasure they are looking for, the more Tuco becomes like Fred C. Dobbs, the Bogart character in *The Treasure of the Sierra Madre*, a major influence on Leone's film. Tuco wants all the gold for himself and assumes that everyone else is trying to cheat him out of his share. Meanwhile, Blondie encounters the young, dying confederate soldier, covers him with his coat, and gives him a last smoke. Afterwards, he puts on the green poncho for the first time. Thus, the poncho actually signifies compassion in the heart of the Man with No Name, a compassion that grows through his relationship with Tuco and later with Colonel Mortimer, and culminates in his decision to liberate the holy family in the first film.

Still, Blondie's compassion is not a psychological development but an allegorical one. Just as Leone saw in Shane "an abstraction, a walking piece of myth" (Frayling 2000: 127), he saw in Clint Eastwood "a block of marble" (137) that he could shape to signify whatever he wanted. Blondie is not so much a real man as the walking manifestation of the dominant subject that has nonetheless been cut loose from its identification with the class system. Ironically, the real meaning of "good" in this film has little to do with virtuous or noble behavior. The dominant subject becomes good to the extent that it subverts its own ideological value by aligning itself with the subaltern like Tuco. It becomes bad when, like Angel Eyes, it puts itself in the service of capital, either by working for the capitalist or by accumulating wealth through any means necessary without regard for the social consequences. Blondie tells Tuco that there are two kinds of men, those with loaded guns and those who dig, which is one way of summing up the class system. Yet the film makes clear in numerous ways that if Blondie does not betray Tuco, as he does Angel Eyes, it is not simply out of paternalistic feeling or compassion. As Tuco says several times in the film, a man who thinks he can betray Tuco and still live does not know Tuco, who uses a train – Leone's symbol of capitalism – to break the chains that bind him to the man escorting him to his own hanging.

In Leone's vision, the Civil War is an apocalyptic event that has transformed the world into a wasteland, and only those like Tuco, who have the strength to survive in the desert and use the mechanical force of the train as an instrument of self-liberation, will be able to transform such a world into a garden, though in all likelihood, given Leone's pessimism, they will merely replicate the same destructive patterns of social existence that produced them. In the battle sequences, Leone insists on both the futility and the comedy of war, the objectives of which never add up to anything more than the occasion for the destruction of human life. He never touches on the issue of slavery, perhaps to emphasize that even the most glorious of causes cannot justify the futility and human cost of war. The fact that it took a war to end slavery does not testify to human greatness but to human stupidity and brutality. By the same token, the pursuit of wealth turns out to be yet another occasion for human beings to slaughter one another; and this rule will hold as long as the class system produces men like Tuco, who are brutalized by the absence of wealth, and men like Angel Eyes, who accumulate wealth out of the desire to dominate others. As for the Man, though he rides off with half the gold, money cannot stick to him; and from one film to the next, viewed in reverse order, he will pursue the chimera of wealth without ever achieving the goal of lasting pleasure or happiness. In *The Good, the Bad and the Ugly*, the only hope for a better world lies in the possibility of a union or true partnership between Tuco and Blondie; but that cannot be as long as the blond-haired, blue-eyed boy remains the archetype of the socially good that reduces the Tucos of the world to ugliness and self-hatred.

Get Out of the Way

Yet Leone does find a way to carve hope out of death's landscape in *Once Upon a Time in the West*. In some ways, Harmonica (Charles Bronson) represents a fusion of the dominant and the subaltern subjects; and the bond he develops with the outlaw Cheyenne (Jason Robards) represents a potentially more progressive and less futile partnership than that between Blondie and Tuco. Leone saw in Bronson another "face made of marble," but this face clearly does not convey the same archetypal racial norm that Clint Eastwood's did. Of the character Bronson plays, Leone remarked, "Since he is an Indian, he already hates the white man" (Frayling 2000: 274). Furthermore, as Sarah Hill comments, Cheyenne's name also suggests possible Native American origins, though "Jason Robard's looks certainly give no indication of this." Hill concedes that in this film Leone intentionally jumbles the ethnicities to reinforce his "view of America as the property of all" and to question "the traditional ethnic divisions of the western." This even applies to the Irish McBains who are portrayed "in the most stereotypical of ways":

along with their red hair and names, the daughter hums and sings "Danny Boy" (1998: 204).

Yet Leone's jumbling of ethnicities is not to dismiss them or their historical significance, but rather to insist on a distinction between realism and reality. Already in the earlier films, Leone had aimed to "nourish my fairy-story with a documentary reality" (quoted in Frayling 2000: 190). For Leone, realism consists of the signifiers or conventional signs by which reality has been coded, but I don't agree with Christopher Frayling that Leone was "into realism, not reality" (2000: 191). Rather, his work presupposes that you approach reality best not through the direct representation of the facts (traditional realism) but by taking the signifiers that ground such a representation, those components of realism, and reshuffling them in such a way that they are exposed as hollow and arbitrary. In *Once Upon a Time*, even more than in the earlier Westerns, race is one more justification for the social divisions produced by the class system and for the inevitable violence that results from that system. The outlaw like Cheyenne and the lone avenger like Harmonica are identified with racial signifiers that seem arbitrary and don't fit them very well; and this drives home the fact that race *is* a signifier that has the social function of naturalizing class divisions and economic injustice. This is not to deny that authentic cultural differences may exist between the groups defined by racial signifiers; but it suggests that beyond such differences, which are dynamic and always interact with one another, the signifiers operate within a larger socioeconomic system as justifications of class.

As virtually every commentary on Leone's fourth Western has pointed out, the most striking displacement of the Hollywood Western lies in the casting of Henry Fonda as Frank. The first time Frank appears on the screen bears some comparison with the opening shot of *The Good, the Bad and the Ugly*. In the latter film, the first shot is of a barren and colorless landscape that epitomizes Leone's vision of the West as the landscape of death. Yet hardly is that vision established in the eye of the spectator before it is interrupted by a face that swings up into the frame. This face offers an obvious human parallel to the background from which it appears to emerge. The eyes are cold, and the contours of face rough and jagged like the Spanish terrain in which Leone shot the scene. In *Once Upon a Time*, after the brutal murder of the McBain family, men emerge once again out of what appears to be a relatively barren landscape, only this time they have been hidden by cactus and yellow prairie grasses from which they are barely distinguishable, as if they too are things that grow in the dry desert. This image is from the viewpoint of the youngest and only surviving McBain, Timmy, who is obviously an allusion to Joey in *Shane*. In one shot, Timmy, in the background left, faces the gunmen at a distance, while the head of their leader is visible from a rear view in the foreground right. Instead of a face swinging up into the frame, this time the camera tracks forward while slowly panning right to reveal the face of Henry Fonda from a side angle. In an extreme close-up, this face reveals at first the same cold brutality and rough exterior that one saw in the opening shot of the earlier film and in the faces of the three iconic gunmen at the train station at the beginning of this one (Jack Elam, Woody Strode, and Al Mulock, the same actor from the opening shot of *The Good, the Bad and the Ugly*). Then, one notices that the eyes are different, because these are the eyes of Henry Fonda, an actor with a long history of playing compassionate and sensitive men in Hollywood films. The eyes light up as the face breaks into a smile at the sight of the boy, like the smile of Shane at Joey. But when one of the men says, "What are we going to do with this one, Frank?," the smile on Fonda's face vanishes with a subtle look of disappointment as he says, "Now that you've called me by name." Just before he pulls the trigger on the boy, his face breaks into another smile (Ill. 24). The use of Henry Fonda as one of the most revolting yet complex villains ever to appear in a Spaghetti Western adds a new sense of depth to the Leone's understanding of evil.

Ironically, though *Once Upon a Time in the West* is the one Leone film that offers the possibility of hope, it is also his most pessimistic work in the sense that it expresses a negative and almost elegiac view of everything that will be lost in the process of creating a new and potentially more just world – in particular, traditional masculine identity (see Landy 1996: 52), though there is definite ambivalence as to how great a loss that really is. Bernardo Bertolucci played a collaborative role in helping Leone develop the story, which has led Frayling to conclude that in this film, "The Marxism of Bertolucci met the melancholy, and the cinephilia, of Sergio Leone" (2000: 250). Dario Argento, who also participated in the collaboration,

ILLUSTRATION 24 Classic Hollywood as a child killer. *Once Upon a Time in the West* (1968). Paramount Pictures. *Producer:* Fulvio Morsella. *Director:* Sergio Leone

commented that they "put [into their treatment of the story] images and sensations rather than a lot of dialogue" (quoted in Frayling 2000: 250). In effect, the film communicates less through words than through the compositions of the shots and the complex facial expressions of the actors, who have been carefully selected for their physical features and the range of emotions that those features signify.

If Fonda is the villain, Claudia Cardinale, who plays Jill McBain, is the emotional center of the film. Brett McBain secretly married her in New Orleans; but when she arrives at Sweetwater expecting to meet her new family, she finds instead their corpses all laid out for burial. After the burial, the camera focuses on her hands tearing open the drawers and closets in the McBain cabin as she tries to find McBain's money and some clue as to why the family was murdered. Her face appears only when she looks in a mirror with a self-judging, self-hating gaze that recalls Marlene Dietrich's similar response to her mirror image in *Destry Rides Again*; and the allusion is meaningful because in New Orleans Jill was a high-class prostitute like Frenchy. Gradually, she is transformed into the symbolic agent of social change, though not without some violent reshaping at the hands of the "good" men in the film. In the last shot, as she brings water to the men laying down the railroad tracks, she represents the possibility of a society based on social collaboration and economic justice; but as the camera pans right to reveal Harmonica riding off alone with the dead body of Cheyenne, the implication is that traditional masculine heroes have no place in such a world. Even the dead Brett McBain was too obsessed with becoming rich to achieve what it may be possible for his widow to achieve in becoming the agent of a new kind of social relationship, one that is not based on the domination and exploitation of others. One could speculate that the final panoramic long shot incorporates the visions of both Leone and Bertolucci. The latter would be responsible for Jill's presence and her centrality in the film as the signifier of communism, understood as a social desire that capitalism generates out of itself through the identities it produces, a desire that ironically brings about the transformation of capitalism into something else. Leone incorporates this vision into his own more pessimistic view that any hope for the future necessarily requires the loss of traditions and values that have mattered in the past. In the exchange between Harmonica and Frank before their final showdown, the latter says that he is "just a man," to which Harmonica responds with a look of sadness and regret, "An ancient race."

Yet from the outset, the film posits the absence of woman and the values associated with the feminine as a root cause of the violence that creates and sustains capitalist social relations. Leone did some location shooting for the film in Monument Valley; but this homage to Ford, particularly to *The Searchers*, merely foregrounds the idea that a masculine world is a world deprived of life, one that substitutes towering rocks – monuments to phallic authority and violence – for the green world that will emerge only after Jill has brought feminine water to the dry masculine landscape. In the sequence leading up the massacre of the McBain family, Leone suggests that Brett McBain is neither an ideal heroic figure like Shane nor an ideal father like Joe Starrett. On the contrary, his relation to family seems at times to be almost ambivalent. While Maureen hums and sings "Danny Boy," her father tells her that soon she'll be able to slice the bread as thick as a door and she'll wear fine clothes and won't have to work anymore; but she seems largely amused when she responds, "We going to get rich, Papa?" Ironically, in a later scene, Jill arrives in McBain's Sweetwater already wearing the fine clothes that McBain dreamed of and that apparently her profession has enabled her to afford. Then Harmonica literally recuts her dress by tearing off the long sleeves and lace in a series of gestures that look like rape but turn out to be his attempt to mold her into some kind of superpeasant, whose now partially exposed breasts suggest her maternal relation to the new social order that is struggling to be born out of the masculine desert. Minutes before Frank murders the McBain family, Brett disciplines his oldest son Patrick for suggesting that the woman who is coming cannot replace his dead mother. McBain pulls his son's head up by the hair and slaps his face. Yet almost immediately his tone becomes gentle as he explains to Patrick how to recognize Jill at the railroad station.

Though these acts are not comparable to Frank's murders, they suggest that a family without a woman to ameliorate masculine authority runs the risk of becoming fascist (Walker 2001: 240) in its reliance on physical intimidation. Like Joe Starrett, McBain has made the mistake of valuing property and material goods over the wealth of family ties and ultimately of his ties to other human beings who would be able to unite with him and resist Frank's fascistic rule. The massacre of the McBains reverses the significance of the massacre at the beginning of *The Searchers* by making predatory capitalism a greater threat to any future civilization than the Native Americans who have been displaced and dispossessed by the process. Still, Brett McBain, recalling Ethan Edwards, has legitimated Frank's violence through his own drive to accumulate superfluous wealth without considering the welfare of the larger community. Though McBain names his property Sweetwater after the water that lies under the ground and will take on economic value when the railroad comes in that direction, he also anticipates with that name the utopian vision that Jill embodies and that he had clearly looked for on his trip to New Orleans where he met her. In distinction from McBain, Jill will become more like Vienna in *Johnny Guitar*, just as the man she is most attracted to, Harmonica, is associated with a musical instrument. Cheyenne could be considered a more philosophical version of the Dancing Kid; and like the Kid, he is accused of a crime he did not commit and will die in the end, though not before he has contributed to Jill's political education. Both men point Jill away from identification with the alienated masculine subjectivities they represent and toward an identification with a collective subject of labor materialized by the multiethnic railroad workers. Such a reading explains Leone's technique of allusion in the film. He refers to other films like *High Noon* and *Johnny Guitar* in order to deploy their symbolic values for his own expressive purposes.

When Frank pulls the trigger on little Timmy McBain, there is a jump cut from the gun firing to the train arriving, which implies that the train itself is the bullet that has taken the life of the innocent (Starrs 1993: 64). As the film will eventually demonstrate, the train, or the technology it represents, is not inherently evil but can be the instrument of evil as long as its social uses are limited by the concept of private property. After the massacre, the next scene with Frank is on the train with Mr. Morton, the magnate who is dying slowly of "tuberculosis of the bones." This man recalls the crippled coal magnates in the novels of D. H. Lawrence; and like those men, symbolically speaking, Morton has been reduced to impotence by his own will to power. He also has an interest in water, though it is radically opposed to the interest Jill will eventually act upon. He says he got on the train in sight of the Atlantic and wants to see the Pacific before his bones rot and he dies. The water Morton dreams about is an abstraction and not something that can nourish human life: it's just another signifier of his desire for power. Ironically, Frank identifies with Morton to the extent that he constantly refers to himself as a businessman and tries to rationalize his decisions, including the massacre of the McBain family, as necessary business transactions. When he sits behind Morton's desk, he comments that "It's almost like holding a gun – only much more powerful." Though Frank suggests that a real man would kill himself if he had a disease like Morton's, the gunman secretly admires the capitalist, which ultimately leads him to make a mistake that is analogous to the fundamental contradiction of the capitalist system. Like Morton, he fails to recognize that the uses to which he puts his power necessarily create an antithesis, an unrelenting force that will pursue him literally to the moment of dying. He believes Morton when the latter says that money is the only weapon that can stop a gun; but when he tries to buy off Harmonica, he learns that money doesn't always work, just as Jill learns that Harmonica is different from Brett McBain when he tells her that he doesn't invest in land or property.

In this film, Harmonica is the most explicit representation of the antithesis of capital, though Jill and Cheyenne are more moderate versions. Ironically, capital's most extreme antithesis cannot survive the transformation of capital itself. Whenever Frank asks Harmonica who he is, the latter reels off the names of Frank's victims; and ultimately he is the primal victim, who comes back from Frank's past as the living dead. The music Harmonica plays repeatedly throughout the movie is a kind of death song; and he represents the power of that which remains unforgiven, the power to produce a revolutionary consciousness that works against the dominant will to power without the same motivation to gain power over others. Harmonica cannot be killed because in some sense he is already dead. But, for the same reason, he is not really capable of love and the communal social identity that love makes possible. Yet he fosters such a community in his attempt to shape Jill into the kind of revolutionary subject he cannot be. After he recuts her fancy dress in the scene that resembles a rape, he tells her to fetch him some water from the well because he likes his water fresh. Though this request is actually a stratagem that enables him to gun down the men Frank has sent to kill Jill, it also articulates symbolically his relation to Jill, since he is part of death's landscape that only Jill's water can revive. Even Frank recognizes a tremendous life force in Jill that makes him regret having to kill her. In this respect, Frank, Cheyenne, and Harmonica share the same death drive that finds its only possible reversal in Jill's vitality, which takes the form of sexual pleasure for Frank, coffee for Cheyenne, and water for Harmonica.

Though Harmonica cannot have a true relationship with Jill, he already has a relationship with Frank. Through a series of flashbacks culminating in an extended flashback just before the two men draw on one another in the final showdown, the spectator learns that Frank lynched Harmonica's brother by having him stand on the shoulders of the boy with his head in a noose. With a smile on his face, Frank shoved a harmonica into the mouth of the boy just before the brother kicked him away to get the lynching over with. Presumably, from that point forward, the harmonica became the primary instrument of the boy's self-expression, the only way he could release his true feelings. Later when the two men face each other, there is an implicit recognition that in some sense they are the same, both members of "an ancient race" who can play no other role in creating a future than to eliminate themselves from the equation that constitutes the social dialectic. By violating the boy that Harmonica was, Frank created a version of himself that eventually destroys him; and Harmonica finally reveals his true identity to Frank by shoving the harmonica into his mouth just when Frank is on the point of dying. Then, just as Cheyenne predicts to Jill, Harmonica announces that he has to move on, even though Jill makes it perfectly clear that she wants him to stay. He has to move on because, though he remains physically alive, his soul has been dead since Frank violated his innocence.

As one of the living dead, Harmonica – or the Man with No Name since we never learn his true name, which would be a Mexican Indian name – can be the agent of change only by enabling Jill to transform herself into a new kind of social being; but he cannot enter into that new world himself. Leone implies that the men who engage in revolutionary violence, no matter how necessary they may be to the process of social change, are themselves part of the problem and will block the real transformation of human social relations unless they can eliminate themselves from the picture. The history of revolutions in the twentieth century more or less supports this view. The composition of the shot in which Frank rides toward Harmonica for the final showdown emphasizes the contradiction between the way of life these men represent and any possible future for the human race. On the left are the railroad workers who are literally creating a future through their labor, on the right sits Harmonica on a fence waiting for Frank, and in the middle rides Frank like death itself in his black outfit (Ill. 25). The most revolutionary act these men can engage in is to remove themselves from history.

ILLUSTRATION 25 Death on a horse. As Blondie said in *The Good, the Bad and the Ugly*, there are two kinds of men: those with loaded guns, like Frank and Harmonica, and those who dig, like the railroad workers. *Once Upon a Time in the West* (1968). Paramount Pictures. *Producer:* Fulvio Morsella. *Director:* Sergio Leone

In *Spaghetti Westerns*, Christopher Frayling notes references in *Once Upon a Time in the West* to the prehistory of the Johnson County War: the lynching of Jim Averell and Cattle Kate or Ella Watson. The name of McBain's town, Sweetwater, alludes to Sweetwater Valley, Carbon County, Wyoming, where the lynching of Averell and Watson took place. In the movie *Heaven's Gate*, Sweetwater becomes the name of the town at the center of the Johnson County War. Though Frayling suggests that Watson was only mistaken for Cattle Kate, the scholarship on this incident, which I referred to earlier, suggests that Watson, whether she was or was not known as Cattle Kate, was murdered for her land. Jim Averell was murdered for challenging the dominant property interests in the region. The actual technique of their lynching, at least as Frayling reports it, bears some resemblance to the lynching of Harmonica's brother. One rope was thrown over the branch of a tree and the two ends tied around the necks of Averell and Watson so that, in effect, when the wagon on which they were standing pulled off, the weight of one was used to bring about the death of the other (Frayling 1981: 125–6). The conflict between the railroad magnate and the small property holder like Brett McBain further echoes the events of the Johnson County War; and the name of Frank probably alludes to the notorious Frank Canton, the former sheriff of Johnson County who, though a small cattleman himself, became a detective for the WSGA, participated in the Johnson County War, and was suspected of several murders and attempted murders (Canton 1966, Smith 1966, DeArment 1996).

The number of parallels between Leone and Bertolucci's story and the Johnson County War are too many to be simply a coincidence. Yet Leone sees his film as a fairy tale, even though it is one for which there is documentary evidence. The ultimate conflict between Jill's unconscious communism – her desire for more collaborative social relations – and Morton's capitalism – his quest for wealth at the expense of the community and human life – is the perennial contradiction of capitalist society. The three men in the middle – Frank, Harmonica, and Cheyenne – represent failed attempts to construct a masculine identity that can transcend these social contradictions. Frank's identification with money and power eventually forces him to realize that he is just as much a cripple as Morton is, because he has relied on his guns to the same extent that

Morton has relied on trains and the accumulated capital they signify. His guns are like Morton's crutches and the other contraptions on the train that enable the magnate to move around. Without his guns, Frank is exactly what he calls Morton at one point, a turtle out of his shell, which is how he appears at the moment of dying. Harmonica is nothing but a shell, a walking embodiment of historical trauma, though he harbors the desire for his own death as the condition of the world that will surpass him and its own traumatic origins. Cheyenne is the more innocent of the three; and he might have survived in the world that Jill will create, if the masculine virtues that drive him to back up Harmonica and realize Brett McBain's dream did not get him killed. After the death of Man, the ancient race, the only struggle that matters is between the Jills and the Mortons of this world.

Leone's final Western, *Duck, You Sucker*, though a more literal translation of *Giù la testa* would be "Keep Your Head Down" or "Get Out of the Way" (Frayling 2000: 319), is the most tragic of all, because there is no redemptive feminine figure, except in the fantasy life of Sean Mallory (James Coburn). The film opens with one of the most vicious and comic portrayals of upper-class pretension and violence ever put on film. Juan Miranda (Rod Steiger) plays a man who appears to be a Mexican peasant when he catches a ride on a fancy stagecoach, the inside of which resembles an elaborately decorated dining car. While he undergoes mockery and humiliation by the passengers, especially the upper-class woman who presumes that all peasants are sexually promiscuous and freely practice incest, the camera zooms in for extreme close-ups of privileged mouths full of chewed-up food, which suggests that beneath the surface of the fancy clothes the rich are as vulgar as the peasants they despise. Though they imagine Juan to be stupid and incapable of grasping their insults, he understands everything; and when his men eventually stop and board the stage, he reveals himself as their leader. While they sack the coach and strip the passengers, Juan takes the woman off and rapes her; and afterwards she looks as if she has enjoyed herself. From that point forward, the feminine presence in the film is signified primarily by its absence. Juan meets up with the Irish Republican Sean Mallory, who has escaped the British authorities by joining the Mexican Revolution, though soon enough it becomes clear that he has lost faith in all revolutions. Juan wants to use Sean's skill with dynamite to rob a bank; but instead Sean consistently tricks Juan into working for the revolution without knowing it, until Juan has literally become a popular hero, a social bandit in Hobsbawm's sense of the word. Through a series of flashbacks, the spectator learns that Sean once had to shoot his closest friend who had informed on his fellow Irish Republicans after apparently being tortured by the British. Sean himself witnesses another betrayal of the revolution in Mexico when he sees Dr. Villega (Romolo Valli), a revolutionary strategist, with the German Mexican Colonel Gunther Reza executing men with a firing squad in the rain. This time he chooses not to eliminate or punish the informer, though he lets the man know what he has witnessed and inadvertently gives him the opportunity to sacrifice himself for the revolution.

Frayling argues that in this film, for the first time, Leone creates a central character in Juan who undergoes a clear development: "he moves from stereotype to human being, from actor on the puppet stage to life-sized person" (2000: 328). In the opening sequence with the rape and the first encounter with Sean, Juan is a stereotype that more or less conforms to the views of the rich who have abused him and toward whom he directs his hatred and revenge. Gradually, however, his rather one-sided friendship with Sean and his involvement in the revolution, which brings about the death of his six children, changes him. The changes in the Irishman are less obvious. In a crucial scene, he throws away his copy of Bakunin after Juan gives a speech on how the people who read the books always persuade the poor people to join the revolution; and then when the changes have been made, the people who read the books sit around talking and eating (like the rich people on the fancy stagecoach) while the poor people are dead. Yet it is clear from the outset that Sean has given up on any future for himself; and the final sequence, in which he brings about the collision of two trains, says that the only true contribution he can make to the future is to get out of the way and take a few of the most reactionary men with him in the process. This is the real meaning of the Italian title, get your head down and get out of the way, because otherwise there will be no future for anyone.

In the train collision scene, Leone offers his most pessimistic view of the future of technology and industrial capitalism. It can only be transformed by subverting it from within, by turning the technology against itself, so that the system implodes. There may be nothing beyond that apocalyptic event, but there is no possibility of a beyond without such an event. Though Sean leaps from the train in the nick of time, he has already sealed his fate by this decision to produce one final explosion instead of heading straight for the United States as he and Juan had dreamed of doing. After he is shot repeatedly by Reza, he apologizes to Juan for having subjected him to such a "royal screwing," though Juan at this point feels no regret or anger for what has happened to him. The homoerotic overtones of this final sequence are unmistakable. In the final flashback, Sean remembers kissing an Irishwoman, who, according to Leone, "represented the revolution everyone wanted to embrace." In the original version of the film, both Irish Republicans, Sean and the comrade he eventually shoots, kiss the girl, though Leone saw this not as "libertarianism and free love" but as a symbolic representation of their mutual longing for social revolution (quoted in Frayling 2000: 330). Yet the sequence also suggests the homoerotic bond between the two revolutionaries, which is disavowed and articulated through the sharing of a woman. Similarly, Sean has been able to develop a relationship with Juan by seducing him into participating in the revolution. The only intimacy of which Sean is now capable is the intimacy that comes from proximity to death.

Sean's last gift to Juan is to blow himself up right in front of him, though at this point in the film there is nothing really to be gained for the revolution by this act. He chooses not to die peaceably but to go out in a holocaust, which recalls the final choice of Pike Bishop and his men in *The Wild Bunch*. After the explosion, the camera cuts to the image of Juan as the spectator hears the words in voiceover that apparently come out of his mind: "What about me?" And the answer should be the original title of the movie that would appear over his image: *Giú la testa* – Get out of the way! Sean's last gift to Juan is to suggest that the only thing he can offer the future is to eliminate himself from the equation as Sean has done. The brutality of the class system has damaged Juan to such an extent that he is incapable of any true relationship except the sort of relationship Sean has offered him, a love based on a mutually shared death drive. Sean has been the victim of British imperialism, although he is clearly one of the people who reads books; and even in his last gesture, his relation to Juan is marked by exploitation to the extent that he always holds the power over the Mexican. In killing himself, he also kills Juan's dream of going to America and getting rich by robbing banks; and he leaves in the place of that dream a revolution that may simply reproduce exploitative social relations and will always suffer from the burden of human weakness that leads even its most ardent supporters, like Dr. Villega, into betraying it. Juan has lost his children and probably his innocence, such as it is, for a revolution that may be of dubious value. He has come a long way since the opening sequence that concludes with the rape of a woman; but unlike the conclusion of *Once Upon a Time in the West*, there is no other woman to represent the possibility of a transformed social being that could be the foundation for a new set of social relationships. Juan's final question cannot be answered.

Transcendence on a Pale Horse

In a 1972 interview, Leone explained the pessimism of his more recent films as that "of a film maker confronted with politics." In the Italian context, he noted, "mankind has let us down . . . Our hypocrisy and our 'politics of compromise' have put us in this crisis situation." Referring to himself as one of those intellectuals who have resigned themselves to the crisis, he asked, "What else can we think of but death?" (quoted in Hill 1998: 205). Elsewhere Leone admitted that he was "a disillusioned socialist. To the point of becoming an anarchist," though he considered himself a moderate who "doesn't go around throwing bombs." He said that in his films "the anarchists are the truthful characters" (quoted in Frayling 2000: 306–7). These remarks suggest that Leone's own political vision comes close to Sean Mallory's in *A Fistful of Dynamite*. They may also help to explain the complexity of Leone's influence on the post-sixties Western, which is ultimately greater than that of Peckinpah, whose influence was primarily on the directors of "action" films. The latter largely ignored the Western as a genre or displaced it onto the genres of science fiction, horror, and thrillers. Obviously, Leone's most direct successor, Clint Eastwood, does not share his anarchistic impulses, though he does seem to buy into Leone's pessimism. According to William Beard, Eastwood came back to

Hollywood after his Spaghetti Western experience "armed with the knowledge (gained with Leone) of how to present heroic power in the total absence of any kind of social project" (2000: 7). This view strikes me as a rather limited reading of Leone that mistakes his pessimism for the absence of any critical consciousness. Leone had little faith in the plans and strategies of "the men who read books"; but he was such a man, whose films are unrelenting in their dissection of the contradictions of capitalist culture; and there is a social project underlying his work that is made explicit at least once at the end of *Once Upon a Time in the West*. It is his pessimism, even downright melancholy, at the possibility of achieving a society based of social collaboration and economic justice that drives his work. Eastwood incorporates much of Leone's vision into at least three of the four key Westerns he directed from the early seventies to the early nineties. While I exclude from this discussion *The Outlaw Josey Wales* (1976), which strikes me as a return to the classical Westerns of Ford and Hawks, the other three, *High Plains Drifter* (1973), *Pale Rider* (1985), and *Unforgiven* (1992), are all attempts to respond to Leone's vision of the West as a landscape of death.

High Plains Drifter is brilliant as an interpretation of Leone's Man with No Name, though it utterly fails to grasp and reproduce Leone's technique of political and historical contextualization. As Beard notes, "What was metaphorical in Leone has become literal in Eastwood" (2000: 24). For the first time, the Man with No Name emerges from the landscape of death as a literal dead man. Though the film never makes this determination completely explicit, the insinuations are so blatant as to be unmistakable and beyond mere symbolism. Furthermore, the overall story reproduces in some ways the central conflict at the heart of *Once Upon a Time in the West*. Instead of a railroad gobbling up public land and eliminating all competitors, there is a mining corporation covertly operating on public land; and when the local sheriff discovers this, the company men hire some outlaws to kill him, which they do in a most brutal fashion. However, when the dead man or his representative returns as the high plains drifter (Eastwood), he exhibits none of the social consciousness of Harmonica or even Cheyenne in *Once Upon a Time*, who want to salvage Brett McBain's dream and to support Jill McBain's transformation into new kind of political subject. Beard sees Eastwood's work as "an expression of alienated individual *ressentiment* and the revenge of each against all, with its origins lying in unknowable subconscious mystery rather than in the discredited rationalist structures of social harmony" (2000: 8). Discredited by whom, one wonders? Social harmony would be an oversimplification of the political vision of collaborative social relations that Leone's last two Westerns postulate as a social goal; and however pessimistic Leone would be about any society ever achieving that goal, the Hobbesian vision of "the revenge of each against all" is hardly the one that would discredit it.

Shortly after arriving in the town of Lago, Eastwood encounters a rather disagreeable young woman, who we learn later witnessed and may have been indirectly involved in the murder of the sheriff, since she is married to one of the conspirators and had some sort of relationship with one of the gunmen who are now in prison and about to be released. Apparently, the drifter offends her by not noticing her when he first arrives; and later, after he has killed the new local gunmen, she intentionally bumps into him and then insults him. The drifter's response is to drag her into a barn and rape her. It's difficult to believe that the decision to put this in the film was not influenced by the rape at the beginning of *Fistful of Dynamite*, though the two incidents could not be more different. First, the motivation for the rape in Leone's film is class hatred; and though this doesn't justify such an act, the opening sequence has at least the effect of giving the act a social context. Second, by the end of the film, one imagines that Juan Miranda has begun to develop the critical consciousness that would recognize the futility of sexual vengeance. In *High Plains Drifter*, Eastwood resorts to a blatant stereotype of the "bitchy" female who wants the thing she says she doesn't want. Later in the movie, after the raped woman tries to shoot him in his bath, he wonders about "what took her so long to get mad." His friend, the dwarf Mordecai, suggests that it's "because maybe you didn't go back for more." Later he takes the wife of the hotel owner to bed; and when he doesn't force her, she practically forces him to make love to her. From that point forward, she seems clearly to take his side in his attempt to punish the town of Lago.

Overall, these acts drive home the idea that the stranger is the embodiment of a social morality that is indistinguishable from bourgeois morality. He punishes hypocritical women with rape, hypocritical businessmen with public humiliation and the loss of their wealth, corporate murderers and their cronies with death, and honest wives with the realization of their true desires. Nothing he does questions capitalist social relations; and far from being the nihilist Beard describes, the drifter is ultimately the instrument of divine retribution, the enforcer of a morality that presupposes the inherent evil − rather than the humanly constructed social injustice − of the world. Eastwood's vision is more Augustinian than Marxist when the drifter has the upright members of the community paint their town red and then renames it Hell. This distinguishes his film not only from Leone's but from two Westerns it clearly refers to, *High Noon* and John Sturges's *Bad Day at Black Rock* (1955). As in those movies, the bad guy is a corrupt community, though in this case the nature of that corruption seems to be metaphysical. After killing the murderers and exposing the hypocrites, the drifter responds to Mordecai's comment that he never did know the drifter's name with the enigmatic remark, "Yes, you do." Most spectators and film critics seem to have concluded that the answer to Mordecai's implicit question is the name of the dead sheriff, even though a close examination indicates that Eastwood's drifter is not the same man in the flashbacks of the sheriff's murder. A better answer would be something like the biblical I-Am-Who-Am. The drifter is the spirit of divine authority and the instrument of transcendent morality.

Given this interpretation, one should not be surprised that the next time Eastwood tries to turn Leone on his head the name of the central character is the Preacher. Overtly, *Pale Rider* is a remake of *Shane*; but instead of the big cattleman there is a corrupt mining corporation, this time engaged in the environmentally vicious process of strip mining and at war with the community of small miners. This film expresses little faith in the community itself, and there is still no strong woman like Jill in *Once Upon a Time* who would symbolize a different kind of society. The character of the Preacher alludes to Harmonica to the extent that he was once the victim of Stockburn and his deputies, who work for the corporation, and there seems to be an element of vengeance in his final showdown. Still, more than in *High Plains Drifter*, the issue here is less personal vengeance than a social reckoning that seems to require divine intervention. At the beginning of the film, the Preacher arrives in answer to the prayer of the teenage girl Megan (Sydney Penny), in a scene that imitates a scene from Leone's 1984 gangster film *Once*

Upon a Time in America. Though there is no vision of a better world, and no anarchistic act of self-destruction, such as we see in *A Fistful of Dynamite* and *The Wild Bunch*, the film does project the view that social justice will eventually win out, not through human actions but through divine providence. Even the book of Revelations promises "a new heaven and a new earth" at the end of time, after the rider on a pale horse has come, the one whose name is death.

Eastwood's final and most successful attempt to revise Leone is the much-celebrated *Unforgiven*. Though the film is dedicated to both Leone and Don Siegel, the issues raised by Leone's cinema are the ones that continue to haunt Eastwood's imagination. First, the film presupposes the return and triumph of the Mortons, as Harmonica pessimistically predicted at the end of *Once Upon a Time in the West*. We know this not because there is a similar character in the film, which there isn't, but because the names of the three central characters, the three gunfighters, signify their commodification by the social system that Morton represented. Will Munny (Eastwood), Little Bill (Gene Hackman), and English Bob (Richard Harris) all have names that allude to currency; and the plot of this film is driven by the desire for money and the need to defend or resist the concept of private property that determines the value of everything, including human life (Krapp 2002: 595). When Little Bill, the sheriff of Big Whiskey, Wyoming, shows up at the local saloon after a cowboy has mutilated the face of a prostitute for laughing at the size of his penis, he primarily addresses the proprietor Skinny's claim that the damage to the whore has adversely affected his investment of capital. "Property!" Little Bill proclaims. Little Bill's identity is subsumed by the concept of property throughout the film. Not only does he ignore the human damage done to the prostitute in lieu of the economic damage done to Skinny's capital investment; but he invests all of his own identity in the house he is building, which, in his mind, makes him a man of high rather low character such as he eventually imagines Munny to be. At the moment of dying, when he looks down the barrel of the Spencer rifle Munny points at him, he says, "I don't deserve this – to die like this. I was building a house." Munny himself wears a gun for the first time in years because he feels that he is losing control over his private property and the social identity that has gone with it since his now deceased wife converted him from the life of a brutal alcoholic killer to that of a pig farmer. By contrast, English Bob is simply a bully in the guise of a gentleman, who, as Harris pointed out in an interview, reverts to a cockney accent after he has been beaten and humiliated by Little Bill (Tibbetts 1993: 16).

Unforgiven posits three alternatives to the mode of social identification represented by the three killers, though in each case these identities fail to one degree or another. The first and least effective social identity is that of the Schofield Kid, whose primary motivation for going after the prostitute's gold is glory, a motive that he quickly surrenders after killing a man and discovering that the experience fails to conform to the fantasy. A second identity is that of the prostitutes. Ethically, their demand for justice and their refusal to accept their status as property in the eyes of men like Skinny and Little Bill is right; but their desire for justice quickly shades into the desire for revenge, even before Little Bill decides on how to settle the issue. When the prostitutes don't get the justice they want from Little Bill, they resort to their own form of arbitrary justice by putting their funds together in order to hire an assassin. The third alternative reveals itself in two different characters. The first is the cut prostitute Delilah (Anna Thomson), who for most of the film says nothing while the others plot their revenge. As one prostitute comments, "If Delilah doesn't care one way or the other, what are we all getting so riled up about?" Strawberry Alice (Frances Fisher) answers that though the men may ride them like horses, it doesn't mean they can brand them like horses. Yet Delilah's facial expressions for the rest of the film and her brief exchange with Munny after his beating by Little Bill (Ill. 26) suggest that, without knowing

ILLUSTRATION 26 The forgiving and the unforgiven. *Unforgiven* (1992). Warner Bros. *Producer and director:* Clint Eastwood

how to articulate it, she is looking for something else besides revenge, something like a different kind of world in which a different kind of social relationship is possible. She believes that Munny has such a relationship with his wife, though she doesn't know at first that his wife is dead. Similarly, Ned Logan (Morgan Freeman) goes along with Munny's quest for the "whore's gold" more out of loyalty to his friend than out of the desire for money. At the critical moment, Ned proves incapable of shooting the young cowboy who is their first victim. After that he tries to leave but is captured by Little Bill and tortured to death. Ironically, as Eastwood makes clear through his use of panoramic shots, while Munny's farm seems barren and destitute, Ned has chosen a location that is green and seemingly fruitful, though the absence of stock or children suggests that he is less ambitious and conventional than his old friend. His Native American wife grows corn; and overall the ethnically mixed couple seem to be more interested in a pleasurable subsistence economy than in raising stock for profit as Munny has unsuccessfully tried to do. Furthermore, during the course of the film, Ned is shown to be less puritanical than his friend about sexuality and other matters. Munny is a man of extremes; and there is a correlation between his Puritanism, which entails a disavowal of desire and fear of pleasure, and his potentially vicious brutality when he finally unlocks his psychic prison by taking a drink after he learns of Ned's death. Tragically, though Ned dies and loses his green world as a result, Munny, at least by rumor, will go on to become a successful small businessman in San Francisco. In this sense, he is the opposite of Frank in *Once Upon a Time in the West*. He discovers that he is not just a man, but a businessman.

Unlike Leone's revolutionary pessimism, *Unforgiven*'s view of the human condition offers no ground for hope. Despite what Beard sees as Eastwood's "virtually Marxist and feminist" positions (2000: 56), the victims of social exploitation either are too weak to stand up against the brutality of social domination or reproduce the identity of the oppressor as the agency of their resistance. The weakness I refer to is not a lack of strength in personal character. On the contrary, Ned's ability to sustain his humanity despite what must have been his history as a black man at this time suggests that personal strength and ethical character translate into social weakness in this context. His history as an African American goes unstated in the film, though it reveals itself symbolically when Little Bill strips Ned to the waist and whips him into confessing. Historically, it has always been African Americans and women who have paid the price for the social supremacy of the white race and the class system founded on the concept of private property. Ned loses his life, the whores gain nothing that would ultimately improve their socioeconomic position or social authority, and Munny "goes free and gets paid too boot." As Beard concludes, "When he walks into Greely's to kill Skinny and Little Bill, he is a creature who has lost salvation, a damned soul, 'unforgiven'" (2000: 54).

Ultimately, what remains unforgiven is any form of debt, whether it be economic or ethical. The prostitutes will never be forgiven for Skinny's capital investment or their loss of the feminine ideal of bourgeois society. The cowboys will never be forgiven for their conformity to the dominant ethos that allows them to treat women as property. Little Bill will never be forgiven for his identification with the concept of private property and the law that defends that concept more than it fosters any socially determined principle of justice. Ned will never be forgiven for the history he represents and for desiring beyond the dominant social system, a desire materialized by the green world of his farm. Finally, William Munny embraces the world of the unforgiven, with the full realization that he can never repair the damage he has done or find forgiveness. He has truly lost salvation through action and is now ready to become a successful businessman with the money he has gained as a result of that loss. The condition of success in such a world is the recognition that justice is impossible. Nothing is ever forgiven.

Eastwood's Augustinian vision is finally transmuted into a Calvinist morality (Sragow 1992). Far from being "an ideologically potent deconstruction" of his own film persona and Western violence in general, as Leighton Grist has argued (1995: 301), *Unforgiven* produces the most absolute justification of violence. Phillip Skerry argues that the movie is "a morality tale: its dark conclusions about the essentially fallen nature of humanity align it with works like Conrad's *Heart of Darkness*." Skerry sees this quality as an example of the film's "postrevisionism," which entails "an apocalyptic moment – a genre-clarifying epiphany" (1996: 282, 290). Such an epiphany suggests that the Western has always been a Calvinist morality tale, which is another way of saying that it justifies violence and the wealth that derives from violence through an appeal to transcendence. This view would be another example of the logic Paul Smith detects in the film when Little Bill assumes the task of telling the true history of the West to W. W. Beauchamp (Saul Rubinek): "the film's discourse in this regard demonstrates that, whatever kinds of revisionism are attempted (even if truthful), the mystified, mythological (and vicious) 'spirit of the West' always returns" (1993: 268). That spirit also happens to be the spirit of the Protestant ethic.

If there is forgiveness, it has nothing to do with our actions or who we are. It is the gift of transcendent authority. As Peter Krapp argues, "while the experience of time, that the past is not erased, is pivotal for the scene of forgiveness, the element of retribution is the return of the past in the moment." The past is not erased in the scene of forgiveness because it must be recalled and recognized as the condition of transcending it. Forgiveness "would not only suspend any law, but also supersede it, for it is not of the order of the law." I would argue that the same is true of justice, which must be distinguished from retribution. Justice is a form of forgiveness. Even when punishment is required under the law, it sets the condition for forgiveness through which the law itself can be superseded. Retribution, by contrast, "suspends the law, and the law of time along with it" (2002: 602). The past becomes the present, and the law becomes an eternal monument. In the final slaughter of *Unforgiven*, "the deadline of the last judgment whose instrument Clint Eastwood's protagonist once again plays is that very due date when all deferrals cease and all debts come due" (594). Though no one is forgiven, sooner or later retribution will come in this Calvinist world; and its instruments are not those who are good or who have been victimized or who have shown wisdom but those capable of the violence retribution requires.

Leone was always pessimistic about the possibility of social change but admired the will that refuses to surrender the desire for a better world. Sometimes that desire can only express itself through the subject's willingness to recognize its participation in the history of exploitation and then, with that knowledge, to get out of the way so that a new form of social being can emerge. Eastwood turns Leone on his head and produces a negative justification of capitalism and the class system. The world is nothing but a landscape of death, and there is no human face that one can give to it. Death is good because it is the passage to another world, and there is no goodness inherent in human actions in this world. That's why Munny says to the dying Little Bill, "Deserve has got nothing to do with it." The reckoning that suspends all time cannot be reduced to a form of social justice. It is simply the expression of transcendent force.

CHAPTER 9

WESTERN ARMAGEDDON

All Men Are Poets

The Johnson County War has been called the war that never happened because most of the people whose names were on the WSGA's death list never met their death at the hands of the men who invaded Johnson County. The invasion failed because the leaders, against the advice of more experienced gunmen like Frank Canton, wasted time besieging the cabin in which Nate Champion and his friends were held up. This allowed the news of their invasion to reach the community they were invading, particularly in Buffalo. Eventually, the regulators found themselves surrounded by the men they had come to kill and had to barricade themselves in some ranch houses until they were saved by US troops under orders from the state governor and the President of the United States (Smith 1966: 220–7). In *Heaven's Gate*, by contrast, the body count seems inordinately high; and the final battle between the WSGA leaders and their gunmen, on one side, and the immigrant population of Johnson County, on the other, is tantamount to Armageddon.

Though historically inaccurate, the message is clear, and it is a message that echoes through a series of films from the early seventies to the various releases of *Heaven's Gate* starting in 1980. Though Peckinpah's *Pat Garrett & Billy the Kid* (1973) and Arthur Penn's *The Missouri Breaks* (1976) both contribute to the apocalyptic vision of the Old West, the most important film of the seventies to anticipate the message and the visual style of *Heaven's Gate* is Robert Altman's *McCabe & Mrs. Miller* (1971). Each of these films could be read as the attempt to re-create what Benjamin called "the sign of a Messianic cessation of happening," while they absolutely refuse the historical methodology that tells history as "the sequence of events like the beads of a rosary" (1969: 263). They implicitly recognize that, as long as the class system exists, the capitalists will always be the winners, no matter who wins this or that particular conflict. In these representations, class struggle is a revolt against time, against history, and against the ideology of progress that says you must put your desires on hold and wait for history to catch up with them. It is a struggle until the end of time because it seeks to put an end to time, or rather to create an apocalyptic event that marks the end of history as we know it.

Altman's *McCabe & Mrs. Miller* is a revisionist Western; and in 1971 it seemed about as offbeat as any Western ever made, though there had been offbeat Westerns before. Paul Arthur has recently noted that, while there is no suppression of "the familiar lineup of characters, situations, settings, and themes," the conventions of the Western are presented from "unfamiliar angles" without the usual "romanticized, dualistic luster." For example, "the archetypal Western town – or in this case, a bleakly soggy Northwest mining outpost in 1902 – is adorned with a grubby miserableness we tend to call 'realistic'" (2003: 19). Yet one needs to be careful about imagining that "realism" of any sort ever truly transcends the conventions of the Western, since even *Shane* was originally considered to be a breakthrough to realism with its minimalist vision of the Western town. Though Altman's West is about as grubby a vision of it as can be imagined, it may not be any more "realistic" than Cimino's polluted urbanscapes and muddy townships in *Heaven's Gate* or Peckinpah's ramshackle outposts, deserted forts, and adobe villages in *Pat Garrett & Billy the Kid*. None of these films is a strict reconstruction of the history it references. Furthermore, though none of them postulates a romanticized dualism between the good guys and the bad guys, they all foreground a conflict between fallible, contradictory human beings who struggle toward some kind of community and a vicious, impersonal corporate system that subordinates human desires to abstract wealth. In that sense, there is no transcendence of dualism.

The most impersonal of all these corporations is the Harrison Shaughnessy Mining Company that John McCabe (Warren Beatty) finds himself up against in Altman's film. Unlike the mining corporations in two Clint Eastwood Westerns, *High Plains Drifter* and *Pale Rider*, or the corporate cattlemen in many other Westerns, there is no face that one can give to this organization; and in fact Altman stresses the banality of evil by suggesting that the different representatives of the corporation have only a limited grasp of the real power that lies behind them. After McCabe has come to the town of Presbyterian Church and, with the partnership and business savvy of Mrs. Miller (Julie Christie), sets up a successful whorehouse, bath, and gambling house, the representatives of the corporation, Sears (Michael Murphy) and Hollander (Antony Holland), abruptly arrive to buy him out at a price that the company wants to dictate. These businessmen in their conventional Eastern suits would be an anomaly in most Westerns; but in this one, every citizen of Presbyterian Church with any property or status tends to wear a suit, at least after McCabe arrives in his black suit and bowler hat. In other words, there is no blatant antithesis here between the iconic representative of Western freedom like Shane, Ethan Edwards, or Harmonica, on the one hand, and the agents of capital, on the other. The latter figures in *McCabe* are certainly cleaner in appearance and represent a bourgeois propriety that has limited tolerance for what Mrs. Miller blithely describes as McCabe's frontier wit; but they refer to themselves and to McCabe as businessmen, and that is exactly what McCabe pretends to be. When he tries to bargain with the corporate agents, old Hollander quickly wants to leave town and hand the problem over to another wing of the corporation, the one that uses force instead of negotiation to make its deals. Sears argues that, with a little more patience and money, they will get McCabe to accept their offer; but Hollander is angry that the company has sent him on such a menial task and won't hear of it.

With this character, the movie implies that the impersonal brutality of the capitalist system can operate because its agents compartmentalize their knowledge of its methods in such a way that they can know without knowing, without taking any responsibility for the real relations of force that underlie the legal façade of private property. Altman participates in the critique of corporate mentalities and a state that serves the interests of business, a critique that emerged in the sixties in response to the Vietnam War and grew throughout the seventies and eighties as the evidence mounted for a US foreign policy that used force to discipline any resistance to the implementation of its so-called free markets by peoples designated first as "insurgents" and later as "fundamentalists." Though Sears and Hollander never overtly threaten McCabe, they clearly insinuate that the only alternative to their offer is something that even they find unspeakable.

McCabe argues that the West was not the haven of rugged individuals and pioneering spirits but the scene of the most brutal assertion of capitalism through the use of raw force. Yet neither McCabe nor Mrs. Miller are revolutionaries, and the community of Presbyterian Church is anything but a model of collaborative social arrangements that would transcend the Hobbesian war of all against all that predatory capitalism fosters. Ironically, McCabe embraces precisely the social identity that modern capitalism constructs for him, and it leads to his destruction. When he arrives in Presbyterian Church, he makes it clear that his goal is to accumulate as much wealth as possible. Once he has established his poker game as an entrance to the community, he immediately makes inquiries about who owns the property in the town. Through a series of cuts that forward the action without transitional scenes that would create a clear sequence of cause and effect, McCabe virtually takes over the town; and one can only conclude that his poker game is the primary means by which he accomplishes this feat. His success can be partially attributed to the rumor that has spread through the town that he is a gunfighter, a man with "a big rep," as Sheehan (Renee Auberjonois) puts it, for killing Bill Roundtree with a derringer when the latter was caught cheating at poker. In the eyes of this mining community, McCabe resembles a Shane figure, especially as Shane appears in the original Jack Schaefer novel with his fancy clothes and rather dandyish manners. Apparently, in the original screenplay by Brian McKay, "McCabe was more of a cocky gunfighter than an antihero playing a shell game of life or death" (McGilligan 1989: 339). Whatever the truth may be, McCabe allows people to think that the rumor is true, a belief that lends force to his presence in the community, which, as the tradition of the Western dictates, could easily have turned against the man who expropriates the wealth of others through a game of chance. In other words, McCabe implicitly accepts the principle that violence determines the right to wealth, at least to the extent that he allows the presumption of his potential violence to stand in the community.

Once she comes to the town, Constance Miller would seem to be the one person who grasps from the outset that McCabe is a poseur. She recognizes that he has little or no business sense; but he does have the means to accumulate enough capital to start a business (primitive accumulation through gambling), and she implicitly goes along with his "big rep" as the necessary condition for the practice of her own considerable business acumen. Therefore, she also accepts the principle that force determines the right of wealth, even on a small scale, though she knows well enough that McCabe's real capacity for violence is no greater than his head for business. The illusion of potential violence is enough until the real thing shows up; and then, as far as Mrs. Miller is concerned, the masquerade is over. Yet, although her goal is to garner enough money to start a boarding house in San Francisco, her drive, along with McCabe's, has a positive effect on the community. As Arthur insightfully comments, "Altman's film suggests that it is not merely capitalism that fuels the advance of civilization . . . but specifically prostitution. In its wake, the burgeoning whorehouse brings better housing, better hygiene and clothing, specialty retail stores, and a modicum of middle-class music and dance" (2003: 19). Mrs. Miller represents what Benjamin saw as the ambiguity of the prostitute as a dialectical image of capitalism: she is "seller and sold in one" (1999: 10). In effect, as such a figure, she demonstrates economically what every individual becomes within the capitalist system, which is why capitalism necessarily generates its own antithesis. Furthermore, she embodies the contradictions of capitalist subjectivity. In struggling for more autonomy and pleasure in life, she recognizes that she has to create an environment in which people can work together and enjoy the same qualities of life that give her pleasure. Consequently, when she takes over the management of McCabe's whorehouse, she transforms it into a little utopia. She requires McCabe to build a bathhouse and will not let anyone enjoy the whorehouse without using the other first. When McCabe argues against these refinements by suggesting that the men of the town don't want them, she points out that they will as soon as they get a taste for them. In other words, Mrs. Miller doesn't simply cater to desires as they exist but actively works at generating new desires and new forms of pleasure.

This image of the frontier woman as prostitute gives a new inflection to Tompkins's thesis about the dominance of the "genteel tradition" of the nineteenth-century middle-class woman. As Limerick has noted about the difference between popular representations of Western women and their reality, "There is no more point in down-grading them [prostitutes] as vulnerable victims than in elevating them [proper married women] as saintly civilizers" (1987: 54). In Altman's vision, the qualities of civilization definitely emerge from the influence of women – but not necessarily as agents of the middle class. Despite the utopian atmosphere of Mrs. Miller's transformed whorehouse, Altman's portrait of Western prostitution articulates the humanity of the exploited without mitigating the brutality of exploitation. It supports Limerick's claim that if you restore Western women to their authentic place in history, "the Western drama gains a fully human cast of characters – males and females whose urges, needs, failings, and conflicts we can recognize and even share" (52). The relationship between the prostitutes and the community of Presbyterian Church actually resembles the situation in a Western mining town like Nevada City, as Limerick describes it:

> the prostitutes' most frequent patrons were wageworkers, miners who risked their lives daily in hard underground labor. The miners, as Marion Goldman has suggested, were themselves "treated like objects rather than individuals" and were thus conditioned to "think of themselves and others that way." The economic elite of the towns often owned the real estate in which prostitution took place; vice districts were among the more rewarding Western investment opportunities. (51)

In this movie, it is not the women of the upper classes who create values and transform society but the woman who recognizes her own commodity status and knows how to exploit it in order to transform her environment. Furthermore, the film suggests that the real agents of this exploitation are not the wageworkers who pay for the utopian pleasures of the whorehouse, and not even the small businessman like McCabe who plays cards and gambles on the capitalist market to escape wage slavery himself. It is the corporation that remains faceless and irresponsible as it transforms human beings, both good and bad, into the instruments of its insane drive toward wealth without any regard for the quality of human life.

Yet the film also pinpoints the constraints on human desires within the capitalist framework and, in particular, the constraints on any form of human relationship. The citizens of Presbyterian Church function as discrete units without social ties to one another. Herein lies the brilliance of Altman's use of sound and the decentered quality of the dialogue in the scenes that focus on the community rather than on individual characters. When the film was released, an error in the transfer from the master made "much of the dialogue . . . incomprehensible"; and this problem, combined with the self-conscious "use of overlapping dialogue," caused some critics to interpret the effect as an intentional insult to the audience (Plecki 1985: 41). Even after the soundtrack had been corrected, the film was not easy to follow in the manner of the traditional Hollywood production. In the recent commentary on DVD, Altman points out that the soundtrack was meant to create for the spectator the real-life situation of being in a crowd of people in which one can't hear everything that is said. Still, even in the scenes that focus on conversations between two characters or in the scenes in which McCabe engages in dialogue with himself, it is not easy to make out every word that is uttered. The effect of this technique, however, is to drive a wedge between the audience and the film, to create the feeling in the spectator that he can't easily project him- or herself into this world – that he or she can't own it. The overlapping dialogue suggests that the individual characters are rarely listening to each other and that this is a world of monologues in which, for the most part, people speak without anticipating the response of the other or even caring whether the other hears them or not. Even in the scenes in which McCabe expresses his passion for Mrs. Miller, either he is alone in his room talking to himself, or he lectures her in her room while she is high on opium, and he interprets the childishly happy expressions on her face as signs of her true affection for him. The only characters who actually talk to each other in a way that suggests dialogical relationship or their implicit recognition of one another are the prostitutes under Mrs. Miller's management. Again, the whorehouse is the one utopian space where the potential for a real community seems to be suggested, but the spectator is shut out of this vision by the depersonalizing techniques Altman employs.

In addition to the overlapping dialogue, there is pervasive use of the telephoto lens and the zoom, which creates, as Robert Kolker remarks, "a tight and enclosed space, peopled with figures who, though contained in that space, seem unconnected to it and, even more, unconnected to each other." They are also unconnected to the spectator, and this style resists the suturing effects that usually bind the spectator to the internal logic of a film through identification with characters and their points of view. As Kolker continues, "There is little eye contact among the various characters in the opening sequence. When McCabe looks, he doesn't get a direct look back. The camera rarely observes the characters squarely, at eye level, centered in the frame. They are rather picked out, seemingly at random, glanced at and overheard" (2000: 341). In that opening sequence, when the camera zooms in on McCabe playing cards, there isn't the feeling of space being annihilated in a way that conduces to the spectator's identification. Rather, the effect is to keep the spectator at a distance, aware that he or she has no relation to these characters or this world.

In this Western, capitalism is not simply a force that exploits and threatens human beings from the outside but disintegrates the ground of their becoming, destroys the possibility of relationship or intersubjective communication, by reducing each individual to the prisonhouse of his or her own self-interests. The only possible transcendence of this war of all against all lies in those spaces that the social system produces as its by-product, spaces like the whorehouse, where the most exploited embrace their commodity status as the condition of their own identification with one another. Kolker argues that the film "mourns . . . the lost possibility of community and the enforced isolation of its members" (340); but ironically the film also reveals the possibility of community in the heart of capitalist exploitation, in those beings who have been most alienated from direct identification with capital. Yet the limitations of this utopia are brutally revealed in the fate of the young cowboy (Keith Carradine) who comes to Presbyterian Church in quest of the utopia of pleasure, "the fanciest whorehouse in the whole territory."

Ironically, after he arrives in town, the film cuts to the first shot of the three gunmen of the mining corporation on their way to Presbyterian Church. In a sense, these are the most classical Western figures in this movie, the cowboy and the hired gunmen; and they represent antithetical modes of relation to capital. The gunmen are instruments of capitalist domination and have internalized the death drive that underlies capital's exploitation of human beings and nature. The cowboy, by contrast, recognizes the utopia of the whorehouse as the real purpose of living. He treats the place as a home, walks around in his socks and long underwear, asks about what's cooking, and wants to sleep with every woman in the house. Though he carries a gun in the classical Western manner, he openly admits that he's no good at shooting it and exhibits absolutely no aggression whatsoever. He earns his money by selling his labor and then spends it in the whorehouse that is the closest thing to a real community he can find in this world. When he encounters the Kid, the most immature of the three gunmen, he is duped into pulling out his gun so that the Kid can look at it. The latter promptly guns him down for no apparent reason, except to demonstrate his capacity for violence to the community.

The death of the cowboy is inserted between two critical scenes between McCabe and Mrs. Miller. In the first, she encourages McCabe to run away because of "something awful" that the gunmen will do to him. He takes this as a conventional sign of womanly affection, but she disavows any such intention. In the second scene, after the killing of the cowboy and with no reference to it, McCabe confesses to Constance that he "ain't never been this close to nobody before." She ends up cradling his head against her breast in a nurturing gesture, though after he goes to sleep she leaves his room so that he wakes up alone to face the gunmen in the morning. As Helene Keyssar notes, the insertion of the cowboy's meaningless death between these two sequences disconcerts the spectator because "neither chronology nor the necessity of descriptive information motivate the sequence of syntagmas [syntactic elements], yet as *McCabe & Mrs. Miller* progresses, connections of meaning manifest themselves." They do so "by accumulation and the gradual disclosure of a pattern, not by any single shot or juxtaposition of shots" (1991: 192).

This technique of privileging patterns of meaning over logical narrative sequencing will be central to the style of *Heaven's Gate,* though without many of the touches that make Altman's style so distinctive. This technique works in tandem with the evocation of what Robert Self calls "the beauty of a painterly West" (2002: 76). He notes that Altman's painterly reference is probably to the impressionists and compares the images of card playing in the opening sequences in Sheehan's saloon to a similar image in Vincent Van Gogh's *The Potato Eaters* (94–5). The director's use of flashing technique, which was an innovation on this film, destroys the normalized gaze of the camera and creates the sense of representational density. As Patrick McGilligan tells it, Altman and his cinematographer Vilmos Zsigmond, who would later work on *Heaven's Gate*, developed this use of the flashing technique, which involves the double-exposure of film to controlled light in order to reduce contrast and mute colors (1989: 343). Altman's images are not the gorgeous, intensely illuminated landscapes that one associates with the Technicolor Westerns of the fifties and early sixties. He intentionally subordinates the visual image to an expressive intention that subverts the classical value of landscape as a utopian image of the freedom that the West is supposed to signify.

Both at the level of story and of visual articulation, Altman's Western should be read in comparison with *Shane*, though the final act replicates the conclusion of *High Noon*. In the opening shot of *Shane*, the hero rides into the frame from the rear and then pauses to take in the panoramic landscape of green trees on the mountain slope with open plains and blue mountains beyond. He rides down into the valley. In *McCabe*, the hero rides up the mountain and enters the frame as the camera pans right across a grainy image of the dark green landscape with rain falling on it. Despite the use of widescreen Panavision, the image of McCabe's ride up the mountain creates the feeling of tightness, as if the landscape were closing in around him rather than opening out in front of him. For Shane, the world is mapped out for him as a known space that he has mastered before he enters it. For McCabe, the world is a dark, unknown space through which he has to find his way as best he can without any clear sense of direction or knowledge of what he actually seeks. As the Leonard Cohen song on the soundtrack suggests, he is *a Joseph looking for a manger*, though this might be a more accurate description of Shane. McCabe is more clueless.

If McCabe looks for a redeemer and some kind of redemption, he doesn't know what form these things will take; and all he finds in the town of Presbyterian Church is the anarchy of capitalist civilization in which the religious justification of the social order is largely ignored while men pursue their self-interests without any serious thought of the other. Though there are more scenes of men congregating together in *McCabe* than in *Shane*, there is no real human relationship or communication between these men. Even the minister, who without anyone's help is building the church after which the town has been named, speaks to no one and wanders around the town like a pariah. Visually, *Shane's* world is clearly illuminated whether it is day or night (since the nighttime scenes are mostly done through day-for-night shooting). In this context, he knows who his friends and who his enemies are. *McCabe's* world, on the other hand, is almost exactly the opposite. The atmosphere up until the final gunfight is dark, with a low contrast that creates grainy textures despite the rich palette of colors. Even the most beautiful compositions serve an expressive purpose. For example, when McCabe is riding up the mountain a second time with the first three prostitutes he brings from Bearpaw, the shots of the figures on horseback, seen from behind foliage as they pass through shadows and the smoky outer limits of the town, are intercut with images of the preacher climbing to the apex of the church steeple to install a cross. The camera is angled in such a way that the steeple rises high in silhouette above the mountains in the background with the sun setting behind them (Ill. 27). On the soundtrack is the

ILLUSTRATION 27 The signifier of desire. *McCabe & Mrs. Miller* (1971). Warner Bros. *Producers*: David Foster and Mitchell Brower. *Director*: Robert Altman

Leonard Cohen song "Sisters of Mercy," which speaks of those women who *"brought me their comfort and later they brought me this song."* The juxtaposition of the symbol of Christian civilization with the image of the prostitutes who bring comfort to a sex-hungry masculine community may seem bizarre, but it suggests that the human desires that lie behind both figures, the cross and the prostitute, are the same. Sexuality and religion are part of the same drive. In this movie, every human desire is holy except those desires that exclude the possibility of desire. Despite its grubby atmosphere and the general materialism of a community that ignores the church until it is burning down, the desire of each individual adds up to the collective desire for a world in which pleasure and joy are no longer at odds with spiritual fulfillment and autonomy.

The critical turning point in *Shane* is the gunning down of Tory by Wilson, which finds another ironic reversal in *McCabe* with the death of the cowboy. Tory is slammed into the mud by Wilson's gunshot and then is carried back to the community by the Swede, who passes by several homesteads in the bright daylight, including Starrett's. The cowboy sinks into the icy river water in a slow-motion shot so grainy and dark that it creates the illusion of the character's virtual disappearance into a cinematic void, the frozen world of meaningless death. McCabe wakes up the next morning to find himself deserted by Mrs. Miller; and unlike the final showdown in *High Noon*, this film doesn't entertain the possibility that the community might be able to help. Though the visual technique in this sequence is consistent with the rest of the film, the white background created by the continuous snowfall causes the illusion of sharp, illuminated contrasts that distinguish the atmosphere here from everything that has preceded it. With the desertion of Mrs. Miller, who does not emulate Amy Kane, McCabe is confronted with the absence of any kind of social relationship that would offer the possibility of resistance to the power of capital manifested in the corporation's gunmen.

Before this event, McCabe met with a lawyer in Bearpaw who promised an escape from such a confrontation through an appeal to the courts and insisted that "this free-enterprise system of ours works" for the small and big businessman; but the free-enterprise system turns out to be a fantasy that has no bearing on the real desire or power of the community. The law deserts McCabe because it is the instrument of capitalist power, even if it does not specifically express the interests of this or that capitalist. Yet the lawyer inadvertently speaks the truth when he responds to McCabe's simple assertion that he "just didn't want to get killed." He says, "Until people stop dying for freedom, they ain't going to be free." Though the lawyer may not actually understand the implications of his own statement, he seems to contradict the progressivist ideology associated with Theodore Roosevelt that he has been espousing to McCabe, which would certainly argue that there is no freedom without the risk of death. His argument about "busting up trusts and monopolies" may be well intended; but in the end, by imagining the law as an institution that transcends particular social interests even as he reveals his own interest in using cases such as McCabe's to bolster his political ambitions, the lawyer has aligned himself with the social system that supports the power of trusts and monopolies. Such a system will not save McCabe from death or produce a world in which freedom without death is possible.

Still, Altman's genius is not to have subverted the classical Western but to have unveiled its apocalyptic truth. At the end of *High Noon*, Will Kane has defeated Frank Miller and his gang and established at least one meaningful social tie, the one with his own wife. It is the marriage of violence and pacifism, which seems to be the contradictory ideal of American Cold War fantasies. At the end *Shane*, the hero has destroyed the enemies of the community, but in the process he has also destroyed himself. The message is clear, though contradictory: Peaceful coexistence in a community can only be achieved through violence, but such violence is tantamount to a death principle that must be expelled from the community if the latter is to be free. McCabe dies alone, without relationship to any individual or to the community as a whole. Yet inadvertently, through the events that lead to his death, he brings about the apocalyptic conditions that could transform the town of Presbyterian Church into a real community. After the preacher has been shot and the church is burning, the community awakens to a sense of its own identity, which also momentarily erases the class distinctions between proper citizens and whores or between men and women. Everyone in the town participates in their first creative action as a community. So while McCabe is killing and dying, the community gives birth to itself without any knowledge of the relation between this new beginning and McCabe's actions.

At the time of the film's release in 1971, it would not have been difficult to see McCabe's killing of Butler (Hugh Millais), the tall and intimidating leader of the corporation's three gunmen, as an allegorical representation of the US defeat in Vietnam that was taking place even as the film was being made. If *The Wild Bunch* responded to the brutality and self-destructive potential of the US presence in Vietnam, which in the public mind culminated in the My Lai massacre, *McCabe* came along at a time when it was more difficult to see the United States in the role of either liberator or tragic actor. Rather, the United States was like the brutal bully Butler who comes after McCabe with his oversized weapon; and though this embodiment of intimidating superpower fatally wounds McCabe, the latter kills his larger enemy with a derringer, which he has kept up his coat sleeve. Butler's arrogance and presumption of superiority makes McCabe's victory possible, though this victory is pyrrhic only. In the end, it isn't Butler who kills McCabe but the absence of social relationships, an absence powerfully captured in the image of a wounded man slowly freezing to death a few feet away from the window of a warm house. The intercutting between the dying McCabe and the self-absorbed Mrs. Miller, who has withdrawn into the warm escape of an opium den, suggests that the desire for community, however anticipated by the momentary intervention of events like the burning of the church, will never be realized as long as relationship is impossible. Relationship is the force that crosses the border between two individuals inside their strongholds of self-interest and personal fantasy. Ironically, though McCabe is murdered by the representative of corporate private property, he might have survived that wound had he and Mrs. Miller not been so thoroughly entranced by their belief that private property and personal wealth guarantee security and social prestige. By implication, previous events in their personal histories have created and reinforced this fantasy, but in the end the fantasy itself kills McCabe and sends Mrs. Miller back to where she started from.

Near the film's beginning, in a long shot through a telephoto lens, McCabe, standing at the end of the long, narrow rope bridge to Sheehan's saloon, lights a small cigar, which produces a bit of clarity in the grainy darkness that engulfs the character from both sides (Ill. 28). The visual logic of the film moves from the grainy

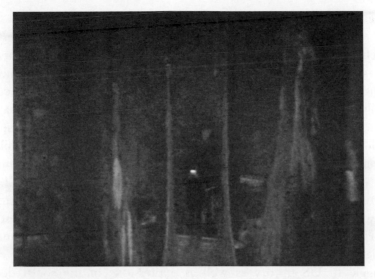

ILLUSTRATION 28 A light in the darkness. *McCabe & Mrs. Miller* (1971). Warner Bros. *Producers:* David Foster and Mitchell Brower. *Director:* Robert Altman

darkness of such opening shots to the relative clarity of the final scenes in the snow. Though McCabe initially responds to Mrs. Miller as someone who costs him "money and pain," she eventually evokes in him the realization that "I got poetry in me," a kind of naïve, utopian self-valorization that contrasts sharply both with Mrs. Miller's alienated pessimism as well as with the view of the corporate agent who wants to reduce McCabe's desire to a "substantial gain in capital." Overall, McCabe's death, despite its futility, represents an unconscious commitment to the Lacanian ethical imperative that one must never let go of one's desire (Lacan 1992: 319). His desire is apocalyptic not in the sense that it can bring about an actual transfiguration of the human reality but in the sense that it articulates a truth about that reality, the truth that *it can be transformed*, through the mediation of desire that has been translated from personal commitment to social collaboration. McCabe ironically manifests the Blakean principles that all men are poets and that the job of the poet is to keep the fires burning during a dark time.

The Multitude at Heaven's Gate

Michael Cimino's *Heaven's Gate* was one of the starting points of this study, though my purpose has not been to redeem the movie from its critical damnation but rather to situate it in the sequence of Hollywood (and Hollywood-inspired) Western movies that enables one to understand the larger cinematic and cultural discourse to which it responds. Numerous explanations of its commercial failure have emerged over the years, while there have been a few attempts to explain its critical failure (Bliss 1985: 240–66; Wood 1986a: 299). I would tell the story in a slightly different way. First, the Westerns to which *Heaven's Gate* responds, a subcategory of the Western movie tradition that includes some of the most popular and influential Westerns ever made, were disguised representations of class struggle in US history as well as expressions of the social desire to transcend or transform the class system. Second, the failure of *Heaven's Gate* lies in its articulation of the truth about that tradition. I don't mean its truth with respect to the history of the Johnson County War, since it misrepresents that history in any number of ways, but rather the truth about the Western movie itself that, as I have shown, often refers back to the Johnson County War or to similar events as a kind of mastertext. *Heaven's Gate* did not emerge out of a void. The seventies Westerns that anticipated it, including *Pat Garrett & Billy the Kid* and *The Missouri Breaks*, were not box-office successes; and the latter film in particular was received by critics and reviewers as a serious disappointment, though like *Heaven's Gate* its reputation has improved over time.

If one keeps in mind the particular Western tradition that I have focused on in this study, then the critical and public reaction to these more recent films begins to make sense. Just as in a psychoanalytic situation the most critical moment comes when a dream or some other disguised or displaced element of an analysand's discourse is made to yield a truth about the unconscious desire of the analysand, so these films bring to the surface a truth about the Western movie tradition. And just as the analysand frequently breaks off the psychoanalytic process at such a moment as a last act of resistance to the truth of the unconscious, so the collective subject of a cultural unconscious may resist the knowledge of threatening social desires when they manage to break through the disguise of a set of generic conventions like the conventions that have dominated the Western movie. In this case, such a breakthrough or breakdown of generic convention may have had the effect of destroying the pleasure that several post-Depression generations derived from viewing Western movies. That pleasure came, in part, from the compartmentalization of feeling and knowledge. The Western movie frequently allowed the spectator to feel the resentment of class and the desire to destroy the class system without having to assume a conscious understanding of that system or its economic impact. It allowed the spectator to contemplate capitalism's use of violence to justify and enforce its commitment to an inequitable distribution of autonomy and free time, even if that violence takes the displaced form of violence against other nations that reinforces the binary logic of nationalism. Though the Western movies I have analyzed reinforce capitalist hegemony by creating nonviolent and apparently anodyne outlets for class resentments and social antagonisms, they also articulate the very contradiction they work so hard to disavow.

Michael Bliss has written at length on the use of the circle as a symbol in *Heaven's Gate*, particularly the interplay of clockwise and counterclockwise movements in four key sequences, two from the film's prologue at the Harvard graduation of 1870 – the dance to the "Blue Danube" and the prelude to the student fight for a symbolic garland of flowers on a centrally positioned tree, both on the same Harvard green – and two from the main body of the film – the roller-skating dance at the uncompleted "Heaven's Gate" meeting hall in Sweetwater, Wyoming, and the final battle between the immigrants and the corporate cattlemen. Furthermore, these circles appear elsewhere in the film – for example, when Ella Watson (Isabelle Huppert) drives her new carriage in counterclockwise circles through the main street of Sweetwater – and usually suggest either conformity to the dominant concept of time as social progress, a clockwise movement, or resistance to such progress that would attempt to reverse time, a counterclockwise movement (Bliss 1985: 196–200). Conformity to progress in this context means identification with the dominant property relations, while resistance refers to the demand for economic justice, even if such justice takes the form of the frontier house of prostitution where Ella and the other prostitutes take stolen cattle in payment for sexual favors.

By demanding attention to symbolic patterns and movements of this sort, the movie produces what Robin Wood has called an assault "on the dominance of the linear codes" and substitutes instead "the semantic (the code of implied meanings out of which the work's thematic structure is developed) and the symbolic (usually functioning in terms of oppositions . . .)" (1986a: 304). With reference to the film's structure of oppositions, Brian Woolland refers to the organizing tension between two perspectives: "the Marxist, materialist view that all these events are underpinned by economic, social and political conditions and result from class-based oppression; and the liberal-humanist view of individuals struggling to do right both for themselves and for each other" (1995: 282). Ultimately, the latter insight refers to the contradiction between human desire – which in some sense is always individual even though any one person's desire must interact with the desire of others – and the material conditions that both solicit and block desire. All of these critics agree that the film refuses, in Woolland's phrase, "the primacy of individual action, a refusal which is in itself a strong critique, not only of the Western, but also of most mainstream Hollywood films" (281). Though I would agree that there is such a critique in the film, there is also, as Bliss stresses, "an implicit existential tone" (1985: 226). If, as I have argued, the gunfighter Western has always been an exploration of the contradictory formation of subjects that either identify or refuse to identify with the dominant viewpoint of capital, then *Heaven's Gate* is perhaps the most complicated version of that critique – the final unveiling or apocalypse of the Western itself as a theory of the political meaning of subjectivity.

In symbolic terms, Jim Averill (Kris Kristofferson) is the embodiment of class contradiction as a contradiction in desire. The opening Harvard sequence that so many reviewers found excessive in either the long or short versions of the film is absolutely essential to establishing the social origin of Jim's desire "to be of important service," a phrase which, in the cut version of the film, he says in voice-over as the film shifts from Harvard in 1870 to Wyoming 20 years later. He also comments that he "saw hundreds leave for the West with nothing but precious dignity and the clothes on their backs." In the long version of the film, these words are absent, but the film conveys even more effectively without them the confused and enigmatic nature of Jim's desire. The first shot in the film signifies spiritual transcendence, as the camera, from a low angle, traces a descent from a red sky, against which the steeple of a cupola appears, into a narrow street in Cambridge, Massachusetts. Because of the low angle of the shot, the steeple itself is isolated from its context in the material world, which distinguishes it from the steeple in *McCabe*. Jim Averill runs into the shot through a narrow arch just beneath the structure of the cupola, and the camera follows him in a pan shot until he disappears around a corner. As Élyette Benjamin-Labarthe notes, this long take suggests the principles of divine mission and Manifest Destiny that became in the nineteenth century the signifiers of America's concept of itself as the annex to an earthly paradise (1998: 130). However, at a more elementary level, the shot expresses such unworldly transcendence as the origin of Jim Averill's concept of himself. Symbolically, Harvard as an institution reinforces this view of transcendence, which is one reason why Cimino may have decided to substitute Oxford, England for Cambridge, Massachusetts in the actual shooting of the scene. This makes emphatic the concept of a cultural tradition that supersedes any specific historical situation and articulates a set of truths and values that cannot be reduced to mere class or personal interests. Unlike the church steeple in *McCabe* – which, based on its context in the film, expresses a desire for *social* transcendence that would resolve contradictions in the material reality of the town Presbyterian Church – Harvard mediates the desire for transcendence by creating the illusion that there is no contradiction between such desire and material social reality. The meaning of social reality *is* spiritual.

The Reverend Doctor (Joseph Cotton) gives verbal articulation to the same logic in his speech to the graduating student body, though there is some irony in his opening phrase, "If it be not a mere farce you are enacting," since farce is exactly what the scene exposes. He speaks about the moral responsibility of the newly educated, their "imperative duty" to transcend the material privileges that their presence in this location signifies, by nurturing "the contact of the cultivated mind with the uncultivated," which amounts to a "high ideal, the education of a nation." However, even as he notes the hostility of American culture at the present time to "all habits of thought and meditation," the graduating students are cutting up and mocking the situation, which they obviously regard as a farce. Billy Irvine (John Hurt), Jim's friend, is the chief clown among the students, though, while the Reverend speaks, Jim flirts and exchanges glances with a young woman in the gallery whose image will continue to embody his Harvard desire for the rest of the film. When Billy, the class orator, gives the valedictory speech, he forgets the high ideals in order to celebrate a social order that is "well arranged," at least for those who are graduating from Harvard in 1870. Still, Billy's fate in the rest of the film subverts the message of his speech. Like Jim he will go to Wyoming, but unlike Jim he will not be able to oppose the Association's war against the immigrants because, as he says to Jim, he is "the victim of our class." Though he goes along with the invasion without commitment, he is killed in the final battle. In the long version of the film, there is no clear indication as to why Jim decides to go out west, and the spectator can only infer the relation between the Harvard scenes and any decision Jim has made after the jump cut from Harvard to Wyoming 20 years later. Before that cut, however, the contradictory nature of his desire is made visible through an image.

In the "Blue Danube" waltz on the Harvard green, Jim dances in the outer circle that moves clockwise around the green. At first, he is not with the young woman who has caught his gaze throughout the day; and while he and this different woman turn, like everyone else, in a clockwise direction, periodically Jim leads her in a counter-clockwise direction, perversely it would seem. Later, when he switches to the woman who is the chief object of his interest, he turns her only clockwise, since this woman is a conservative principle in his life, a part of that which is "well arranged." This waltz anticipates the roller-skating dance in Wyoming in the "Heaven's Gate" meeting hall where the immigrants move in a predominantly counterclockwise direction (Ill. 29). Curiously, Jim hesitates to enter the circle of skaters until J.B. (Jeff Bridges) and Ella drag him in. Later, after Jim has gone outside to load the drunk J.B. into the wagon, he reenters the hall, which is now suddenly empty without any visual indication as to where the people have gone. They have simply disappeared. Some critics see this as a sign that the whole dance sequence is a fantasy, a kind of utopian dream of social coalescence, in which Ella is fully accepted by a community that previously has judged her rather harshly, particularly the women who resent her relation to the men. If so, it is a dream in which Jim hesitates to participate. However, when he comes back into the empty hall, he dances with

ILLUSTRATION 29 An image of community. *Heaven's Gate* (1980). United Artists. *Producer:* Joann Carelli. *Director:* Michael Cimino

Ella, this time turning and spinning her clockwise while they move together in a counterclockwise direction. As the dance progresses, he occasionally turns her counterclockwise.

The symbolic significance of these parallel sequences, including the significance of their cinematic composition, is rather complex. In the "Heaven's Gate" sequence, after the drunk J.B. stumbles outside the building, the coloring is reduced to a sepia tint, while throughout the dance sequence there is an extreme use of "flashing." The whole sequence suggests that time has stopped; but there is enough contrast between the outside and the inside of the building to signify that the interior of "Heaven's Gate," despite its simulation of reality, is actually a world of possibilities, including the possibility of communal solidarity and happiness, represented by the dance of the immigrants, as well as the possibility of Jim's individual resolution of the class contradiction that exists between himself and Ella, represented by their dance. In the Harvard sequence, Jim is clearly seduced by the fantasy of a communal identity in the form of a natural aristocracy, which recalls the Wisterian distinction between the quality and the equality, though he symbolically flirts with the idea of going in another direction, a flirtation that is quickly brought under control by his "dream" woman, who seems to embody the seductions of social class. However, the jump cut to Wyoming 20 years later implies that the subversive element in his makeup never dies and leads him to pursue a different kind of identity in the West. Ella is the object of a desire that supports this other identity, which is why her presence at the "Heaven's Gate" dance is required even if the possibility of her presence there is counterintuitive. Ella represents a radical social identity not because of her espousal of a political ideology that would criticize capitalism but because of her insistence on self-valorization and her demand for autonomy, which would include her sexual freedom.

Though Ella's desire may sometimes seem conventional enough (for example, when she tells Jim that Nate has proposed marriage to her), a close analysis shows something both contradictory and subversive. Ella descends from heroines like Frenchy in *Destry Rides Again*, Pearl in *Duel in the Sun*, Vienna in *Johnny Guitar*, and Jill McBain in *Once Upon a Time in the West*. Like Pearl and Vienna, she is courageous and not afraid of using a gun in the final battle between the immigrants and the corporate cattlemen. Like Frenchy, she becomes an organizing catalyst for the community when she reports to the immigrants, once again gathered inside "Heaven's Gate," on the death of Nate Champion (Christopher Walken), and virtually leads them toward a direct confrontation with the cattlemen. Like Jill McBain, who implies that she has learned from experience how to survive a rape, Ella endures rape and humiliation and survives as a kind of "Eve/Venus" figure and mother of the community (Lindroth 1989: 225–6), because her desire is stronger than anything that can be done to her. Though she accumulates some property and wealth in ways that are not legal, she nonetheless turns capitalism's values against itself as a means of self-valorization, which aligns her with women like Vienna and Jill. Just as the latter two want to use their wealth to construct an alternative community, Ella not only serves the community in a number of instances, but also, like Mrs. Miller, has constructed a kind of material utopia in her whore-house. Finally, though she seems pleased by Nate's proposal of marriage and by Jim's ambivalent hint that he might have wanted to propose, she also articulates her desire more directly when she says to Jim, "Can't a woman love two men?" Ella sometimes appears passive in response to Jim or Nate, but in point of fact she never surrenders or subordinates her desire to either man; and though she may be a prostitute, the rape scene is "particularly shocking" (226) because it violates her well-established autonomy.

Jim's attraction to Ella is attraction to an alternative social identity, but his relation to that identity is ambivalent at best. If Ella appears to accept Nate's proposal of marriage, it is only because she recognizes the ambivalence in her relation to Jim. Since she charges Nate for sexual intimacy and does not charge Jim, the spectator may assume that Jim is the true object of her desire; but that discrimination between the two men may have more to do with the fact that money is meaningless to Jim, since, by his own admission, he can buy her all the things she wants whenever she wants. In this case at least, Ella is not interested in money as the power to buy things but rather as a symbolic expression of an emotional commitment and as a form of valorization. Because money means nothing to Jim, it conveys nothing of his inner feelings and no sense of her own worth to Ella. In Nate's case, money means everything because he has never had any, and in giving it to Ella, he expresses her value in his eyes. Though Ella may seem indecisive in choosing between the two men, she is actually quite decisive in choosing both men and realizing the differences between what they have to give her.

As Robin Wood stresses, "*Heaven's Gate* violates some of the basic principles of classical narrative," particularly those of classical Hollywood, which insisted on transparent cause and effect relationships between the scenes (1986a: 300). For example, we only discover halfway through the film that Jim is Nate's friend, when he prefaces his warning to Nate that he wants Ella to leave the territory with the remark, "You're a friend, Nate, so I'll come straight to it." Later, after Ella rides into town and informs the immigrants at "Heaven's Gate" about the imminent invasion of the cattlemen, she goes to Jim's room to tell him that Nate is dead. Initially, Jim says nothing and continues to look at himself in the mirror while shaving, but Ella's eye wanders to the picture of Averill with the Harvard woman that he keeps in his room. Interestingly, the scene never suggests that Ella is jealous of the other woman; and when Jim's only response to Nate's death is to say, "I told you so," she quietly responds after a long hesitation, "He loved you. He thought you were his friend." Still looking in the mirror, Jim responds, "I'm not responsible."

Ultimately, that phrase defines Jim. Despite his desire to be of service, he takes no responsibility for the current social order that has produced the conflict in Johnson County. In some ways, he always imagines that he transcends every situation, and by focusing on his mirror image in the scene with Ella, he aligns himself with his own hegemonic identity based on the ideology of the Harvard experience and his passion for the Harvard woman. Even in his conflict with the corporate cattlemen, he never leaves behind that identification, for, as he says to Frank Canton (Sam Waterston), "You're not in my class, Canton. You never will be." Presumably, Jim's class is the class of those who transcend class. The reality, however, is that, despite his attraction to Ella, Nate, and J.B., Jim never can forget his class origin. He flirts with the idea of moving in a counterclockwise direction, but in the end he can never completely give himself over to the reversal of time and the sort of apocalyptic event that would represent the total transformation of this social context.

As every interpreter of the film has pointed out, Jim is always late: he is late for his graduation at Harvard, late in warning Ella and the community of Sweetwater that the corporate cattlemen are about to invade Johnson County with a death list, late in proposing marriage to Ella (if indeed his ambivalent suggestion is a proposal), late in making the decision to join the immigrants in their war against the cattlemen, and finally late in getting Ella, or Nate, or J.B. out of harm's way. When he first asks Ella to leave Wyoming, he makes it clear that he will not go with her and says nothing about joining her later. At the end of the film, they are leaving Wyoming together, but it is again too late. As Wood points out, his ambivalence toward the immigrants he supposedly means to protect is made clear in the early scenes in Casper and on the road to Sweetwater (1986a: 303–4). In town, he witnesses an immigrant being beaten to death by a hired gunman of the Association. Jim asks the man to stop since he has already won and gets the response, "Says who, old man?" Jim takes it as a personal insult (since, as we later learn, he is sensitive to the issue of aging) and knocks the man down, but then he walks away. Later, he encounters the woman pulling the wagon on her own and learns that the Association's men came after them and killed the husband and animals. Though he expresses concern and sympathy, advising her to go back, he nonetheless offers her no real help when she insists that she will stay and work the land. He exchanges concerned glances with the children but then rides off in his horse and carriage, leaving the woman to pull the wagon on her own. Jim is not responsible because he believes that his social identity transcends the realm of particular interests that drives the class war in Johnson County.

The fiction of transcendence that governs Jim's social identity is also what binds him to the members of the Association, despite his scorn for them and opposition to their invasion. In the end, they also believe in the transcendence of their social class, particularly in relation to the law. As Frank Canton puts its in his confrontation with Nate Champion, "You were hired to enforce the law. We are the law." There is a distinction to be made between the outlaw, like Peckinpah's Billy the Kid, and those who transcend the law to the extent that they can rewrite it to suit their interests because they see the law as nothing more than the expression of their legitimate social authority. In this film, Nate Champion is the Billy the Kid figure, and Cimino has altered the historical Nate Champion to conform to such an archetype. The historical Nate Champion was never a regulator, though in the early 1880s he rode the range for the corporate outfits, many of which were headed by British or Irish investors like Horace Plunkett, who described Champion as a good man (Smith 1966: 155). By 1891, Champion was presumably the leader of a number of blackballed cowboys (146). After he had been murdered during the invasion almost exactly as depicted in Cimino's movie, the WSGA defended itself unofficially by insisting on his status as an outlaw and a rustler. Helena Smith has concluded that the "bad man story is bunk" (155). Though it is not beyond the realm of possibility that Champion did rustle some maverick cattle, this would have been in a context in which the WSGA made the situation of the small cattleman impossible. From the mid-1880s on, they enforced the policy of blacklisting cowboys with their own cattle and any cattleman who hired them. Since blacklisted cowboys and ranchers could not participate in roundups, they could not legally recover their own cattle from the open range (27–8). Despite changes in the law and the Wyoming legislature, the WSGA maintained control over the roundups after the repeal of the Maverick Law in 1891 (82–9). Even without the law the mavericks were to be divided up in a way that "excluded the small owners from participation" (88).

The historical Nate Champion was considered to be a fearless man who was "lightning with a gun" (155). Cimino's Champion is seemingly fearless and good with a gun, but otherwise he is a more contradictory figure than the real man was and has operated on both sides of the law, as embodied in the Association. When Jim asks him what he wants, he responds, "How the hell do I know?" but then adds, "Get rich, like you." Though Jim considers this a good answer, it's never clear that he really understands the difference between Nate and himself, or, for that matter, between Ella and himself. Neither Nate nor Ella can afford the illusion of spiritual transcendence that nourishes Jim's social identity. They recognize that the only possible autonomy they can achieve is through some degree of wealth, and Nate further recognizes that the foundation of wealth lies in the use of force. His first appearance in the film is through the hole in a sheet made by the blast of his shotgun when he executes Michael Kovach for stealing and slaughtering a steer. Later we learn that Nate himself is an immigrant, someone who is seen as a traitor by the other members of that community. Far from being a leader, therefore, he has become the local embodiment of the Association's rule by force. Ironically, the real historical figure on whom this fictional Nate's character would be based is Frank Canton, the Association's gunman and not, as he is in this movie, a corporate cattleman. Yet, as Woolland points out, Nate is "the character who changes most in the course of the film," and there can be little doubt that the source of this change derives from his passion for Ella (1995: 280). Ultimately, Nate is willing to embrace the radical social position that Ella embodies in a way that Jim cannot. He can do this because he never has the illusion that a social identity can be anything more than a material relation, a function of the distribution of wealth; and unlike Jim, he can learn from his errors, including his work for the Association, because he has no "high ideal" of which he imagines himself to be the expression.

When Ella visits Nate's cabin, she witnesses his material efforts to "civilize the wilderness" by wallpapering it with old newspapers. Though early reviewers and critics of *Heaven's Gate* found the characters cartoonish and unconvincing, Christopher Walken conveys the complexity of Nate Champion through his body gestures and facial expressions. In these scenes with Ella in the cabin, Nate (whose name, despite its historical origin, alludes to the founding archetype of Western myth, Natty Bumpo) betrays an innocence that stands in marked contrast to the brutality he displayed in his first scene in the film. In working for the Association, Nate has identified with the viewpoint of capital and, ironically, with the man who would seem to be a sort of hero to him, namely Jim. When Nate tells Jim at one point that he can't understand him, he reveals a confusion as to why Jim judges him so harshly for his work with the Association because he can see more clearly than Jim can that Jim's identity derives from his economic privileges and that the only visible and explainable justification of his wealth lies in his capacity for violence. Jim, after all, resorts to violence in response to whatever threatens or insults him, including Nate. Nevertheless, the interior of Nate's cabin betrays a creative impulse that is altogether lacking in Jim and that we find no sign of in the room he occupies in the town of Sweetwater. As Benjamin-Labarthe has pointed out, Nate is almost feminine when he expresses, through his work on the cabin, "the universal desire to take refuge in a chrysalis" (1998: 135). Herein lies the attraction between Nate and Ella, for they both work at transforming their environment through specific material alterations. Furthermore, if we draw out the metaphor of the chrysalis further, they are both seeking a material process by which they can transform themselves into something more than what they already are.

Jim, on the other hand, despite his desire to achieve some degree of economic justice for the dispossessed, never questions the material foundation of the class system that privileges him. He shows absolutely no impulse toward real creativity, and he never recognizes that the kind of justice on earth he wants to achieve cannot be derived from the realm of transcendent values. As the cavalry captain says to him, "You can't force salvation on people, Jim. It doesn't work." In the next scene at Ella's place, while Nate is trying to learn how to write by copying out an encyclopedia article on Nathaniel Hawthorne, Jim storms in and physically attacks Nate for not telling Ella about the list, though he has known about the list himself throughout the first half of the film and told no one except Eggleston (Brad Dourif) and J.B. Throughout the film, he never once tries to communicate with Nate as a peer or to share his education with this man who so desires to become more than what he is. Jim's tone to Nate and even to Ella is almost always condescending. Jim's one creative act in the film is to teach the immigrants how to make moveable forts out of logs, a technology based on his knowledge of Roman history (see Smith 1966: 221–2). Bliss sees Jim's character, as well as the characters of Nate and Ella, as the outcome of economic determination in the raw sense that "money dictates one's politics." Even for the characters without Jim's class status, "their ownership of 'goods' converts them into people who are virtually compelled by the nature of the capitalist system to forsake their friends and associates and, if necessary, eventually to compromise their integrity in the name of a form of self-protection that in the film is usually capitalistically defined" (1985: 229–31). Yet this argument fails to recognize each character's singularity and the dynamics of the subjective processes that distinguish them from one another.

Though Jim is the ostensible hero of this story, his commitment to anyone is never stable. In Wyoming, he cannot commit to Ella because he has the Harvard woman on his mind; back east on a yacht in Newport, he cannot commit to the Harvard woman because he has the memory of Ella on his mind. His friendship with Nate cannot accede to the latter's demand for equality; and while Nate accepts, to some extent, Jim's relation to Ella, Jim cannot accept Nate as his competitor for her love. His relation to the homesteading community is cinematically expressed in the scene before he finally rides out to join them in their battle with the cattlemen. He moves his horse in one direction and then in another, as if his will to move has been paralyzed. Finally, he joins the immigrants after stopping by Nate's where Ella has retreated from the battle to mourn the latter's death. After virtually commanding her to go back to her place and wait for him, Jim finally joins the immigrants in time to direct their suicidal attack on the invaders. By the time the cavalry arrive to rescue the remnants of the cattlemen, the film has created the illusion that nearly all the immigrants have been wiped out, even though they seemed to have the advantage in the final sequences of the battle. One of the few surviving women, who has to shoot her husband after his legs are mangled by one of the moveable forts, shoots herself in the mouth. The spectator sees this image from J.B.'s perspective as he wanders around the field with a look of disbelief on his face before the camera cuts to a long shot of Jim, a speck of a figure wandering away from the field toward the trees as the camera zooms back to reveal the mountains in the distance. This allusion to the ending of *Shane* could not make more emphatic the film's deconstruction of the Western hero.

If Shane is the mysterious stranger who saves the homesteading community, Jim is not a mystery except insofar as we never know where his real commitment lies. He is not a mystery because everyone – Nate, Ella, and even the cavalry captain – knows the truth about him, which is that he's a rich man who has come to Wyoming on some sort of mission to redeem those who are implicitly beneath him. Nate tells Ella at one point that Jim isn't her friend, "he ain't nobody's friend." Later, Ella says to Jim, "I am grateful to you, Jim, for everything. And I love you [*pause*] for it." But then she adds that her feelings derive from her debt to him for "the protection at the beginning and now." Jim clearly has feelings for Ella and the community, but all too frequently his ambivalence cancels out those feelings. Though there is no strict cause-and-effect relationship between Jim's decisions and the tragic end of the film with the virtual destruction of the community and the specific deaths of Nate, Ella, and J.B., there can be no avoiding the symbolic relationship between Jim's ambivalence and the death that descends on everyone close to him. Whereas Shane sacrifices his own life for the redemption and life of the community, Jim symbolically brings about the death of the community and everyone he loves in it. Though he saves Ella after she has been raped, he could have prevented the rape by marrying her and taking her out of Wyoming. He sends her away from the battle that in some ways she started but then naively lets her be killed in an ambush by Frank Canton. Still, in this movie the Shane figure cannot be limited to one character.

Nate is also not a mystery, and if spectators have always wondered about what lies behind Shane's loneliness and disillusionment, Nate makes that clear in his first appearance when he murders Michael Kovach for the Association. Nate has become the instrument of death in the hands of the capitalist class; but unlike Jim he never identifies with the transcendence of that class and its system of moral values, its "high ideals." Ironically, Nate's death becomes the event that warns the community of the impending disaster, which is one of the few historically accurate representations in this film. Nate represents the feminine dimension of the Shane figure, and he is capable of the commitment that Jim is not. He implicitly criticizes Jim's patriarchal and aristocratic attitude toward Ella and the community as a whole. But his death before the final battle even begins reminds us that redemption, if there is any, can never come from a single individual.

At the end of the film, Jim's arrival to support the immigrants in their war with the Association alters their strategy and their movements. Initially, when they are led into battle by Ella, the majority of them move in a counterclockwise direction around the cattlemen (Ill. 30). In that instance, their struggle is visually identified, according to Hollywood conventions, with the struggle of Native Americans

ILLUSTRATION 30 Immigrants as Indians, class war as race war. *Heaven's Gate* (1980). United Artists. *Producer:* Joann Carelli. *Director:* Michael Cimino

against those forces that would seize their lands and destroy their way of life. It points to the identity of race war and class war as struggles over economic justice. Before Jim's arrival, they make a tactical retreat that might suggest the possibility of reorganizing their forces into a defensive action that would enable them to survive as a community. Jim transforms that retreat into a new offense, though he never explains what the immigrants can possibly achieve by such an aggressive action. After Jim teaches them how to build moveable forts and devises a strategy of attack, they move directly into the circle of the cattlemen, hurling sticks of dynamite over the forts as they get closer and closer. In symbolic terms, the first impulse of the immigrants, under Ella's inspiration, is to reverse time against the brutal progress that the cattlemen represent, but Jim effectively pushes them toward the destruction of time that would take advantage of the apocalyptic moment, Benjamin's "messianic cessation of happening." The result, however, is not victory but holocaust.

Ironically, in his leadership of the immigrants, Jim is at his most revolutionary and his most reactionary. Though he is right to encourage them to exploit the apocalyptic moment of their self–empowerment as a community in order to achieve a real social transformation, he fails to see that their self-empowerment is more important than his military strategy or knowledge of Roman history. He values himself as the spiritual subject that transcends material history over the collective subject of the community that has been achieved through negotiation and compromise. In the real Johnson County War, there was no holocaust such as we see in this film. The cattlemen held up in some ranch houses, fortified their situation such as it was, and held out against the homesteaders until the cavalry arrived to rescue them (Smith 1966: 210–28). In the movie, if Jim wants to lead the immigrants in a way that will bring about their survival as well as their victory, he should probably advise them to avoid a direct attack on the cattlemen that will necessarily wipe out so many of the attackers. Yet, like most of the events in this movie, these decisions are more symbolic than logical. Jim imagines himself in control of the community, when in reality he has become the instrument by which the community expresses the truth of its own desire, which is to destroy time and transform their land into the place of transition on the way to a new heaven and a new earth. This is the real meaning of their earlier dance and of their meeting place that bears the name "Heaven's Gate."

Though the film shows the failure of the heroic individual to save his friends and to save the community, the real significance of these events lies in the failure of the individual to save himself by transforming his social consciousness and self-understanding into something that would be the ground of a new world through the formation of a new kind of human relationship. However, something comes out of Jim's failure, which must be seen as the failure of the classical Western to articulate a political subject that can truly liberate the masses and bring about a resolution of the contradiction between the individual and the community in capitalist society. The thing that emerges for a moment in the apocalyptic conclusion to the film is "the multitude," in Hardt and Negri's sense – "an internally different, multiple social subject whose constitution and action is based not on identity or unity . . . but on what it has in common" (2004: 100). In *Heaven's Gate*, Cimino has intentionally constructed the community of Johnson County as one characterized by differences that cannot be incorporated into the national identity as it is posited by the members of the Association. The film has sometimes been criticized for creating the false impression that the Johnson County War was a conflict between Eastern European immigrant farmers and Anglo-American cattlemen, when in fact the conflict was primarily between corporate cattlemen and small ranchers, mostly Anglo-American, who had formerly been cowboys. Still, there is some basis for the belief that a significant number of immigrants settled in Wyoming in the 1880s, though they were mostly from Northern Europe (Smith 1966: 22–3). According to Osgood, "By

1888, Wyoming ranchers were feeling the full force of this invasion" by a significant number of Germans, Russians, and Swedes (1957: 243). The historical Jim Averell, who was lynched some years before the Johnson County War, had published an article in the *Casper Weekly Mail* on February 7, 1889, which described the corporate cattleman as a land grabber who "*advances the idea that a poor man has no say in the affairs of this country*" (quoted in Meschter 1996: 103; original emphasis). Cimino put that statement into his screenplay. In other words, Cimino chooses to shape the historical reality of the Johnson County War in order to dramatize a conflict between the social desires of the multitude, whom he identifies as the poor, and the desire of the dominant class for superfluous wealth.

The final chapter of *Heaven's Gate* represents the possibility of the multitude not as an ideal that transcends the individual but as a social force that emerges only with great difficulty out of the conflicts and divisions between individuals. In the debates at the "Heaven's Gate" meeting hall, the community of immigrants comes together in response to the news about the imminent invasion and the death list. In earlier sequences, this community has already revealed its internal divisions, including divisions over property and the law. In their final debate, a conflict emerges between the small entrepreneurs, including the Mayor and his allies, and the more radical members of the community, particularly J.B. and Mr. Eggleston. J.B. calls on the community to stand together in order "to protect what we have," but Eggleston is the one who uses the words of the historical Jim Averell about land speculators and the exclusion of the poor from any voice in the affairs of the country. Eggleston, though his role in this film is minimal, recognizes the possibility of the immigrants to shape themselves into a "posse" – into a collective force that can "have power" through the "organization of the multitude as a political subject" (Hardt and Negri 2000: 411). When the Mayor of Sweetwater tries to inhibit the emergence of such a subject in the interest of his own "private property," he is shot by Mrs. Kovach, an event that consolidates the formation of the new political subject in opposition to private property.

This formation is the meaning of the final battle, which, even though it fails to transfer power from the masters of private property to the masses of ordinary men and women, nonetheless apocalyptically reveals the ever-present ground of such a transformation in the force of the multitude. In this film, Eggleston is the theorist of the multitude, and he demonstrates the point made by Marx long ago: "Material force can only be overthrown by material force; but theory itself becomes a material force when it has seized the masses" (1964: 52). In the end, *Heaven's Gate* is nothing more than a visual articulation of this theory, which would shape the masses into a political identity that does not negate the individual – though it negates the ideology of possessive individualism – but rather constructs "forms and instruments of association through cooperation" and moves "towards the (ontological) recognition of the common" (Negri and Zolo 2003: 36). The common is what the unfinished "Heaven's Gate" meeting hall has symbolized all along. It is the minimal public wealth required so that individuals can collaborate on the production of their own freedom.

In this movie, the multitude is something that we can only glimpse as a social possibility. It is the revolutionary chance that has been missed, and that Western movies are constantly looking for in their quest for a resolution to the contradiction between the individual and the community. It is what Jim Averill has tragically lost at the end of the film after he has returned to the woman from Harvard. Through his facial expressions, while he sits in a luxurious room on his yacht off the coast of Newport, Rhode Island, he conveys the emptiness of his life and his absolute distance from any other human being, including this woman of his dreams, as he listens to the beating of the ship's engine like the sounding of a death knell. That sound recalls one of the most subtle effects in this film that no other critic has ever commented on so far as I know. During the scenes of intimacy at Ella's house – lovemaking between Ella and Jim, then between Ella and Nate, the aftermath of the rape, and the final scene in which Jim and Ella are dressing to leave Wyoming after the battle – you can hear the ticking of a clock in the background. To me, this means that time is running out on the revolutionary possibilities signified by the relationship of these men to Ella. In the early scenes, Jim makes love to Ella without warning her of the impending invasion. Later, in her room, Nate can barely stay awake long enough to make love to Ella, a condition that takes on political significance when he wakes up too late to the possibility of transforming himself. Ultimately, Ella's death, after the brief emergence and disappearance of the multitude, represents the triumph of time that becomes the death knell on Jim's yacht, the coffin in which he is buried at sea.

Yet the desires that Ella solicited from these men, and even from the community of Sweetwater, still live, if only as the reverse measure of Jim's unhappiness. The pounding of the ship's engine is also the knocking on heaven's door (to recall the title of Bob Dylan's song in the released version of *Pat Garrett & Billy the Kid*). Jim realizes too late that he should have followed his desire all the way and given himself over completely to Ella, Nate, and the multitude of which they were a part. As he says about Nate and Ella earlier in the film when he bows out of the triangle, "Well, you take it all, both of you. It's more your country than mine, anyway." At Newport, he must realize how right he was in saying that. It's more their country because they refuse to surrender their desire for something better. As Cully the Irish stationmaster (Richard Masur) says to Jim near the beginning of the Wyoming sequence in Casper, "If the rich could hire the poor to do their dying for them, the poor could make a good living." Living up to his vision, Cully is killed trying to warn the community of Johnson County about the invasion. He reminds us that as long as the poor fear death they remain victims of the organized violence of capital. But when they lose their fear of death, nothing is impossible. In the end, the only way to heaven is through the revolutionary transformation of the material world.

CONCLUSION: *KILL BILL*, OR WHY SHANE ALWAYS COMES BACK

Periodically since the early seventies, the Western has been pronounced dead only to be resurrected by some particular reinvention of the genre. For a while, it seemed as if Clint Eastwood would have to carry the tradition forward alone after it had been nearly buried by the avalanche of negative criticism over the failure of *Heaven's Gate*. Though the Western is no longer the central American film genre, it has nonetheless experienced a series of amazing reinventions since the middle of the eighties, sometimes successfully and sometimes not: *Silverado* (1985), *Young Guns* (1988), *Lonesome Dove* (1989), *Dances with Wolves* (1990), *Unforgiven* (1992), *Tombstone* (1993), *Posse* (1993), *The Ballad of Little Jo* (1993), *Wyatt Earp* (1994), *Bad Girls* (1994), *Dead Man* (1995), *The Quick and the Dead* (1995), *The Missing* (2003), *Open Range* (2003), and *Deadwood* (2004 and continuing). These films, even when they failed at the box office, attempted to redefine the genre by aiming at a new audience from different genders, races, age groups, and social backgrounds. All of them, in one way or another, explore the relation between wealth and violence; and some of them focus on class conflict, even if the conflict is between women demanding autonomy and economic justice and a masculinist society that denies it to them. Perhaps none of them explores the origin of wealth with more critical vision than the recent *Deadwood*. This HBO series offers one of the more original reinventions not because it tells the truth about the West, as so many "revisionist" Westerns have claimed to do in the past, but because it deconstructs the system of Western characters by lending more complexity to the "bad guys" like Al Swearengen (Ian McShane) than to the "good" Shane-like figure of Seth Bullock (Timothy Olyphant). It reveals the interimplications of good and evil that lie at the foundation of capitalist culture, while it makes a parody of Adam Smith's famous theory of the "invisible hand" through which the pursuit of self-interest by the multitude of individuals is supposed to add up to the general good. Though this series may be attempting to do with Western language what Peckinpah did with Western violence, its most critical vision amounts to a vivisection of the origin of capital and the damaging effect the war for wealth has on any kind of human relationship.

To me, one of the most interesting revivals of the Western is not a Western: Quentin Tarantino's fourth film, *Kill Bill*. This movie reshuffles the elements of the classical Hollywood Western, along with elements of other genres of mass culture, in complicated ways that suggest an allegory appropriate to the age of globalization. As I have argued of the Western tradition that finds its archetypal form in the movie *Shane*, class struggle in the Hollywood Western is primarily a struggle over the identification of the social individual with either the power of the capitalist class or the struggles of the multitude. The social individual has the power of self-valorization, and this symbolically takes the form of a gun in most Westerns. In *Kill Bill*, the symbol of this power is less the gun than the samurai sword; and the maker of those swords, Hattori Hanzo (Sonny Chiba), is himself a Shane figure, a man who has perfected his own creative autonomy in the production of a weapon but has withdrawn from the practical use of weapons to the purely aesthetic contemplation of his own work. Apparently, Hanzo once taught Bill (David Carradine) how to use the samurai sword; but when Bill betrayed his learning by selling his skill to the highest bidder, Hanzo swore never to make another such weapon. Like Shane, however, he breaks his own vow in agreeing to make a weapon for the Bride (Uma Thurman). When she meets Hanzo in his cheap sushi bar in Okinawa, she meets the antithesis of Bill. First, by comparison with Bill, Hanzo is a relatively poor man, almost a clownish figure, who keeps his power a secret. He represents the singularity of the multitude, the creative autonomy of the individual that must be realized as the condition of collective action that could bring about social change. He becomes the conscience of the Bride.

At the moment when Bill shoots the Bride, a scene which opens both volumes of the film, he informs her that there is nothing sadistic about this act, though there may be toward the other nine people that he and his Deadly Viper Assassination Squad have killed. On the contrary, he says, "At this moment, this is me at my most masochistic." Allegorically, Bill kills the Bride as a reflection of himself he can no longer own; and the Bride sets out to kill Bill as the embodiment of the social identity from which she has tried unsuccessfully to separate by running away to El Paso, Texas, to start a family. At the beginning of Volume 2, Tarantino re-creates the massacre at the Two Pines Wedding Chapel that the Bride is out to revenge. Most of the reviewers have noted the direct allusions to John Ford's *The Searchers* in this sequence, but in fact Tarantino has fused together elements of *Shane* and Ford's film with the glue of spaghetti-Western techniques of distantiation. As the Bride approaches the door of the chapel to take a break from the wedding rehearsal, she hears the sound of a flute playing and the expression on her face shows that she recognizes the player. From her viewpoint, the world outside the chapel is a desert like the one from which Ethan Edwards emerges at the beginning of *The Searchers*; but the Bride herself occupies the interior world of domestic family relations, like Martha Edwards in the first shot from Ford's film (Ills. 31–32). Just as Ethan unconsciously desires the destruction of his brother's family so that he can expropriate his wealth and his wife, Bill very consciously kills the family and friends of the Bride, in order to expropriate her future.

Bill is the patriarchal subject and the subject of capital. As the former, he is literally presented to the wedding party as the Bride's father, which technically he is not, though he is the father of her child; but he shoots the Bride and kills her friends in order to take possession of the child, which he claims as property. As an iconic

ILLUSTRATION 31 Martha Edwards on the eve of a massacre. *The Searchers* (1952). Warner Bros. *Producer:* Merian C. Cooper. *Director:* John Ford

ILLUSTRATION 32 The Bride on the threshold of another massacre. *Kill Bill*, Vol. 2 (2004). Miramax Films. *Producer:* Lawrence Bender. *Director:* Quentin Tarantino

Hollywood actor who started his career by playing Shane in a short-lived television series in the mid-sixties and then redefined that role for his successful *Kung Fu* series in the seventies, Carradine inverts his iconic significance in *Kill Bill* by becoming an Ethan Edwards figure, the man who cannot enter the interior space of the family or the community without bringing death and destruction with him. Yet this reading oversimplifies the actual structure of the relationship between Beatrix Kiddo, the Bride's real name, and Bill. For her pursuit of Bill, her "roaring rampage of revenge," as she puts it, makes her as dark a figure as Bill himself, a feminine Ethan who in the end discovers the child she thought she had lost. Ultimately, this revenge is a revolt of the self against the various possibilities of what it must be in a world where the privileged form of the subject is Bill. To kill Bill is to transform that subject into something else, but this process is not without its own contradictions. One of these contradictions lies in the ethnocentrism of the story, which is particularly emphatic in Volume 1.

The first victim of the "white" Bride's roaring rampage, in terms of the film's presentation rather than its narrative, is a black woman. The fight with Vernita Green, aka "Copperhead" (Vivica A. Fox), makes perfectly visible the Bride's ultimate refusal of the middle-class nuclear family, which is signified by the house in which Vernita now plays the role of Mrs. Jeanne Bell, the wife of Dr. Lawrence Bell. The green house looks like something out of a fairy tale; and though green isn't exactly the color of ginger bread, this sweet façade harbors something corrupt, a social identity that will consume anything innocent that enters its space – in this case, Vernita's own child. In the last act of Volume 2, Bill asks Beatrix if she really thought that her marriage to Tommy Plimpton would have worked, and she admits that it wouldn't have, but she would have had her child. But already when she encounters Vernita, the Bride deconstructs the fantasy of the family as a nonviolent utopia. Precisely to the extent that Vernita's new lifestyle has disavowed her past and her participation in the murder of the Bride's people, she has created the conditions of a return of the repressed – the eruption of violence that her own child will inadvertently witness, despite the Bride's offer to meet Vernita away from the house. One can only wonder what kind of violence may be visited on Beatrix when Vernita's child grows up. This sequence and other images of the corruption of children in this film subvert the idealization of the child as a figure of innocence in a movie like *Shane*, though there is the insistence on a form of innocence that survives beneath the corruption.

Even before the fight with Vernita Green, however, the Bride has already annihilated O-Ren Ishii, aka "Cottonmouth" (Lucy Liu), and her Tokyo gang. Interestingly, O-Ren is the only character whose history we learn, and one cannot help but assume that she embodies yet another facet of the Bride's desire and that her history also reflects the things we never learn about the Bride. She is half-Japanese and half-Chinese-American and was born on an American base in Tokyo. Through the use of Japanese *anime* style, Tarantino re-creates the murder of her parents by a yakuza boss; and in this sequence, the Spaghetti-Western-style music echoes the massacre of the McBain family at the beginning of *Once Upon a Time in the West*. After this event, the child O-Ren goes on her own rampage of revenge, killing the pedophiliac yakuza boss who murdered her family, an event which effectively turns her into a monster, another corrupted child. The racial ambiguity of the figures in this sequence, which is a feature of Japanese anime, underscores the link between the violence that erupts within and destroys the family institution across different cultures and the subject of capital, whose archetype is Bill. This form of subjectivity, which virtually colonizes O-Ren and all of Bill's gang, including the Bride, is what Hardt and Negri might call the subject of empire, the new order of global capital. In some sense, the relationship between the United States and Japan is replicated in the relationship between Bill and O-Ren, while the latter's racial hybridity foregrounds the hybrid subjectivity of empire, even as it suggests that the United States is the archetype of that subject-form.

The Bride virtually destroys O-Ren's posse, the Crazy 88, in a show of force as unreal as it is brutal; and though one can criticize the problematic social effects of such film violence, it nonetheless operates as a hyperbolic representation of the force it takes to withdraw from identification with a dominant social archetype. If O-Ren embodies the desire for power and domination, and if Vernita embodies the flipside of that in the desire for family and convention, Michael Madsen's Budd, Bill's brother, represents something quite different. Given Budd's cruel and sexist behavior toward the Bride, one should keep in mind something that Tarantino mentions on the DVD release of Volume 2 – namely, that in some ways Budd is the most sympathetic member of the Deadly Vipers, the only one of them to express regret over having murdered the Bride's people. He says that she deserves her revenge and the members of the assassination squad deserve to die. Furthermore, Budd is the only character besides the Bride who seems to have broken with Bill. The sequence at the strip club where Budd works as a bouncer and is ordered by a stripper to clean a flooded toilet drives home the fact that Budd has returned to something resembling the working class. Though he secretly keeps his Hanzo sword while letting everyone think he has hocked it, he nonetheless is willing to accept his subaltern status rather than work for Bill.

The landscape surrounding Budd's trailer evokes Leone's landscapes, as does the Bride's emergence out of the desert, which recalls the Henry Fonda flashbacks in *Once Upon a Time in the West*. Budd is probably a direct reference to Eli Wallach's Tuco in *The Good, the Bad and the Ugly*, a man fully capable of sadistic behavior but who nonetheless represents a form of class subjectivity through his resentment. As Jean-Paul Sartre noted, "to resent is already to go beyond, to move toward the possibility of an objective transformation" (1968: 97). Budd, like Tuco, wants wealth, but he wants it on his own terms, not Bill's. The Man himself would correspond with Clint Eastwood's Blondie, the Good or hegemonic subject; but to the extent that the blond Bride is herself a reflection of that dominant subject, Tarantino inverts the ending of Leone's Western in which the Good puts a noose around the Ugly's neck but leaves him a chance to survive. In this case, the Ugly, Budd, buries the Good alive and takes her wealth, which is her sword. Still, in several Leone-esque close-ups, Budd's viewpoint seems more ambivalent than this scenario suggests. Ironically, his sadism in shooting the Bride in the chest using a shotgun loaded with rock salt and then burying her alive along with a flashlight is probably what enables her to survive, since he could have shot her dead in the first place. In turn, he is killed by Elle Driver (Darryl Hannah), who puts a Black Mamba snake in the suitcase full of money with which she is supposed to buy the Bride's Hanzo sword. Since Black Mamba is the codename of the Bride, you could argue that Elle, a generic "she," acts in her place.

The Bride's blinding of Elle is the final deconstruction of her own feminine identity before she meets Bill. As the woman who supposedly has taken the Bride's place with Bill, Elle combines a girlish silliness, which causes her to giggle whenever Bill expresses affection for her, with the qualities of a femme fatale. She is also the Cyclops of this Odyssey, having already lost one eye for insulting Pai Mei, the Bride's Kung Fu teacher. In return for this act, she poisoned the man's food, which, from the Bride's viewpoint, compounds Elle's blindness with stupidity for not recognizing someone who could have taught her a life-transforming art. Since Elle's one-eyed viewpoint is egocentric and monological, she naively instructs the Bride on how to defeat her, and the Bride simply plucks out the other eye. Implicitly, through this act, the Bride is destroying her own blindness and the "drive" to be a "girl" for Bill.

The Bride's story is about an awakening, a coming back from the dead, which she does twice. First, in Volume 1, she awakens from the coma into which Bill's bullet has sent her; and then, after she has been buried alive by Budd in Volume 2, she breaks out of the coffin and digs her way out of the earth, using the Kung Fu techniques learned from Pai Mei. After the Bride's second rebirth, she doesn't actually kill anyone except for Bill, and even that seems more symbolic than real. In a Mexican heart of darkness, she finally

ILLUSTRATION 33 Child's play and the violence of the nuclear family. *Kill Bill*, Vol. 2 (2004). Miramax Films. *Producer:* Lawrence Bender. *Director:* Quentin Tarantino

confronts Bill with B.B., the child of Bill and Beatrix, playing with toy guns (Ill. 33). This image reduces the whole film to the status of a horrifying child's game that has been developed within the nurturing space of the family. Everything that Bill stands for finds its logical origin and natural justification in that institution. His accumulation of wealth through force, his policing of the social relations of capital through his agents like O-Ren and her yakuza lords, his alienation from his working-class brother, his seduction of Elle, Vernita, Beatrix, and all the other women in his life, for which he has earned the codename "Snake Charmer," and, most of all, his ownership of a woman's body asserted through the expropriation of her child – these acts enable Bill, like Ethan Edwards, to define the family as the natural form and justification of private property and as the foundation of the class system as a naturalized social hierarchy, which is the real meaning of Bill's monologue on superheroes. Yet if The Man who was the ultimate goal of The Bride's roaring rampage was evil, the figure we find in this location turns out to be something more contradictory. When Beatrix finally kills Bill, it's more like an act of love than an act of violence. Though Bill calls the Five-Point-Palm-Exploding-Heart Technique the deadliest blow in all of martial arts, it looks to the naked eye like the act of stealing someone's heart.

Once his heart has been taken, Bill's Ethan Edwards identity gives ground to the Shane persona he really is and that David Carradine symbolizes; and his expression before he turns away to die is almost beatific. Beatrix, by contrast, is virtually in mourning for the social identity she has given up, though later in a motel room with B.B., this mourning is transformed into a more ambivalent *jouissance*, a mixture of pleasure and pain. The truth is that Shane must die so that Mommy, the Bride's last and final identity, can be born. This Mommy, however, is not a real resolution but the fantasy of resolution. Neither Beatrix nor B.B. can be imagined or understood without Bill, and their motel stop is perhaps only the first of a series of false resolutions that leave the family behind but find nothing that will take its place. The motel is where you go to wait for the possibility of return.

Shane never comes back because he must die in order to transform the thing he stands for – the subject under capital, whether it identifies with or against that social force. Yet Shane always comes back in new forms because he represents the possibility of self-transformation under capital, the ongoing struggle for autonomy, freedom, and the social wealth that makes those conditions possible. Shane has had many names and no name in any number of films. But perhaps his most promising name, the one that captures the essence of a future that escapes our social imagination, is Mommy. The future of the Western in the twenty-first century may lie in the way it continues to feed the productions of mass culture with desires that we struggle to recognize and refuse to surrender.

REFERENCES

Abbott, E. C. "Teddy Blue," and Helena Huntington Smith. 1991. *We Pointed Them North: Recollections of a Cowpuncher*, ed. Ron Tyler. Chicago: Lakeside Press. [First published in 1939.]

Adorno, Theodor W. 1992. *Negative Dialectics*, trans. E. B. Ashton. New York: Continuum.

——. 1997. *Aesthetic Theory*, ed. Gretel Adorno and Rolf Tiedemann, trans. Robert Hullot-Kentor. Minneapolis: University of Minnesota Press.

Allen, Ruth. 1941. "A Cowboy Strike, 1883." In *Chapters in the History of Organized Labor in Texas*. Austin: University of Texas Press, pp. 33–41.

——. 1942. *The Great Southwest Strike*. Austin: University of Texas Press.

Arendt, Hannah. 1973. *The Origins of Totalitarianism*, new edn., with added prefaces. New York: Harcourt Brace Jovanovich.

Arthur, Paul. 2003. "How the West Was Spun: *McCabe and Mrs. Miller* and Genre Revisionism." *Cinéaste* 28.3: 18–20.

Bach, Steven. 1985. *Final Cut: Dreams and Disaster in the Making of "Heaven's Gate."* New York: William Morrow.

Badiou, Alain. 2001. *Ethics: An Essay on the Understanding of Evil*. London and New York: Verso.

Baughman, James L. 2000. "'That'll Be the Day': Response to Freedman." *American Literary History* 12.3: 605–9.

Bazin, André. 1971. "The Evolution of the Western." In *What Is Cinema?*, vol. 2, trans. Hugh Gray. Berkeley: University of California Press, pp. 149–57. [First published in 1955.]

Beard, William. 2000. *Persistence of Double Vision: Essays on Clint Eastwood.* Edmonton: University of Alberta Press.

Benjamin, Walter. 1969. *Illuminations*, trans. Harry Zohn. New York: Schocken Books.

——. 1999. *The Arcades Project*, trans. Howard Eiland and Kevin McLaughlin. Cambridge, MA: Belknap Press of Harvard University Press.

Benjamin-Labarthe, Élyette. 1998. "L'espace au cinéma: *La Porte du Paradis* de Michael Cimino." *Cycnos* 15.1: 127–50.

Biskind, Peter. 1983. *Seeing Is Believing: How Hollywood Taught Us to Stop Worrying and Love the Fifties.* New York: Pantheon Books.

Bliss, Michael. 1985. *Martin Scorsese and Michael Cimino.* Metuchen, NJ: Scarecrow Press.

——. 1993. *Justified Lives: Morality and Narrative in the Films of Sam Peckinpah.* Carbondale and Edwardsville: Southern Illinois University Press.

——. 1999. "'Back Off to What?' Enclosure, Violence, and Capitalism in Sam Peckinpah's *The Wild Bunch*." In Prince 1999b: 105–29.

Bliss, Michael, ed. 1994. *Doing It Right: The Best Criticism on Sam Peckinpah's "The Wild Bunch."* Carbondale and Edwardsville: Southern Illinois University Press.

Bogdanovich, Peter. 1978. *John Ford*, rev. edn. Berkeley: University of California Press.

Brecht, Bertolt. 1978. *Brecht on Theatre*, ed. and trans. John Willet. New York: Hill & Wang.

Brooks, James F. 2004. "'That Don't Make you Kin!' Borderlands History and Culture in *The Searchers*." In Eckstein and Lehman 2004: 265–87.

Brown, Jeffrey A. 1995. "'Putting on the Ritz': Masculinity and the Young Gary Cooper." *Screen* 36.3: 193–213.

Brown, Richard Maxwell. 1991. *No Duty to Retreat: Violence and Values in American History.* Norman: University of Oklahoma Press.

Buhle, Paul, and Dave Wagner. 2002. *Radical Hollywood: The Untold Story Behind America's Favorite Movies.* New York: The New Press.

Burgoyne, Robert. 1997. *Film Nation: Hollywood Looks at U.S. History.* Minneapolis: University of Minnesota Press.

Buscombe, Edward. 1992. *Stagecoach.* London: BFI.

——. 1993. "*The Magnificent Seven*." In *Mediating Two Worlds: Cinematic Encounters in the Americas*, ed. John King, Ana M. López, and Manuel Alvarado. London: BFI, pp. 15–24.

——. 2000. *The Searchers*. London: BFI.

Buscombe, Edward, ed. 1988. *The BFI Companion to the Western*. London: André Deutsch/BFI.

Buscombe, Edward, and Roberta E. Pearson, eds. 1998. *Back in the Saddle Again: New Essays on the Western*. London: BFI.

Butler, Judith. 1991. "Imitation and Gender Subordination." In *Inside/Out: Lesbian Theories, Gay Theories*, ed. Diana Fuss. New York and London: Routledge, pp. 13–31.

Cameron, Ian, and Douglas Pye, eds. 1995. *The Book of Westerns*. New York: Continuum.

Canton, Frank. 1966. *Frontier Trails*, ed. Edward Everett Dale. Norman: University of Oklahoma Press.

Carroll, Noël. 1998. "The Professional Western: South of the Border." In Buscombe and Pearson 1998: 40–62.

Cawelti, John G. 1976. *Adventure, Mystery and Romance: Formula Stories as Art and Popular Culture*. Chicago: University of Chicago Press.

——. 1999. *The Six-Gun Mystique Sequel*. Bowling Green, OH: Bowling Green State University Popular Press.

Colonnese, Tom Grayson. 2004. "Native American Reactions to *The Searchers*." In Eckstein and Lehman 2004: 335–42.

Corkin, Stanley. 2004. *Cowboys as Cold Warriors: The Western and U.S. History*. Philadelphia: Temple University Press.

Countryman, Edward. 1996. *Americans: A Collision of Histories*. New York: Hill & Wang.

Countryman, Edward, and Evonne von Heussen-Countryman. 1999. *Shane*. London: BFI.

Coyne, Michael. 1997. *The Crowded Prairie: American National Identity in the Hollywood Western*. London and New York: I. B. Tauris.

Cumbow, Robert C. 1987. *Once Upon a Time: The Films of Sergio Leone*. Metuchen, NJ and London: Scarecrow Press.

DeArment, Robert K. 1996. *Alias Frank Canton*. Norman: University of Oklahoma Press.

Denning, Michael. 1987. *Mechanic Accents: Dime Novels and Working-Class Culture in America*. London: Verso.

——. 1998. *The Cultural Front: The Laboring of American Culture in the Twentieth Century*. London and New York: Verso.

Dixon, Wheeler Winston. 1999. "Re-Visioning the Western: Code, Myth, and Genre in Peckinpah's *The Wild Bunch*." In Prince 1999b: 155–74.

Drago, Harry Sinclair. 1970. *The Great Range Wars: Violence on the Grasslands*. New York: Dodd, Mead & Co.

Drummond, Phillip. 1997. *High Noon*. London: BFI.

Durgnat, Raymond, and Scott Simmon. 1998. "Six Creeds That Won the West." In Kitses and Rickman 1998: 69–83.

Eckstein, Arthur M. 1998. "Darkening Ethan: John Ford's *The Searchers* (1956) from Novel to Screenplay to Screen." *Cinema Journal* 38.1: 3–24.

——. 2004. "Introduction." In Eckstein and Lehman 2004: 1–45.

Eckstein, Arthur M., and Peter Lehman, eds. 2004. *"The Searchers": Essays and Reflections on John Ford's Classic Western.* Detroit: Wayne State University Press.

Etulain, Richard W. 2001. "Introduction" and "Broncho Billy, William S. Hart, and Tom Mix: The Rise of the Hollywood Western." In *The Hollywood West: Lives of Film Legends Who Shaped It,* ed. Richard W. Etulain and Glenda Riley. Golden, CO: Fulcrum Publishing, pp. viii–xiii, 1–19.

Evans, Martha Noel. 1991. *Fits and Starts: A Genealogy of Hysteria in Modern France.* Ithaca and London: Cornell University Press.

Felson, Richard. 2000. "Mass Media Effects on Violent Behavior." In *Screening Violence,* ed. Stephen Prince. New Brunswick, New Jersey: Rutgers University Press, pp. 237–66.

Fine, Marshall. 1991. *Bloody Sam: The Life and Films of Sam Peckinpah.* New York: Donald I. Fine.

Fink, Leon. 1983. *Workingmen's Democracy: The Knights of Labor and American Politics.* Urbana: University of Illinois Press.

——. 1994. *In Search of the Working Class: Essays in American Labor History and Political Culture.* Urbana and Chicago: University of Illinois Press.

Flagg, Oscar H. 1969. *A Review of the Cattle Business in Johnson County, Wyoming Since 1892 and the Causes That Led to the Recent Invasion.* Mass Violence in America. New York: Arno Press and *The New York Times.* [First published in 1892.]

Ford, John. 2001. *Interviews,* ed. Gerald Peary, with Jenny Lefcourt. Jackson: University Press of Mississippi.

Foster, Gwendolyn. 1999. "The Women in *High Noon*: A Metanarrative of Difference." In Nolletti 1999: 93–102.

Frayling, Christopher. 1981. *Spaghetti Westerns: Cowboys and Europeans from Karl May to Sergio Leone.* London: Routledge & Kegan Paul.

——. 2000. *Sergio Leone: Something to Do with Death.* London and New York: Faber & Faber.

Freedman, Jonathan. 2000. "The Affect of the Market: Economic and Racial Exchange in *The Searchers.*" *American Literary History* 12.3: 585–99.

French, Philip. 1977. *Western: Aspects of a Movie Genre,* rev. edn. New York: Oxford University Press.

Freud, Sigmund. 1963. *Dora: An Analysis of a Case of Hysteria*. New York: Collier Books.

——. 1964. *Leonardo da Vinci and a Memory of His Childhood*, trans. Alan Tyson. New York: Norton.

Gallagher, Tag. 1986. *John Ford: The Man and His Films*. Berkeley: University of California Press.

Gibbons, Luke. 1996. "Synge, Country and Western: The Myth of the West in Irish and American Culture." In *Transformations in Irish Culture*. Notre Dame, IN: University of Notre Dame Press, pp. 23–34.

Graham, Allison. 1983. "The Final Go-Around: Peckinpah's Wild Bunch at the End of the Frontier." *Mosaic* 16.1–2: 55–70.

Graulich, Melody, and Stephen Tatum, eds. 2003. *Reading "The Virginian" in the New West*. Lincoln and London: University of Nebraska Press.

Grimsted, David. 2004. "Re-searching." In Eckstein and Lehman 2004: 289–334.

Grist, Leighton. 1995. "*Unforgiven*." In Cameron and Pye 1995: 294–301.

Hardt, Michael, and Antonio Negri. 2000. *Empire*. Cambridge, MA: Harvard University Press.

——. 2004. *Multitude: War and Democracy in the Age of Empire*. New York: Penguin.

Hawks, Howard. 1982. *Hawks on Hawks*, ed. Joseph McBride. Berkeley: University of California Press.

Heath, Stephen. 1981. *Questions of Cinema*. Bloomington: Indiana University Press.

Henderson, Brian. 2004. "*The Searchers*: An American Dilemma." In Eckstein and Lehman 2004: 47–73.

Hill, Sarah. 1998. "Sergio Leone and the Myth of the American West: *Once Upon a Time in the West*." *Romance Languages Annual* 9: 202–10.

Hine, Robert V., and John Mack Faragher. 2000. *The American West: A New Interpretive History*. New Haven and London: Yale University Press.

Hobsbawm, Eric. 2000. *Bandits*. New York: The New Press.

Horne, Gerald. 2001. *Class Struggle in Hollywood 1930–1950: Moguls, Mobsters, Stars, Reds, and Trade Unionists*. Austin: University of Texas Press.

Hufsmith, George W. 1993. *The Wyoming Lynching of Cattle Kate, 1889*. Glendo, WY: High Plains Press.

Hutson, Richard. 2003. "Early Film Versions of *The Virginian*." In Graulich and Tatum 2003: 120–47.

——. 2004. "Sermons in Stone: Monument Valley in *The Searchers*." In Eckstein and Lehman 2004: 93–108.

Jefferson, Thomas. 1984. *Writings*. The Library of America. New York: Viking.

Kaminsky, Stuart M. 1980. *Coop: The Life and Legend of Gary Cooper*. New York: St. Martin's Press.

Kermode, Frank. 2000. *The Sense of an Ending: Studies in the Theory of Fiction*, with a New Epilogue. Oxford: Oxford University Press.

Keyssar, Helene. 1991. *Robert Altman's America*. New York and Oxford: Oxford University Press.

Kitses, Jim. 1970. *Horizons West: Anthony Mann, Budd Boetticher, Sam Peckinpah: Studies of Authorship within the Western*. Bloomington and London: Indiana University Press.

Kitses, Jim, and Gregg Rickman, eds. 1998. *The Western Reader*. New York: Limelight Editions.

Kittrell, William H. 1954. "Foreword." In *The Banditti of the Plains, or The Cattlemen's Invasion of Wyoming in 1892 (The Crowning Infamy of the Ages)*, by A. S. Mercer. Norman: University of Oklahoma Press, pp. xiii–l.

Kolker, Robert. 2000. *A Cinema of Loneliness: Penn, Stone, Kubrick, Scorsese, Spielberg, Altman*, 3rd edn. Oxford: Oxford University Press.

Krapp, Peter. 2002. "Unforgiven: *Fausse Reconnaissance*." *South Atlantic Quarterly* 101.3: 589–607.

Kreidl, John Francis. 1977. *Nicholas Ray*. Boston: Twayne.

Kuenz, Jane. 2001. "The Cowboy Businessman and 'The Course of Empire': Owen Wister's *The Virginian*." *Cultural Critique* 48.1: 98–128.

Lacan, Jacques. 1992. *The Ethics of Psychoanalysis 1959–1960*, book 7 of *The Seminar*, ed. Jacques-Alain Miller, trans. Dennis Porter. New York: W. W. Norton.

Lamont, Victoria. 2003. "History, Gender, and the Origins of the 'Classic' Western." In Graulich and Tatum 2003: 148–74.

Landy, Marcia. 1996. "'Which Way Is America?': Americanism and the Italian Western." *Boundary 2* 23.1: 35–59.

Lehman, Peter. 1981. "Looking at Look's Missing Reverse Shot: Psychoanalysis and Style in John Ford's *The Searchers*." *Wide Angle* 4.4: 65–70.

——. 1990. "Texas 1868/America 1956: *The Searchers*." In *Close Viewing: An Anthology of New Film Criticism*, ed. Peter Lehman. Tallahassee: Florida State University Press, pp. 387–414.

——. 2004. "'You Couldn't Hit It on the Nose': The Limits of Knowledge in and of *The Searchers*." In Eckstein and Lehman 2004: 239–63.

Lenihan, John H. 1985. *Showdown: Confronting Modern America in the Western Film*. Urbana and Chicago: University of Illinois Press.

Leyda, Julia. 2002. "Black-Audience Westerns and the Politics of Cultural Identification in the 1930s." *Cinema Journal* 42.1: 40–70.

Liandrat-Guigues, Suzanne. 2000. *Red River*. London: BFI.

Limerick, Patricia Nelson. 1987. *The Legacy of Conquest: The Unbroken Past of the American West*. New York: Norton.

Lindroth, James. 1989. "From Natty to Cymbeline: Literary Figures and Allusions in Cimino's *Heaven's Gate*." *Literature/Film Quarterly* 17.4: 224–30.

Manso, Peter. 1994. *Brando: The Biography*. New York: Hyperion.

Marx, Karl. 1964. *Early Writings*, trans. T. B. Bottomore. New York: McGraw Hill.

——. 1973. *Grundrisse: Foundations of the Critique of Political Economy*, trans. Martin Nicolaus. New York: Vintage.

——. 1977. *Capital: A Critique of Political Economy*, vol. 1, trans. Ben Fowkes. New York: Vintage.

Marx, Karl, and Frederick Engels. 1947. *The German Ideology, Parts I & III*. New York: International Publishers.

——. 1968. *Selected Works*. New York: International Publishers.

McBride, Joseph. 2001. *Search for John Ford: A Life*. New York: St. Martin's Press.

McBride, Joseph, and Michael Wilmington. 1975. *John Ford*. New York: Da Capo Press.

McCarthy, Todd. 1997. *Howard Hawks: The Grey Fox of Hollywood*. New York: Grove Press.

McCormick, Thomas J. 1995. *America's Half-Century: United States Foreign Policy in the Cold War and After*, 2nd edn. Baltimore: Johns Hopkins University Press.

McElrath, Frances. 2002. *The Rustler: A Tale of Love and War in Wyoming*, intro. Victoria Lamont. Lincoln and London: University of Nebraska Press.

McGee, Patrick. 1999. "Terrible Beauties: Messianic Time and the Image of Social Redemption in James Cameron's *Titanic*." *Postmodern Culture* 10.1: 45 paras.

McGilligan, Patrick. 1989. *Robert Altman: Jumping Off the Cliff*. New York: St. Martin's Press.

McGilligan, Patrick, and Paul Buhle. 1997. *Tender Comrades: A Backstory of the Hollywood Blacklist*. New York: St. Martin's Press.

McKinney, Doug. 1979. *Sam Peckinpah*. Boston: Twayne.

McKinney, Devin. 1999. "*The Wild Bunch*: Innovation and Retreat." In Prince 1999b: 175–99.

Meschter, Daniel Y. 1996. *Sweetwater Sunset: A History of the Lynching of James Averell and Ella Watson near Independence Rock, Wyoming, on July 20, 1889*. Wenatchee, WA: D. Y. Meschter.

Mitchell, Lee Clark. 1996. *Westerns: Making the Man in Fiction and Film*. Chicago and London: University of Chicago Press.

Mulvey, Laura. 1989. *Visual and Other Pleasures*. Bloomington: Indiana University Press.

Muscio, Giuliana. 1997. *Hollywood's New Deal*. Philadelphia: Temple University Press.

Navasky, Victor S. 1991. *Naming Names*, rev. edn. New York: Penguin.

Neale, Steve. 2000. *Genre and Hollywood*. London and New York: Routledge.

Negri, Antonio. 1984. *Marx Beyond Marx: Lessons on the "Grundrisse"*, trans. Harry Cleaver, Michael Ryan and Maurizio Viano, ed. Jim Fleming. South Hadley, MA: Bergin & Garvey.

Negri, Antonio, and Danilo Zolo. 2003. "Empire and the Multitude: A Dialogue on the New Order of Globalization." *Radical Philosophy* 120: 23–37.

Nichols, Mary P. 1998. "Law and the American Western: *High Noon*." *Legal Studies Forum* 22.4: 591–605.

Nobles, Gregory H. 1997. *American Frontiers: Cultural Encounters and Continental Conquest*. New York: Hill & Wang.

Nolletti, Arthur, ed. 1999. *The Films of Fred Zinnemann: Critical Perspectives*. Albany: State University of New York Press.

Norwood, Stephen. 1996. "Ford's Brass Knuckles: Harry Bennett, the Cult of Muscularity and Anti-Labor Terror, 1920–1945." *Labor History* 37.3: 365–91.

Osgood, Ernest Staples. 1957. *The Day of the Cattleman*. Chicago and London: University of Chicago Press. [First published in 1929.]

Oswalt, Conrad E., Jr. 1995. "Hollywood and Armageddon: Apocalyptic Themes in Recent Cinematic Presentation." In *Screening the Sacred: Religion, Myth, and Ideology in Popular American Film*, ed. Joel W. Martin and Conrad E. Oswalt, Jr. Boulder, CO: Westview Press, pp. 55–63.

Perkins, V. F. 1995. "*Johnny Guitar*." In Cameron and Pye 1995: 221–8.

Peterson, Jennifer. 1998. "The Competing Tunes of *Johnny Guitar*: Liberalism, Sexuality, Masquerade." In Kitses and Rickman 1998: 321–39.

Plecki, Gerard. 1985. *Robert Altman*. Boston: Twayne.

Prats, Armando José. 2002. *Invisible Natives: Myth and Identity in the American Western*. Ithaca and London: Cornell University Press.

Prince, Stephen. 1998. *Savage Cinema: Sam Peckinpah and the Rise of Ultraviolent Movies*. Austin: University of Texas Press.

———. 1999a. "Historical Perspective and the Realist Aesthetic in *High Noon*." In Nolletti 1999: 79–92.

Prince, Stephen, ed. 1999b. *Sam Peckinpah's "The Wild Bunch."* Cambridge: Cambridge University Press.

Pye, Douglas. 1995a. "The Collapse of Fantasy: Masculinity in the Westerns of Anthony Mann." In Cameron and Pye 1995: 167–73.

——. 1995b. "Double Vision: Miscegenation and Point of View in *The Searchers*." In Cameron and Pye 1995: 229–35.

——. 1995c. "Genre and History: *Fort Apache* and *The Man Who Shot Liberty Valance*." In Cameron and Pye 1995: 111–22.

Rapf, Joanna E. 1990. "Myth, Ideology, and Feminism in *High Noon*." *Journal of Popular Culture* 23.4: 75–80.

Ray, Robert B. 1985. *A Certain Tendency of the Hollywood Cinema, 1930–1980*. Princeton, NJ: Princeton University Press.

Robertson, Pamela. 1996. "Camping under Western Stars: Joan Crawford in *Johnny Guitar*." In *Guilty Pleasures: Feminist Camp from Mae West to Madonna*. Durham, NC and London: Duke University Press, pp. 85–114.

Rogin, Michael. 1987. *Ronald Reagan, The Movie and Other Episodes in Political Demonology*. Berkeley: University of California Press.

——. 1996. *Blackface, White Noise: Jewish Immigrants in the Hollywood Melting Pot*. Berkeley: University of California Press.

Rosenzweig, Roy. 1983. *Eight Hours for What We Will: Workers and Leisure in an Industrial City, 1870–1920*. Cambridge: Cambridge University Press.

Ross, Steven J. 1998. *Working-Class Hollywood: Silent Film and the Shaping of Class in America*. Princeton, NJ: Princeton University Press.

Sarris, Andrew. 1975. *The John Ford Movie Mystery*. Bloomington: Indiana University Press.

Sartre, Jean-Paul. 1968. *Search for a Method*, trans. Hazel E. Barnes. New York: Vintage Books.

Schaefer, Jack. 1975. *Shane*. New York: Bantam Books. [First published in 1949.]

Schatz, Thomas. 1981. *Hollywood Genres: Formulas, Filmmaking and the Studio System*. New York: Random House.

Schrader, Paul. 1994. "Sam Peckinpah Going to Mexico." In Bliss 1994: 17–30.

Self, Robert T. 2002. *Robert Altman's Subliminal Reality*. Minneapolis: University of Minnesota Press.

Seydor, Paul. 1999. *Peckinpah: The Western Films – A Reconsideration*. Urbana and Chicago: University of Illinois Press.

Sharrett, Christopher. 1999. "Peckinpah the Radical: The Politics of *The Wild Bunch*." In Prince 1999b: 79–104.

Shulman, Robert. 1998. "Introduction." In Wister 1998: vii–xxix.

Silverman, Kaja. 1983. *The Subject of Semiotics*. New York: Oxford University Press.

——. 1992. *Male Subjectivity at the Margins*. New York: Routledge.

Simmon, Scott. 2003. *The Invention of the Western Film: A Cultural History of the Genre's First Half-Century*. Cambridge: Cambridge University Press.

Simons, John L. 1994. "The Tragedy of Love in *The Wild Bunch*." In Bliss 1994: 90–106.

Skerry, Philip K. 1996. "*Dances with Wolves* and *Unforgiven*: Apocalyptic, Postrevisionist Westerns." In *Beyond the Stars 5: Themes and Ideologies in American Popular Film*, ed. Paul Loukides and Linda K. Fuller. Bowling Green, OH: Bowling Green State University Popular Press, pp. 281–91.

Sklar, Robert. 1996. "Empire to the West: *Red River*." In *Howard Hawks: American Artist*, ed. Jim Hillier and Peter Wollen. London: BFI, pp. 152–62. [First published in 1978.]

Slotkin, Richard. 1973. *Regeneration Through Violence: The Mythology of the American Frontier, 1600–1860*. Middletown, CT: Wesleyan University Press.

———. 1985. *The Fatal Environment: The Myth of the Frontier in the Age of Industrialization, 1800–1890*. New York: Atheneum.

———. 1992. *Gunfighter Nation: The Myth of the Frontier in Twentieth-Century America*. New York: Atheneum.

Smith, Andrew Brodie. 2003. *Shooting Cowboys and Indians: Silent Western Films, American Culture, and the Birth of Hollywood*. Boulder: University Press of Colorado.

Smith, Carlton. 2000. *Coyote Kills John Wayne: Postmodernism and Contemporary Fictions of the Transcultural Frontier*. Hanover and London: Dartmouth College and University Press of New England.

Smith, Helena Huntington. 1966. *The War on Powder River: The History of an Insurrection*. Lincoln and London: University of Nebraska Press.

Smith, Henry Nash. 1970. *Virgin Land: The American West as Symbol and Myth*. Cambridge, MA: Harvard University Press. [First published in 1950.]

Smith, Paul. 1993. *Clint Eastwood: A Cultural Production*. Minneapolis: University of Minnesota Press.

Spivak, Gayatri Chakravorty. 1988. "Can the Subaltern Speak?" In *Marxism and the Interpretation of Culture*, ed. Cary Nelson and Lawrence Grossberg. Urbana and Chicago: University of Illinois Press, pp. 271–313.

Sragow, Michael. 1992. "Outlaws." *New Yorker*, August 10: 70–3.

Stanfield, Peter. 2001. *Hollywood, Westerns and the 1930s: The Lost Trail*. Exeter: University of Exeter Press.

———. 2002. *Horse Opera: The Strange History of the 1930s Singing Cowboy*. Urbana and Chicago: University of Illinois Press.

Starrs, Paul F. 1993. "The Ways of Western Death: Mor(t)ality and Landscape in Cormac McCarthy's Novels and Sergio Leone's Films." *Wide Angle* 15.4: 62–74.

Taylor, Quintard. 1998. *In Search of the Racial Frontier: African Americans in the American West, 1528–1990*. New York: Norton.

Thomas, Deborah. 1995. "John Wayne's Body." In Cameron and Pye 1995: 75–87.

Tibbetts, John C. 1993. "Clint Eastwood and the Machinery of Violence." *Literature/Film Quarterly* 21.1: 10–17.

Tompkins, Jane. 1992. *West of Everything: The Inner Life of Westerns.* New York: Oxford University Press.

Torry, Robert. 1993. "Therapeutic Narrative: *The Wild Bunch, Jaws,* and Vietnam." *Velvet Light Trap* 31 (Spring): 27–38.

Walker, Janet. 2001. "Captive Images in the Traumatic Western: *The Searchers, Pursued, Once Upon a Time in the West,* and *Lone Star.*" In *Western Films through History,* ed. Janet Walker. New York and London: Routledge, pp. 219–51.

Weddle, David. 1994. *"If They Move . . . Kill 'Em!": The Life and Times of Sam Peckinpah.* New York: Grove Press.

White, G. Edward. 1968. *The Eastern Establishment and the Western Experience: The West of Frederic Remington, Theodore Roosevelt, and Owen Wister.* New Haven: Yale University Press.

Williams, Raymond. 1977. *Marxism and Literature.* Oxford: Oxford University Press.

Wills, Garry. 1998. *John Wayne's America.* New York: Touchstone.

Wister, Owen. 1958. *Owen Wister Out West: His Journals and Letters,* ed. Fanny Kemble Wister. Chicago: University of Chicago Press.

——. 1998. *The Virginian: A Horseman of the Plains,* ed. Robert Shulman. Oxford and New York: Oxford University Press. [First published in 1902.]

Wister, Owen, and Kirke La Shelle. 1958. *The Virginian: A Play in Four Acts,* intro. and notes by N. Orwin Rush. Tallahassee, FL: n.p.

Wood, Robin. 1981. *Howard Hawks,* rev. edn. London: BFI.

——. 1986a. *Hollywood from Vietnam to Reagan.* New York: Columbia University Press.

——. 1986b. "Ideology, Genre, Auteur." In *Film Genre Reader,* ed. Barry Keith Grant. Austin: University of Texas, pp. 59–73.

——. 1988. *"Rancho Notorious*: A Noir Western in Colour." *CineAction!* 13–14: 83–93.

——. 1995. *"Duel in the Sun*: The Destruction of an Ideological System." In Cameron and Pye 1995: 189–95.

——. 1998. *Sexual Politics and Narrative Film: Hollywood and Beyond.* New York: Columbia University Press.

Woolland, Brian. 1995. "Class Frontiers: The View through Heaven's Gate." In Cameron and Pye 1995: 277–83.

Worland, Rick, and Edward Countryman. 1998. "The New Western American Historiography and the Emergence of the New American Westerns." In Buscombe and Pearson 1998: 182–96.

Wright, Will. 1975. *Six Guns and Society: A Structural Study of the Western.* Berkeley: University of California Press.

Zinnemann, Fred. 1986. "Fred Zinnemann." *American Film* 11.4: 12–13, 62, 60–7.

——. 1992. *A Life in the Movies: An Autobiography.* New York: Scribner's.

Žižek, Slavoj. 1992. *Looking Awry: An Introduction to Jacques Lacan through Popular Culture.* Cambridge, MA: MIT Press.

INDEX

hysteria, revolutionary implications
    of, 61–2, 67–72, 76, 80, 110,
    140

In Old California, see Griffith, D. W.
Ince, Thomas H., 26
International Alliance of Theatrical
    Stage Employees (IATSE),
    115–16
Iron Horse, The, see Ford, John
Jarmusch, Jim
    Dead Man, 76, 235
Jefferson, Thomas, 22–3, 45, 46
Jeffries, Herb, 32
Jesse James, see King, Henry
Johnny Guitar, see Ray, Nicholas
Johnson County War (1892), x, 2,
    20–5, 38–9, 41, 52, 64, 66,
    70, 72–3, 97, 115, 130, 138,
    175, 187, 201, 216, 230–2
Jones, Jennifer, 67–8, 79

Kazan, Elia
    Gentlemen's Agreement, 68
    Pinky, 68
    Viva Zapata, 68
Kermode, Frank, 147–8, 168
Keyssar, Helene, 209
Kill Bill, see Tarantino, Quentin
King, Henry
    Gunfighter, The, 113–14
    Jesse James, 50
Kitses, Jim, 150
Kolker, Robert, 208
Krapp, Peter, 199
Kuenz, Jane, 23
Kurosawa, Akira
    Seven Samurai, 143, 145, 149
    Yojimbo, 169
Kyne, Peter B., 27

La Shelle, Kirk, 25
Lacan, Jacques, 3, 215
Ladd, Alan, 1–2, 110
Landy, Marcia, 167

Lang, Fritz
    Rancho Notorious, 73
Last Train from Gun Hill, see Sturges,
    John
Lehman, Peter, 95, 102, 104–5
Leone, Sergio, xii, 5, 75, 167–9, 179,
    191–5, 197, 199, 240
    Fistful of Dollars, A, 168–73
    Fistful of Dynamite, A, also known
        as *Duck, You Sucker*, 169,
        188–91, 193, 195
    For a Few Dollars More, 168, 173–5
    Good, the Bad and the Ugly, The,
        168–9, 172, 179–80, 174–80,
        240–1
    Once Upon a Time in America,
        194–5
    Once Upon a Time in the West, 75,
        141, 167, 169, 178–88, 191–2,
        194–5, 197, 222, 239–40
Liandrat-Guigues, Suzanne, 87, 91
Limerick, Patricia, xi, 12, 46, 57–8,
    97, 206
Lonesome Dove, 235

Magnificent Seven, see Sturges, John
Man Who Shot Liberty Valance, The,
    see Ford, John
Mann, Anthony, 129
Marsh, Mae, 105
Marshall, George
    Destry Rides Again, 40, 45–51, 59,
        61, 133–4, 181, 222
Marx, Karl, 33–6, 95–6, 103, 233
McBride, Joseph, 134, 138
McBride, Joseph, and Michael
    Wilmington, 79
McCabe & Mrs. Miller, see Altman,
    Robert
McCarthy, Todd, 83
McElrath, Frances
    Rustler, The, 20
McGilligan, Patrick, 210
McKay, Brian, 204
McQueen, Butterfly, 65, 67–8

Wister, Owen (*cont.*):
  1929 film version, *see* Fleming,
    Victor
  1946 film version, 25
  stage version, 25
Wood, Robin, ix–x, xii–xiii, 60–1, 66,
    68, 71, 73, 131–2, 218, 223–4
Woolland, Brian, 218, 226
Wright, Will, 39
Wyatt Earp, 235
Wyler, William
  Big Country, The, 129
  Friendly Persuasion, 53–4
  Westerner, The, 52–8, 72, 108

Wyoming Stock-Growers' Association
  (WSGA), 22–3, 41, 85, 135,
  146, 175, 187, 201, 225

Yordan, Philip, 70
Young Deer, James, 26
Young Guns, 235

Zinnemann, Fred, 115
  High Noon, 44, 53–4, 56, 112–15,
    117–31, 133–5, 144, 150, 162,
    183, 194, 210, 212–13
Žižek, Slavoj, 3
Zsigmond, Vilmos, 210